SELF-PROECTION A fawn uses its color and spots on its fur to hide.

YOUNG A doe spends little time with her fawns. She hides the fawns in tall grass.

CHARACTERISTIC The fur of a white-tailed deer changes color with the season.
CHARACTERISTIC A buck is a male deer.
Bucks grow antlers in spring.

HSP Georgia Science

Visit *The Learning Site!*
www.harcourtschool.com

HSP Georgia Science

White-tailed deer

Science and Technology features provided by

Printed in the United States of America

ISBN 13: 978-0-15-358536-4
ISBN 10: 0-15-358536-6

3 4 5 6 7 8 9 10 048 16 15 14 13 12 11 10 09 08

Series Consulting Authors

Michael J. Bell, Ph.D.
Associate Professor of Early Childhood Education
College of Education, West Chester
University of Pennsylvania
West Chester, Pennsylvania

Michael A. DiSpezio
Curriculum Architect
JASON Academy
Cape Cod, Massachusetts

Marjorie Frank
Former Adjunct, Science Education
Hunter College
New York, New York

Gerald H. Krockover, Ph.D.
Professor of Earth and Atmospheric Science Education
Purdue University
West Lafayette, Indiana

Joyce C. McLeod
Adjunct Professor
Rollins College
Winter Park, Florida

Barbara ten Brink, Ph.D.
Austin Independent School District
Austin, Texas

Carol J. Valenta
Senior Vice President
Saint Louis Science Center
Saint Louis, Missouri

Barry A. Van Deman
President and CEO
Museum of Life and Science
Durham, North Carolina

Georgia Curriculum and Classroom Reviewers

Amy Benson
Tritt Elementary
Marietta, Georgia

Joyce Brooks
Alpharetta Elementary
Alpharetta, Georgia

Julie B. Burns
Blandford Elementary
Runcon, Georgia

Shelley Crittenden
Grantville Elementary
Grantville, Georgia

Calandra Eineker
Alpharetta Elementary
Alpharetta, Georgia

Jennie Haynes
A. B. Merry School
Augusta, Georgia

Gail Hines
A. B. Merry School
Augusta, Georgia

Dawn M. Hudson
Paulding County Schools
Dallas, Georgia

Valerie E. King
Big Shanty Intermediate
Kennesaw, Georgia

Sondra M. Lee
Grantville Elementary
Grantville, Georgia

Stacey N. Mabray
Augusta, Georgia

Heather L. Nix
Berrien Primary School
Nashville, Georgia

Lisa E. Reynolds
Holsenbeck Elementary
Winder, Georgia

Vicki Roark
Little River Elementary
Woodstock, Georgia

Karol H. Stephens
Northeast High School/ Bibb County Board of Education
Macon, Georgia

Karen W. Sumner
G.O. Bailey Primary School
Tifton, Georgia

Beth Thompson
Alpharetta Elementary
Alpharetta, Georgia

Gina A. Turner
Troup County Schools
LaGrange, Georgia

Nannette R. Ward
Lake Park Elementary
Albany, Georgia

Dianne Wood
Woody Gap School
Suches, Georgia

Georgia HSP Science and the Georgia Performance Standards for Science

Dear Students and Parents,

The Georgia Performance Standards for Science (GPS), shown here for your reference, were designed to provide students with the knowledge and skills necessary for science proficiency at the first grade. Therefore, the GPS will drive science instruction. Since science is a way of thinking and investigating, as well as a body of knowledge, students need an understanding of both the Characteristics of Science and its Content. The GPS require that instruction treat these together, so they are shown here as co-requisites.

Georgia HSP Science was developed to provide complete coverage of the GPS. Throughout the book you will find exciting investigations, engaging text, and ties to Georgia people and places. These help ensure mastery of the GPS, while providing a rewarding science experience for all students.

Harcourt School Publishers

Co-Requisite—Characteristics of Science

Habits of Mind

S1CS1 Students will be aware of the importance of curiosity, honesty, openness, and skepticism in science and will exhibit these traits in their own efforts to understand how the world works.

a. Raise questions about the world around them and be willing to seek answers to some of the questions by making careful observations and measurements and trying to figure things out.

S1CS2 Students will have the computation and estimation skills necessary for analyzing data and following scientific explanations.

a. Use whole numbers in ordering, counting, identifying, measuring, and describing things and experiences.

b. Readily give the sums and differences of single-digit numbers in ordinary, practical contexts and judge the reasonableness of the answer.

c. Give rough estimates of numerical answers to problems before doing them formally.

d. Make quantitative estimates of familiar lengths, weights, and time intervals, and check them by measuring.

S1CS3 Students will use tools and instruments for observing, measuring, and manipulating objects in scientific activities.

a. Use ordinary hand tools and instruments to construct, measure, and look at objects.

b. Make something that can actually be used to perform a task, using paper, cardboard, wood, plastic, metal, or existing objects.

c. Identify and practice accepted safety procedures in manipulating science materials and equipment.

S1CS4 Students will use the ideas of system, model, change, and scale in exploring scientific and technological matters.

a. Use a model—such as a toy or a picture—to describe a feature of the primary thing.

b. Describe changes in the size, weight, color, or movement of things, and note which of their other qualities remain the same during a specific change.

c. Compare very different sizes, weights, ages (baby/adult), and speeds (fast/slow) of both human made and natural things.

S1CS5 Students will communicate scientific ideas and activities clearly.

a. Describe and compare things in terms of number, shape, texture, size, weight, color, and motion.

b. Draw pictures (grade level appropriate) that correctly portray features of the thing being described.

c. Use simple pictographs and bar graphs to communicate data.

The Nature of Science

S1CS6 Students will be familiar with the character of scientific knowledge and how it is achieved.

Students will recognize that:

a. When a science investigation is done the way it was done before, we expect to get a similar result.

b. Science involves collecting data and testing hypotheses.

c. Scientists often repeat experiments multiple times, and subject their ideas to criticism by other scientists who may disagree with them and do further tests.

d. All different kinds of people can be and are scientists.

S1CS7 Students will understand important features of the process of scientific inquiry.

Students will apply the following to inquiry learning practices:

a. Scientists use a common language with precise definitions of terms to make it easier to communicate their observations to each other.

b. In doing science, it is often helpful to work as a team. All team members should reach individual conclusions and share their understandings with other members of the team in order to develop a consensus.

c. Tools such as thermometers, rulers, and balances often give more information about things than can be obtained by just observing things without help.

d. Much can be learned about plants and animals by observing them closely, but care must be taken to know the needs of living things and how to provide for them. Advantage can be taken of classroom pets.

Co-Requisite—Content

EARTH SCIENCE

S1E1 Students will observe, measure, and communicate weather data to see patterns in weather and climate.

a. Identify different types of weather and the characteristics of each type.

b. Investigate weather by observing, measuring with simple weather instruments (thermometer, wind vane, rain gauge), and recording weather data (temperature, precipitation, sky conditions, and weather events) in a periodic journal or on a calendar seasonally.

c. Correlate weather data (temperature, precipitation, sky conditions, and weather events) to seasonal changes.

S1E2 Students will observe and record changes in water as it relates to weather.

a. Recognize changes in water when it freezes (ice) and when it melts (water).

b. Identify forms of precipitation such as rain, snow, sleet, and hailstones as either solid (ice) or liquid (water).

c. Determine that the weight of water before freezing, after freezing, and after melting stays the same.

d. Determine that water in an open container disappears into the air over time, but water in a closed container does not.

PHYSICAL SCIENCE

S1P1 Students will investigate light and sound.

a. Recognize sources of light.

b. Explain how shadows are made.

c. Investigate how vibrations produce sound.

d. Differentiate between various sounds in terms of (pitch) high or low and (volume) loud or soft.

e. Identify emergency sounds and sounds that help us stay safe.

S1P2 Students will demonstrate effects of magnets on other magnets and other objects.

a. Demonstrate how magnets attract and repel.

b. Identify common objects that are attracted to a magnet.

c. Identify objects and materials (air, water, wood, paper, your hand, etc.) that do not block magnetic force.

LIFE SCIENCE

S1L1 Students will investigate the characteristics and basic needs of plants and animals.

a. Identify the basic needs of a plant.

1. Air
2. Water
3. Light
4. Nutrients

b. Identify the basic needs of an animal.

1. Air
2. Water
3. Food
4. Shelter

c. Identify the parts of a plant—root, stem, leaf, and flower.

d. Compare and describe various animals—appearance, motion, growth, basic needs.

Contents

Chapter 1

Big Idea
Scientists find out about things by asking questions and doing investigations.

Big Idea
Weather patterns help you observe, measure, and communicate about weather.

Big Idea
You can observe and record changes in water with the weather.

UNIT

B PHYSICAL SCIENCE 116

Big Idea

Light can make shadows. Vibrations make sound.

Big Idea

Magnets can attract objects made of iron, and can pull through some materials.

magnet pulling through a hand

UNIT C LIFE SCIENCE 186

Big Idea
Plants need air, water, light, and nutrients to live and grow. Different parts of plants help plants get what they need.

Big Idea
Animals need air, water, food, and shelter to live and grow. You can compare animals.

References

field of sunflowers

CHAPTER 1

Getting Ready for Science

Georgia Performance Standards in This Chapter

Characteristics of Science

S1CS1 Students will be aware of the importance of curiosity, honesty, openness, and skepticism in science and will exhibit these traits in their own efforts to understand how the world works.

S1CS2 Students will have the computation and estimation skills necessary for analyzing data and following scientific explanations.

S1CS3 Students will use tools and instruments for observing, measuring, and manipulating objects in scientific activities.

S1CS4 Students will use the ideas of system, model, change, and scale in exporting scientific and technological matters.

S1CS5 Students will communicate scientific ideas and activities clearly.

S1CS6 Students will be familiar with the character of scientific knowledge and how it is achieved.

S1CS7 Students will understand important features of the process of scientific inquiry.

What's the Big Idea?

Scientists find out about things by asking questions and doing investigations.

Essential Questions

for student eBook www.hspscience.com

Dear Malcolm,

Our class went to Imagine It! I observed with a hand lens. I explored like a real scientist. I wish you could have been there!

Your friend,

Maddie

Read Maddie's postcard. What did Maddie learn about being a scientist? How do you think that helps explain the **Big Idea?**

Georgia Performance Standards in This Lesson

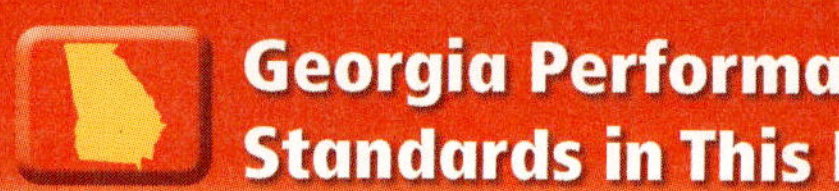

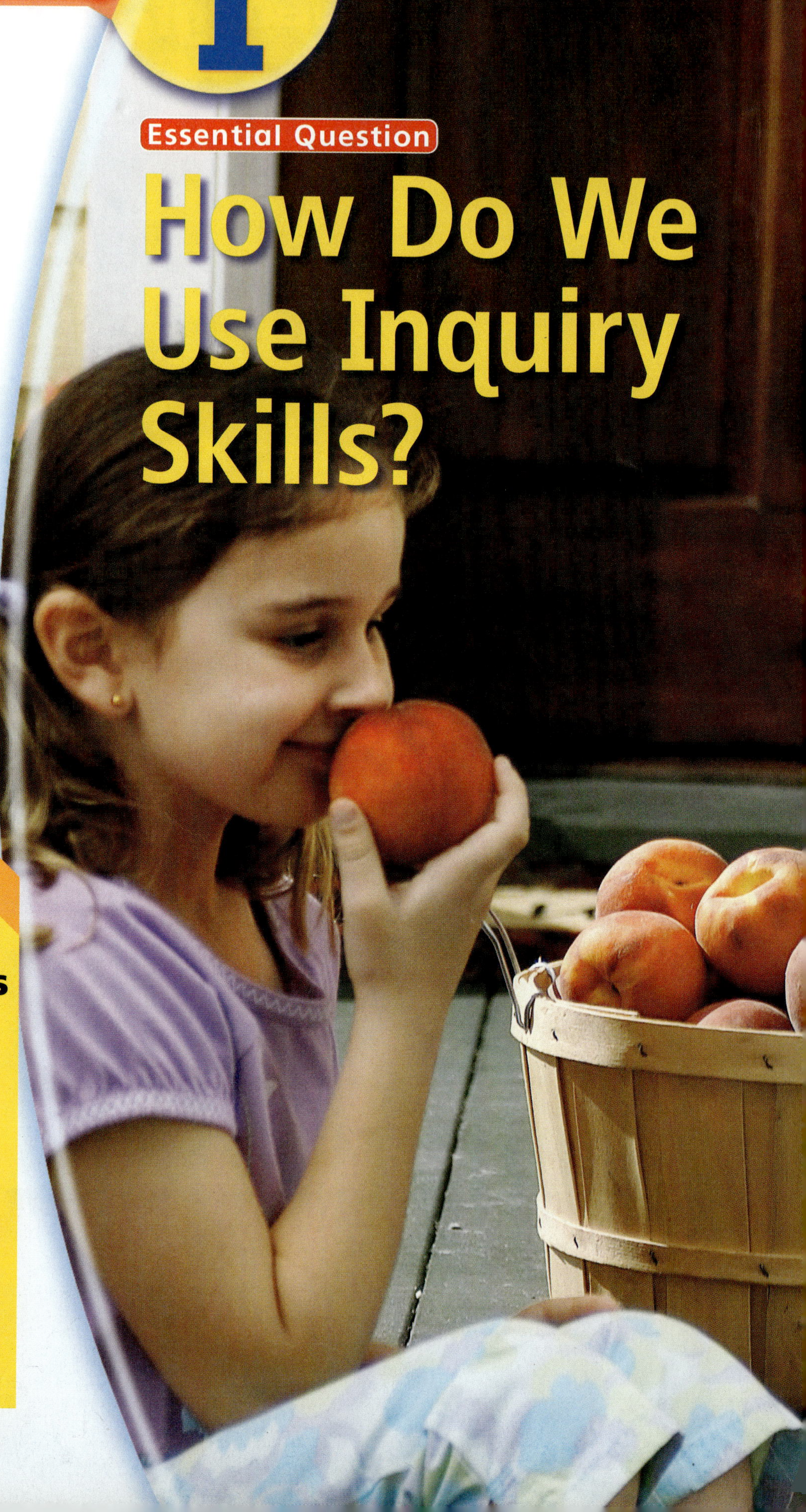

Characteristics of Science

S1CS1a Raise questions about the world around them and be willing to seek answers to some of the questions by making careful observations and measurements and trying to figure things out.

S1CS2a Use whole numbers in ordering, counting, identifying, measuring, and describing things and experiences.

S1CS3a Use ordinary hand tools and instruments to construct, measure, and look at objects.

S1CS4a Use a model—such as a toy or a picture—to describe a feature of the primary thing.

S1CS4c Compare very different sizes, weights, ages (baby/adult), and speeds (fast, slow) of both human made and natural things.

S1CS5a Describe and compare things in terms of number, shape, texture, size, weight, color, and motion.

S1CS5b Draw pictures . . . that correctly portray features of the thing being described.

Georgia Fast Fact

Georgia Peaches
You can compare peaches. The fruit of some peaches breaks away from the seed. The fruit of other peaches clings to the seed. What are some other ways you can compare peaches?

LESSON 1

Essential Question

How Do We Use Inquiry Skills?

Vocabulary Preview
inquiry skills p. 6
observe p. 10
Georgia peaches

Fruit Protection

Guided Inquiry

Ask a Question

Observe and compare the peels of these fruits. How are they alike? How are they different? Investigate to find out. Then read to find out more.

Get Ready

Inquiry Skill Tip

When you observe, you use your senses to find out about things. You can use pictures, numbers, or words to record what you see.

You need

fruits

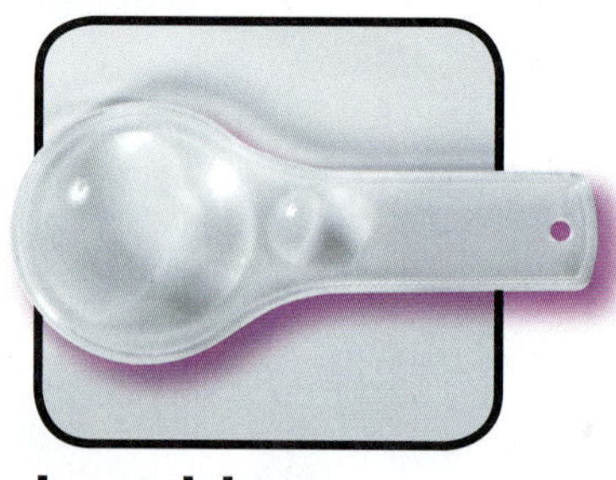

hand lens

What to Do

Step 1

Observe some fruits with a hand lens. Look at their peels.

Step 2

Observe the cut fruits with the hand lens. What is inside the fruits?

Step 3

Draw a picture to record what you see.

Draw Conclusions

How do peels protect the insides of fruits? S1CS1a

Independent Inquiry

Find pictures of plants that have thorns or bark. **Draw a conclusion** about why plants have these kinds of coverings. S1CS1a S1CS5b

S1CS1a, S1CS4a,c, S1CS5a

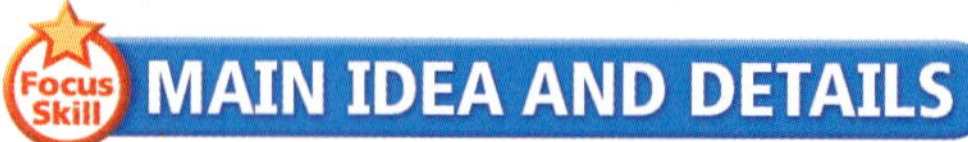

VOCABULARY
inquiry skills
observe

Focus Skill **MAIN IDEA AND DETAILS**

Look for details about the inquiry skills scientists use.

Using Inquiry Skills

Scientists use inquiry skills when they do tests. **Inquiry skills** help people find out about things. You can use these skills, too.

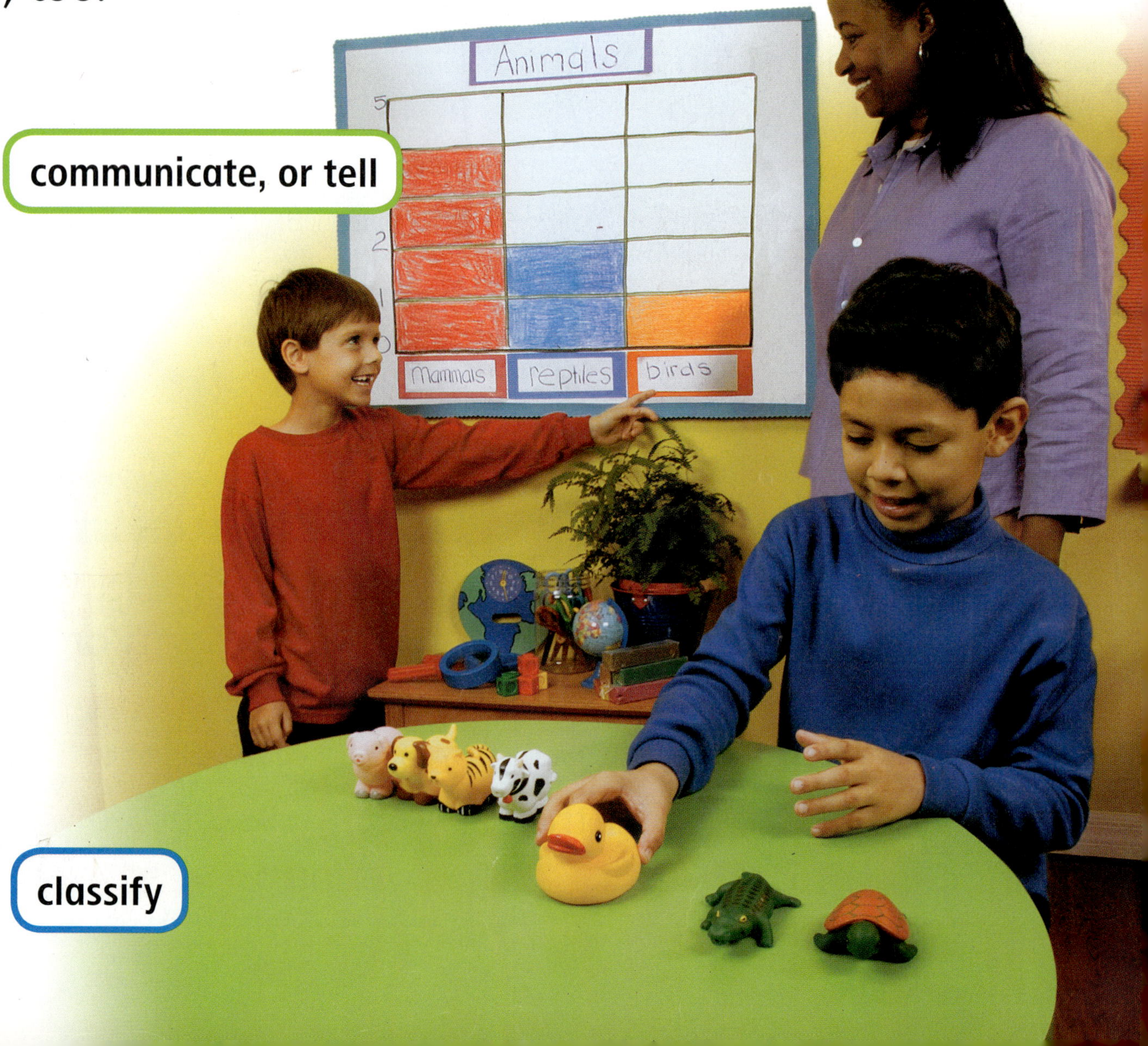
Animals
5
2
1
0
mammals
reptiles
birds
communicate, or tell
classify

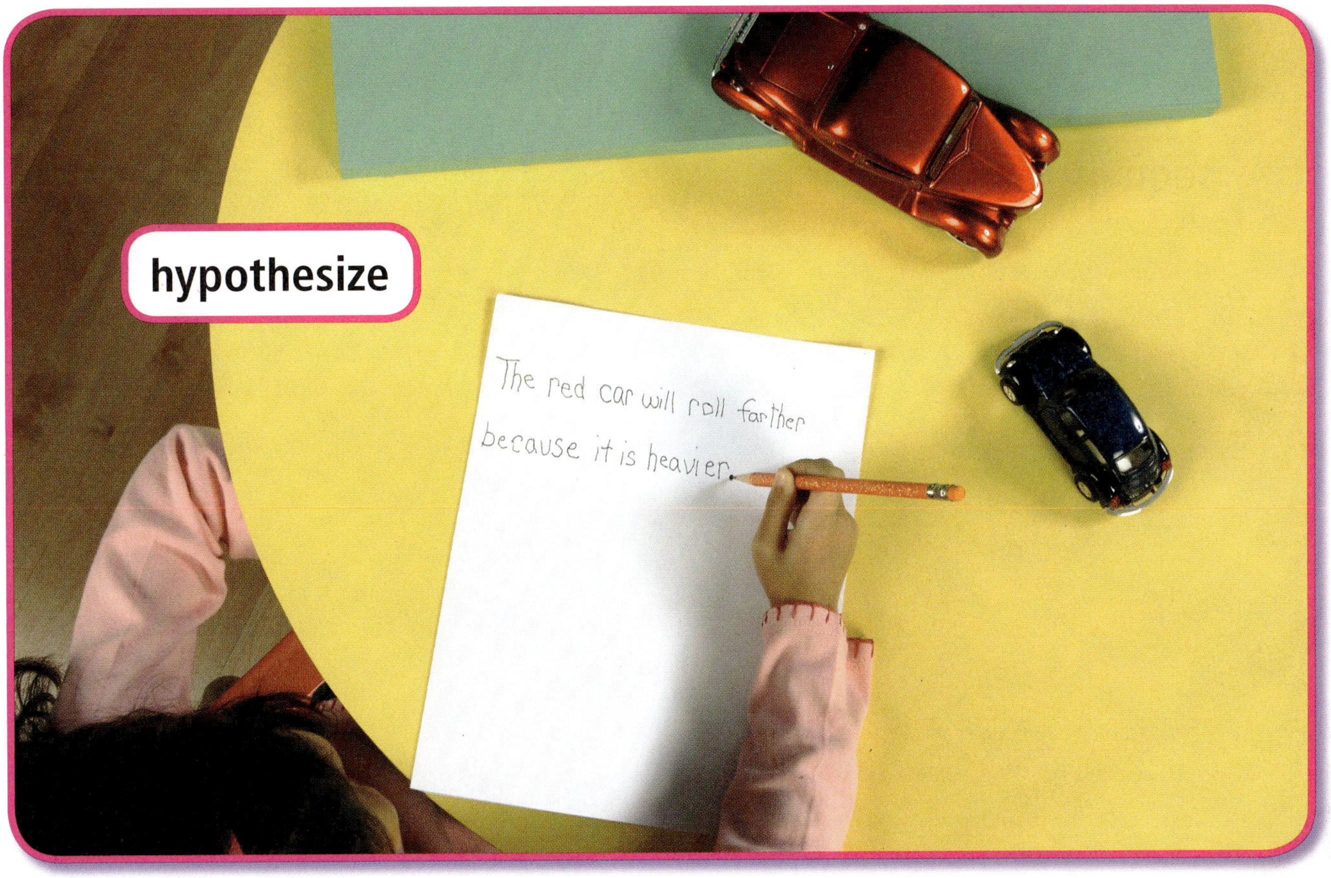

hypothesize

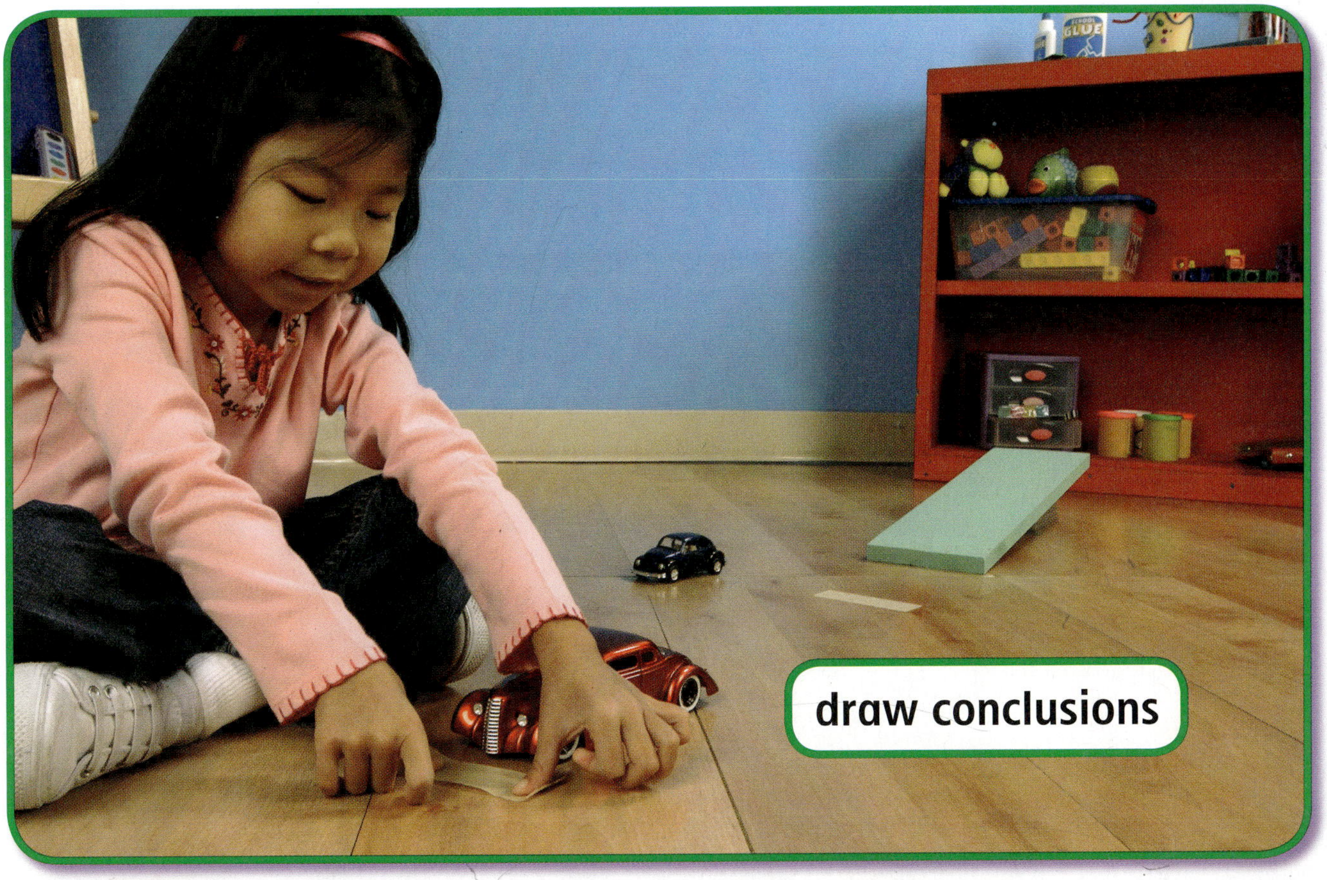

draw conclusions

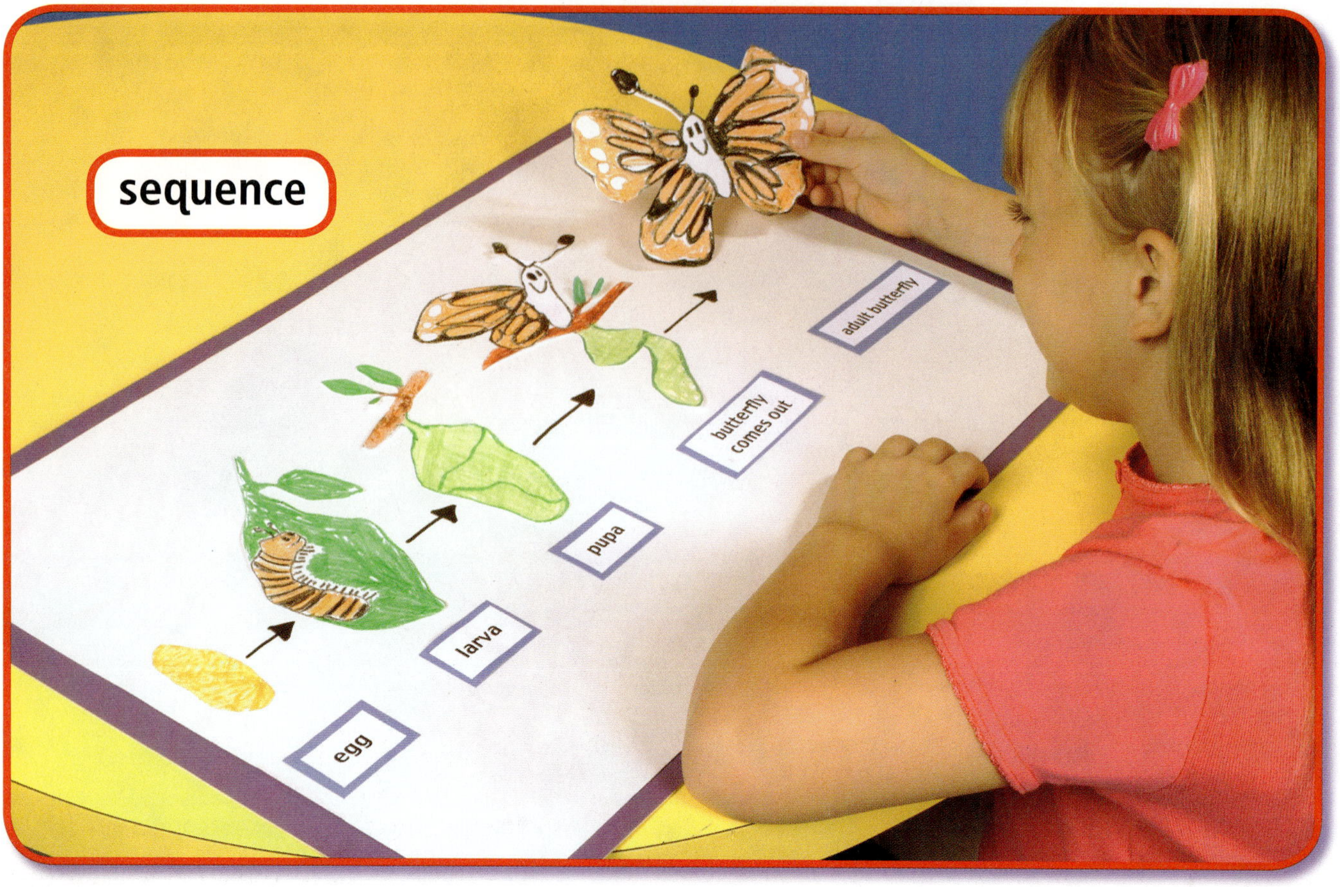
sequence
egg
larva
pupa
butterfly comes out
adult butterfly

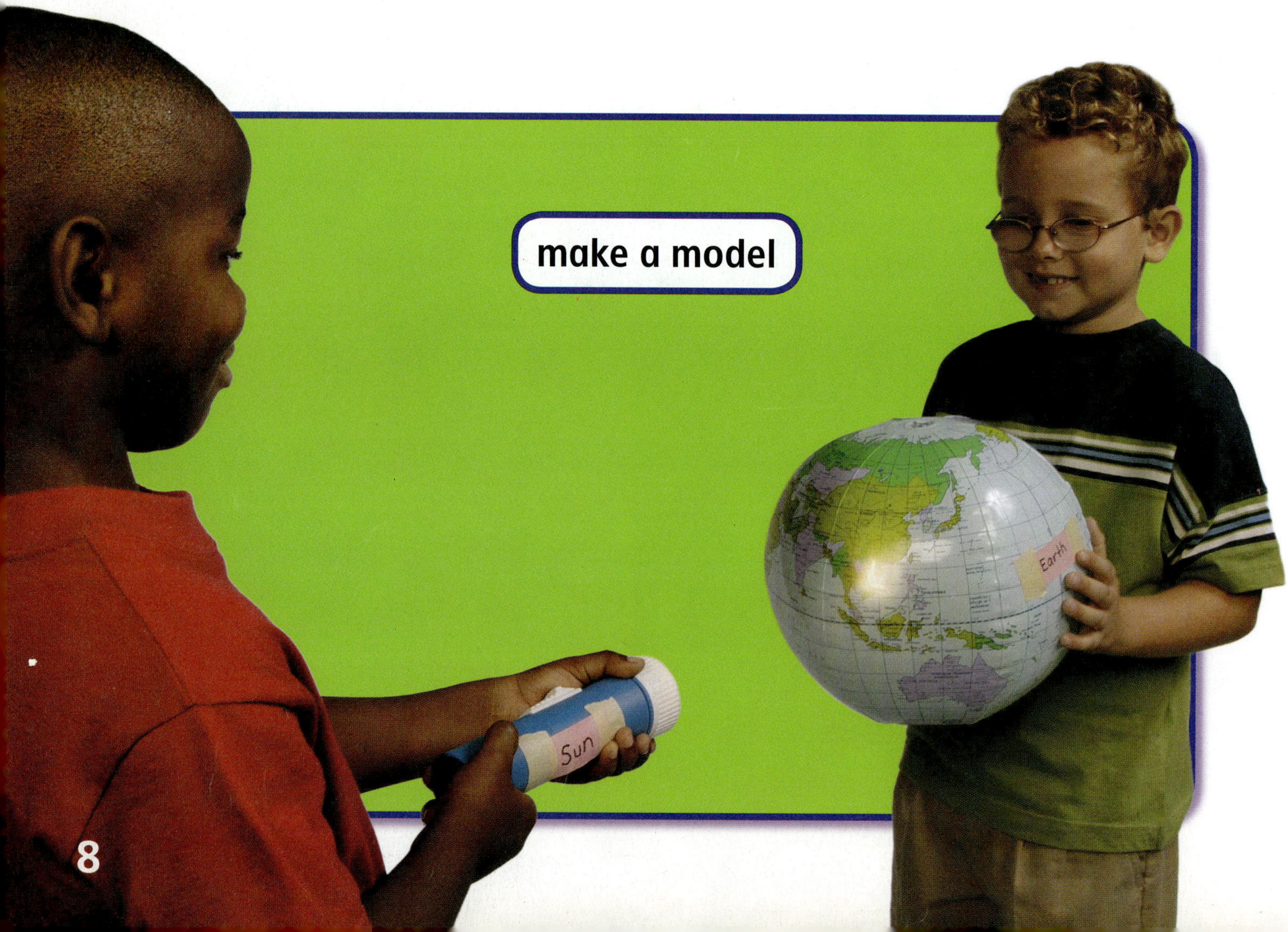
make a model
Sun
Earth

compare
measure
GO TEAM!

When you **observe**, you use your senses to find out about things.

observe

predict

plan an investigation

infer

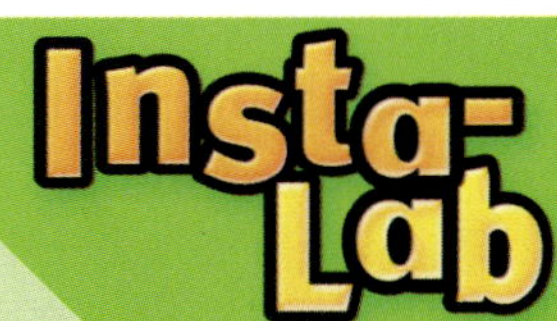

How Far Will It Roll?

Get a ball. Predict how far it will go if you roll it across the floor. Mark that spot with tape. Then roll the ball. Was your prediction correct?

Focus Skill **MAIN IDEA AND DETAILS**

What skills do scientists use when they do tests?

GPS Wrap-Up and Lesson Review

Essential Question

How do we use inquiry skills?

In this lesson, you learned about inquiry skills that help scientists observe, find out about things, and test ideas.

1. **MAIN IDEA AND DETAILS** Make a chart like this one. Show details for this main idea. **Inquiry skills help people find out about things.** S1CS1a

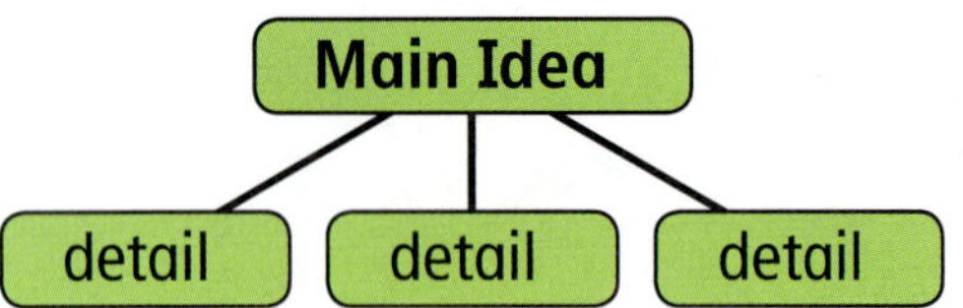

2. **DRAW CONCLUSIONS** How can a model help you find out about something? S1CS4a

3. **VOCABULARY** Use the words **inquiry skills** to tell about this picture. S1CS1a

4. What should you do to find out how long a pencil is? S1CS2a

CRCT Practice

5. What do you do when you observe?
   A group things
   B make a guess
   C use your senses S1CS1a

The Big Idea

6. How do inquiry skills help you observe, find out about things, and test ideas? S1CS1a

Writing

ELA1W1b

Write to Describe

1. Use clay to make a model of your favorite animal.
2. List words that describe your animal.
3. Share your model and your list with the class.

Math

M1G2

Grouping Blocks

1. Get some blocks that are different sizes and colors.
2. Classify the blocks by both size and color.
3. Draw a picture that shows how you classified the blocks.

For more links and activities, go to **www.hspscience.com**

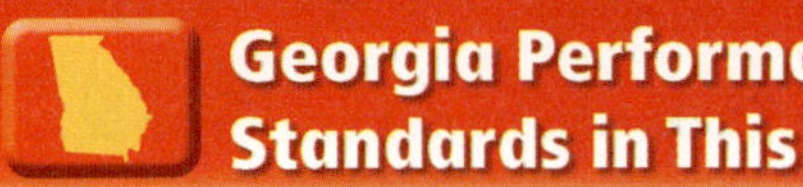

Georgia Performance Standards in This Lesson

LESSON 2

Essential Question

How Do We Use Science Tools?

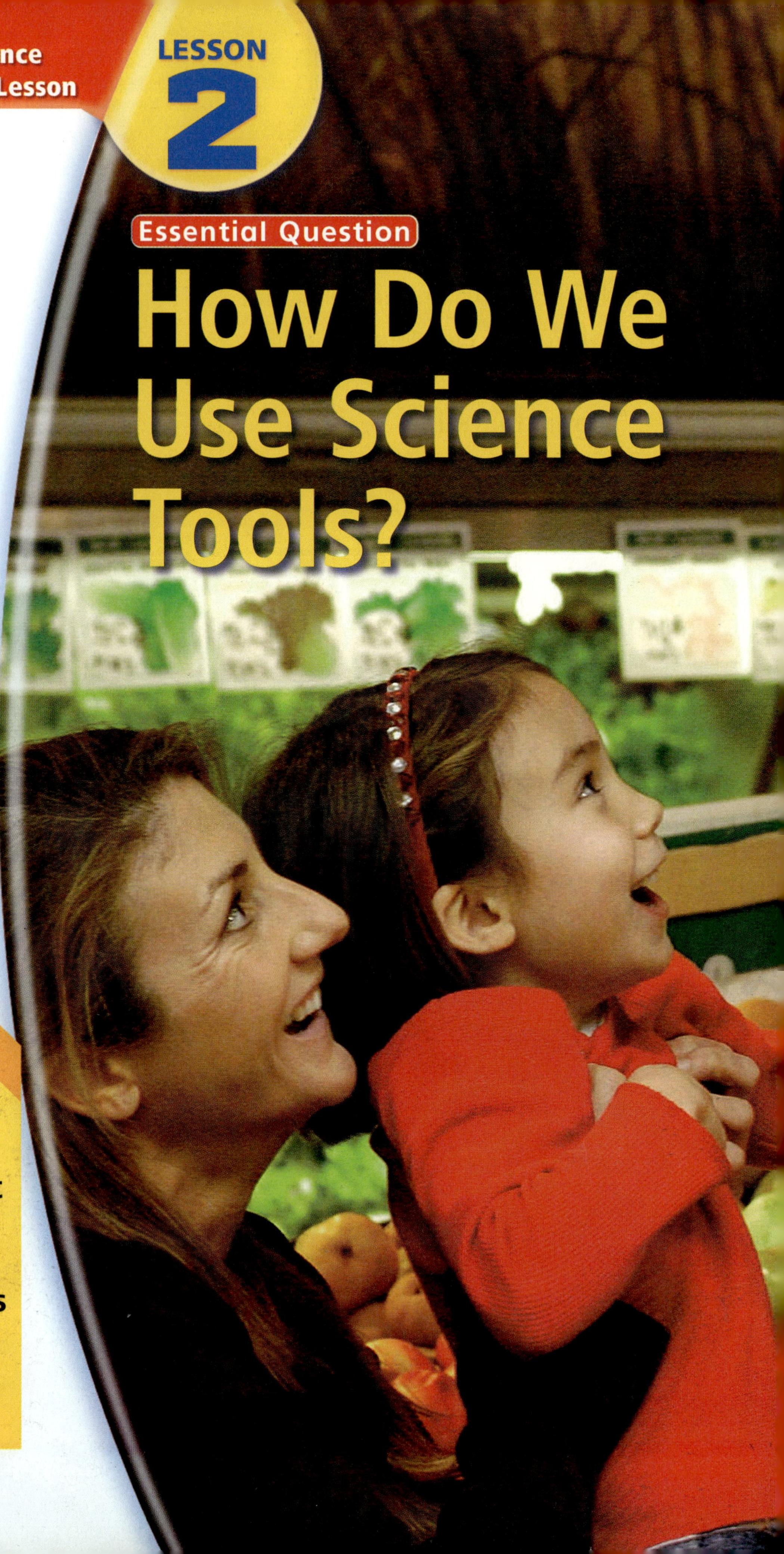

Characteristics of Science

S1CS2a Use whole numbers in ordering, counting, identifying, measuring, and describing things and experiences.

S1CS2c Give rough estimates of numerical answers to problems before doing them formally.

S1CS2d Make quantitative estimates of familiar lengths, weights, and time intervals, and check them by measuring.

S1CS3a Use ordinary hand tools and instruments to construct, measure, and look at objects.

S1CS3c Identify and practice accepted safety procedures in manipulating science materials and equipment.

S1CS4c Compare very different sizes, weights, ages (baby/adult), and speeds (fast/slow) of both human made and natural things.

S1CS5a Describe and compare things in terms of number, shape, texture, size, weight, color, and motion.

S1CS7c Tools such as thermometers, rulers, and balances often give more information about things than can be obtained by just observing things without help.

Georgia Fast Fact

Weighing Fruit

People can buy fruit at markets. They can weigh the fruit on a scale. A scale is a tool used to find out how heavy an object is.

Vocabulary Preview

science tools p. 18

weighing fruit at a Georgia market

Investigate

Compare Fruit

Guided Inquiry

Ask a Question

What tool are these people using? Investigate to find out. Then read to find out more.

Get Ready

Inquiry Skill Tip

When you compare objects, you see how they are alike and different. You can draw pictures to show how you compare objects.

You need

strawberry

pear

balance

What to Do

Step 1

Put one piece of fruit on each side of a balance.

Step 2

Compare the masses of the fruits.

Step 3

Draw a picture to record what you see.

Draw Conclusions

Which fruit has less mass? Which fruit has more mass? S1CS3a S1CS4c S1CS5a

Independent Inquiry

Measure around two fruits. **Compare** the measurements. Which fruit is bigger around? S1CS3a S1CS4c S1CS5a

VOCABULARY
science tools

MAIN IDEA AND DETAILS
Look for details about science tools.

Using Science Tools

Scientists use tools to find out about things. You can use tools to find out about things, too. **Science tools** help people do investigations. They help you observe, compare, and measure things. Be sure to follow all safety rules when using science tools.

Some things have parts that are too small to see. You can use a hand lens or a magnifying box to help you see them.

hand lens and magnifying box

You can use forceps to help you hold or separate things.

You can use a dropper to place drops of liquid.

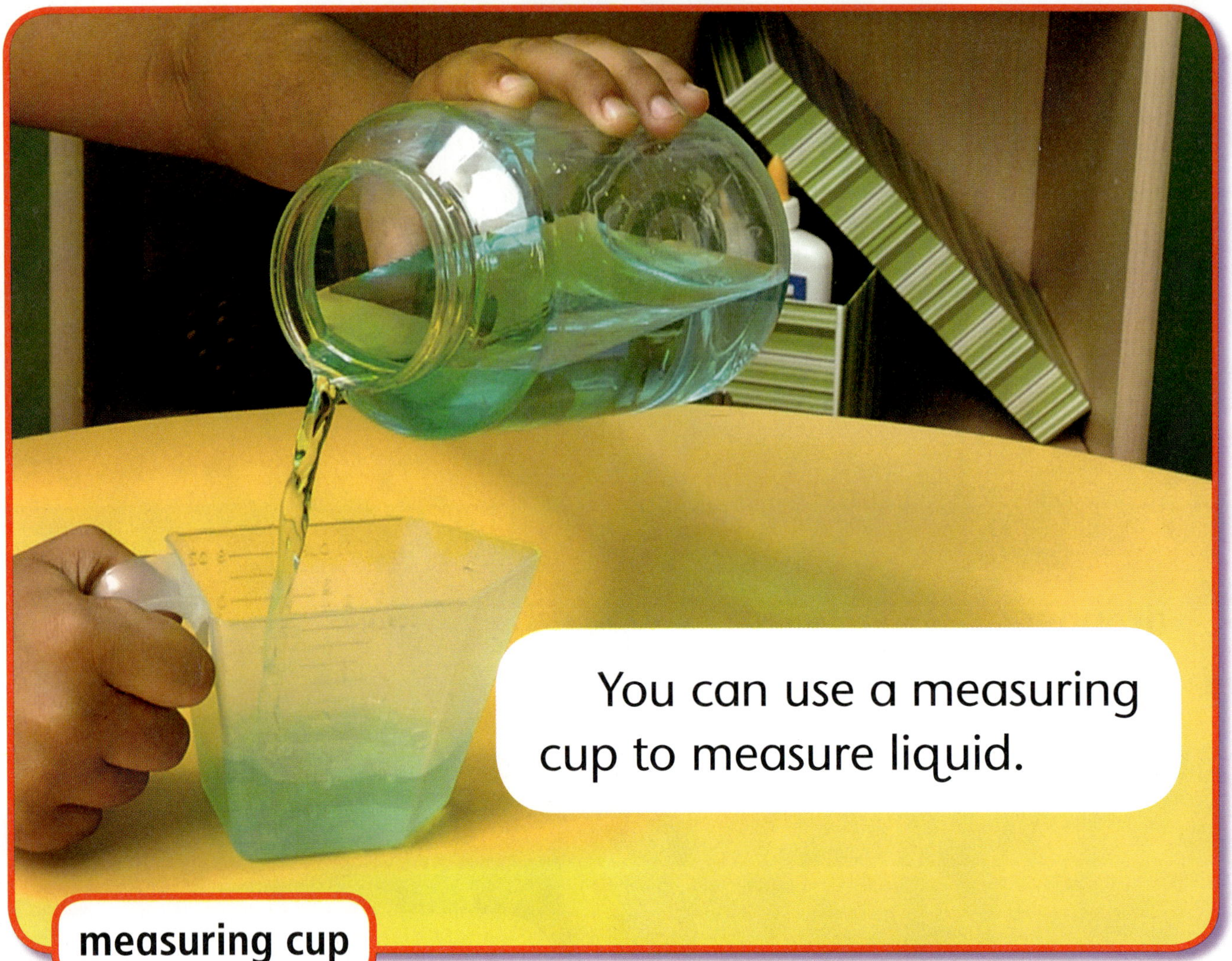

You can use a measuring cup to measure liquid.

measuring cup

You can use a thermometer to measure how warm or cold something is.

thermometer

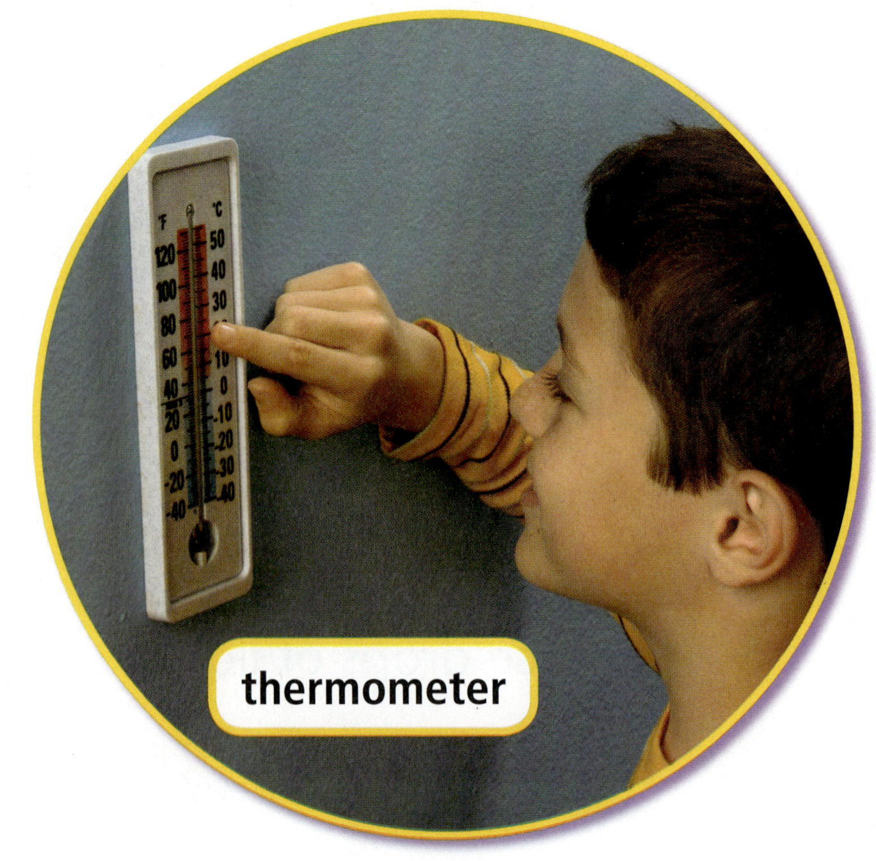

You can use a ruler to measure how long or tall an object is. You can use a tape measure to measure around an object.

You can use a balance to measure the mass of an object.

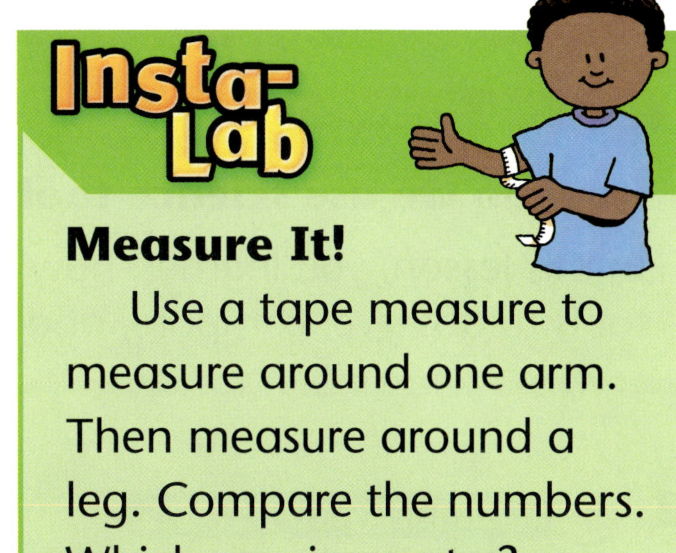

Measure It!

Use a tape measure to measure around one arm. Then measure around a leg. Compare the numbers. Which one is greater?

Focus Skill MAIN IDEA AND DETAILS

How can you use science tools to find out information?

balance

ruler

tape measure

GPS Wrap-Up and Lesson Review

Essential Question

How do we use science tools?

In this lesson, you learned how to use science tools to observe, compare, and measure things.

1. **MAIN IDEA AND DETAILS** Make a chart like this one. Show details of this main idea. **You can use science tools.** S1CS7c

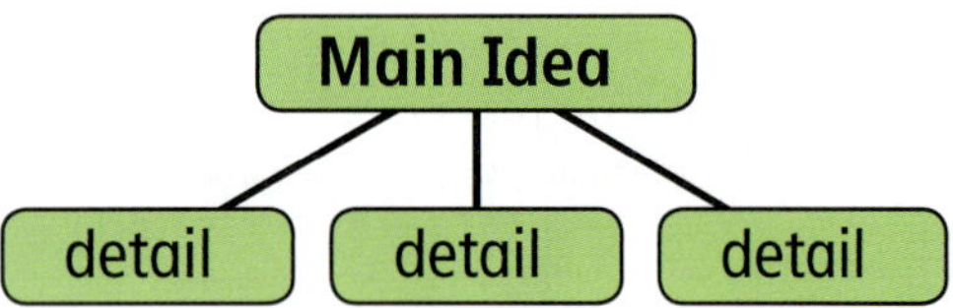

2. **SUMMARIZE** Tell ways to use science tools to find out about things. S1CS7c

3. **VOCABULARY** Use the words **science tools** to tell about the picture. S1CS3a

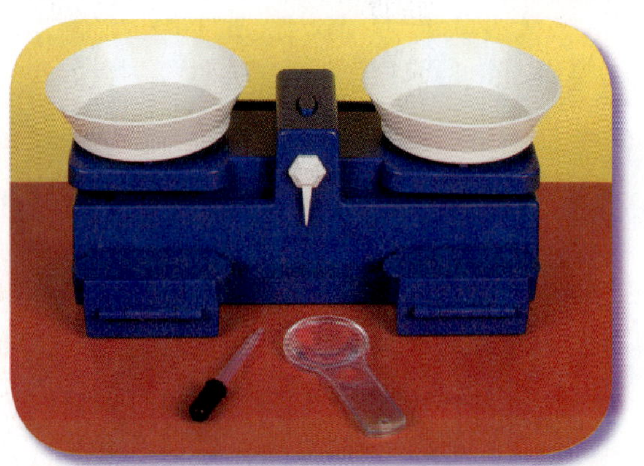

4. Look at these science tools. Which one would you use to make something look larger? S1CS7c

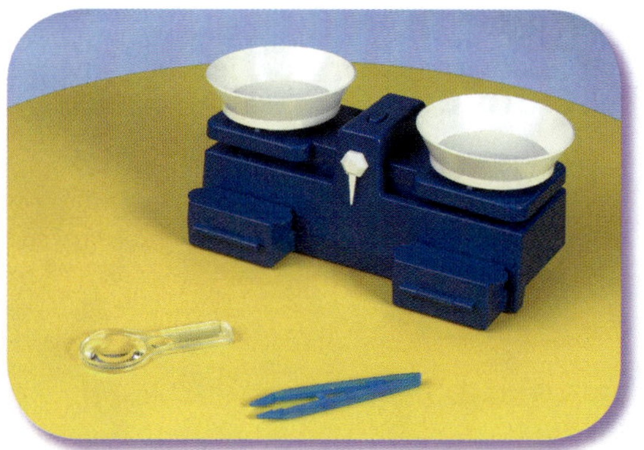

CRCT Practice

5. How are a ruler and tape measure alike? How are they different? S1CS3a

The Big Idea

6. How do science tools help you observe, compare, and measure things? S1CS3a

Writing

ELA1W1b

Write to Describe

1. Name a science tool you have used.
2. Draw a picture of the tool.
3. Write one sentence about how you used the tool.

I use a ruler to measure things.

Math

M1M1b

Estimate and Count

1. Estimate how many cotton balls it will take to fill a measuring cup. Then fill the cup with cotton balls.
2. How many cotton balls did you need? Use > or < to tell if the number of cotton balls was greater or less than the number you estimated.

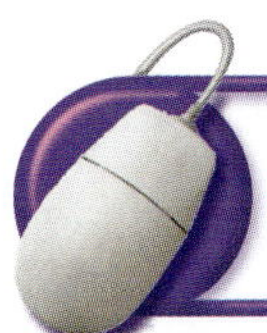

For more links and activities, go to **www.hspscience.com**

Georgia Performance Standards in This Lesson

LESSON 3

Characteristics of Science

S1CS1a Raise questions about the world around them and be willing to seek answers to some of the questions by making careful observations and measurements and trying to figure things out.

S1CS5c Use simple pictographs and bar graphs to communicate data.

S1CS6a When a science investigation is done the way it was done before, we expect to get a similar result.

S1CS6b Science involves collecting data and testing hypotheses.

S1CS6c Scientists often repeat experiments multiple times, and subject their ideas to criticism by other scientists who may disagree with them and do further tests.

S1CS7a Scientists use a common language with precise definitions of terms to make it easier to communicate their observations to each other.

S1CS7b In doing science, it is often helpful to work as a team. All team members should reach individual conclusions and share their understandings with other members of the team in order to develop a consensus.

Essential Question

How Do Scientists Work?

Georgia Fast Fact

Pumpkin Growing Contest

Some pumpkins weigh more than 350 pounds (158 kilograms). That is about as much as a young elephant! Why do you think this pumpkin grew so big?

Vocabulary Preview
Fruits
pictograph p. 32
Number of Fruits
Kinds of Fruits
bar graph p. 33
Georgia 4-H Pumpkin
Growing Contest

Measure Fruits

Guided Inquiry

Ask a Question

Look at these things. Which one would you measure with a tape measure? Which one would you measure with a ruler? Investigate to find out. Then read to find out more.

Get Ready

Inquiry Skill Tip

When you plan an investigation, you think of what you need to do to find out what you want to know.

You need

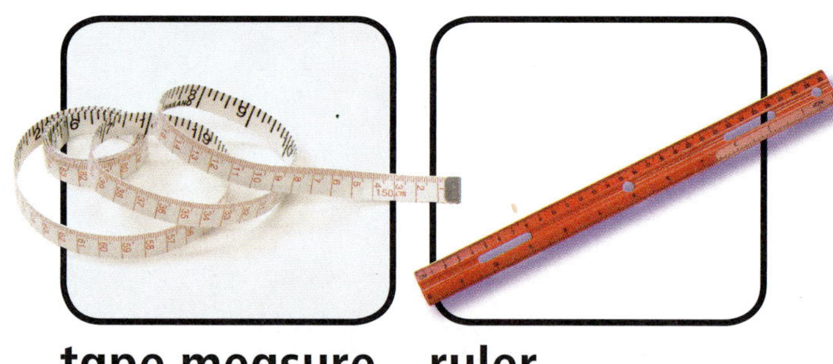

tape measure ruler

fruits

What to Do

Step 1

How can you measure fruits? Think about it. **Plan an investigation.** Write a plan to find out.

Step 2

Follow your plan to investigate your ideas.

Step 3

Record what you observe. Share with the class what you learned.

Draw Conclusions

What did you find out about how to measure fruits? S1CS3a

Independent Inquiry

How can you use a straw, a string, and a craft stick to move a block? **Plan an investigation** to find out. S1CS1a

S1CS1a, S1CS5c, S1CS6a,b,c, S1CS7b

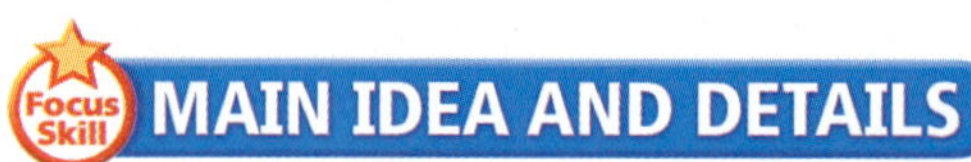

VOCABULARY
pictograph
bar graph

MAIN IDEA AND DETAILS

Look for the main ideas about the steps that scientists use to work.

Investigating

Scientists follow steps to test the things they want to learn about.

1 Observe. Then ask a question.

Think of a question you want to answer. What do you want to know?

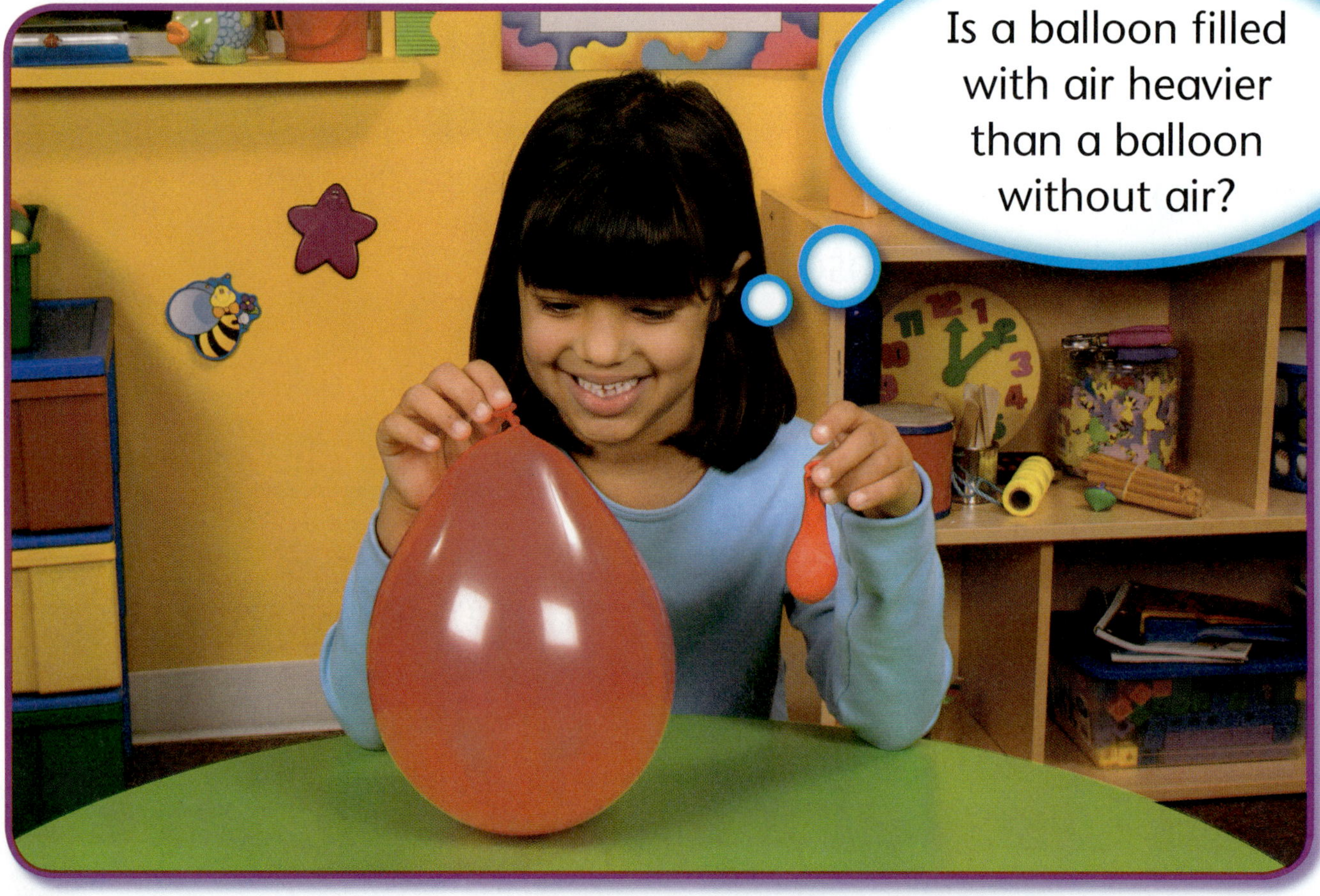
Is a balloon filled with air heavier than a balloon without air?

2 Form a hypothesis.

What do you think will happen? Write an idea that you can test.

3 Plan a fair test.

What do you want to learn? Write a plan. List the things you will need to do your test. List the steps you will follow.

4 Do the test.

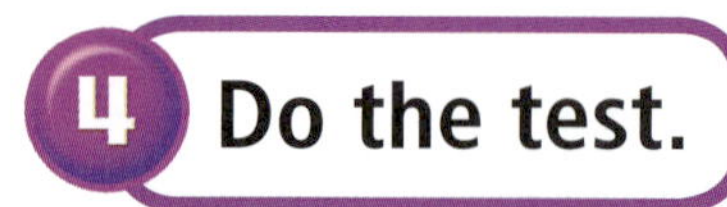

Follow the steps of your plan. Observe. Record what happens.

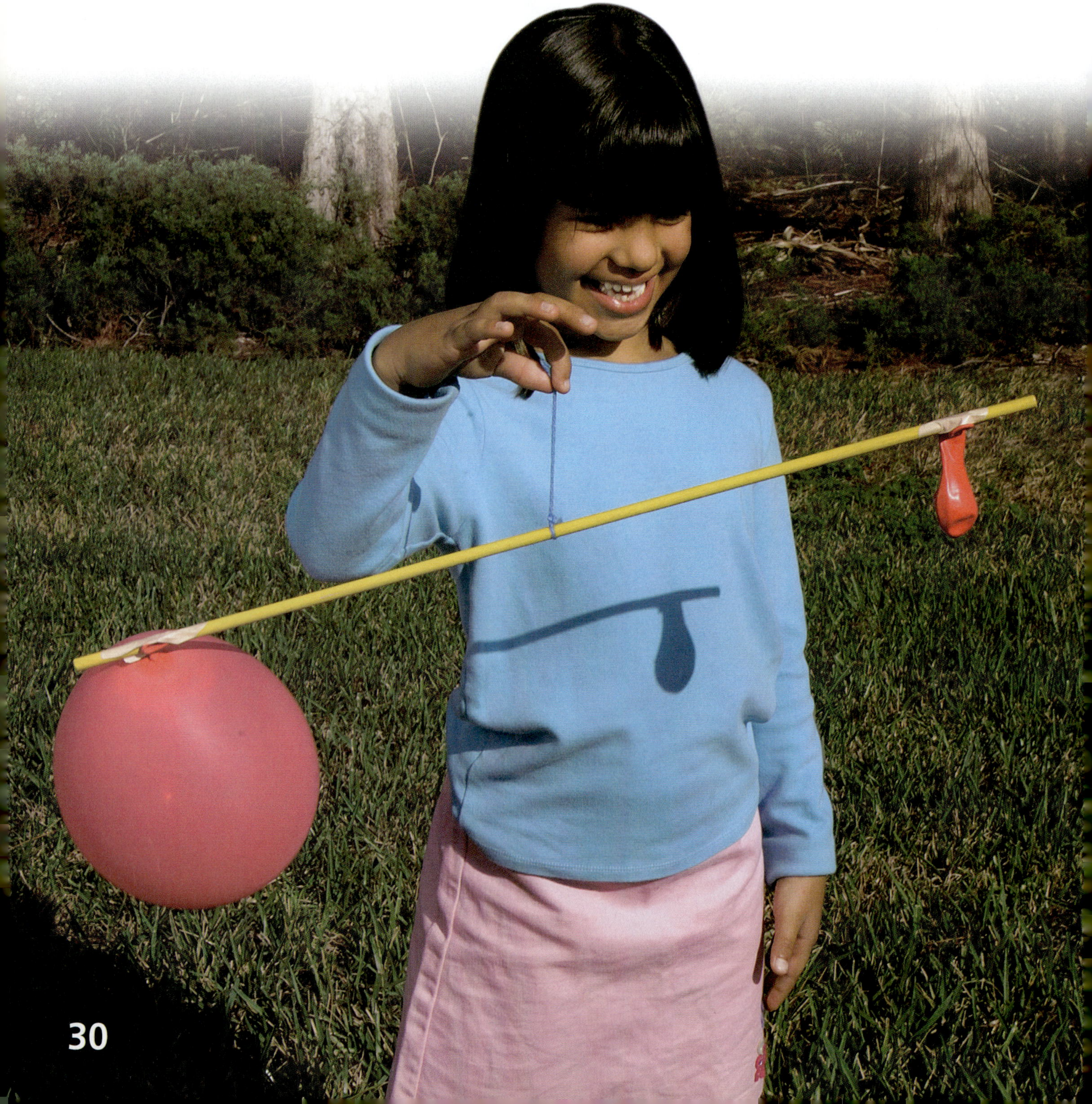

5 Draw conclusions. Tell what you learn.

What did you find out? Was your idea correct? Share your answers. Compare your answers with those of classmates. If you get different answers, do your test again.

Focus Skill **MAIN IDEA AND DETAILS**

What steps do scientists follow to test things?

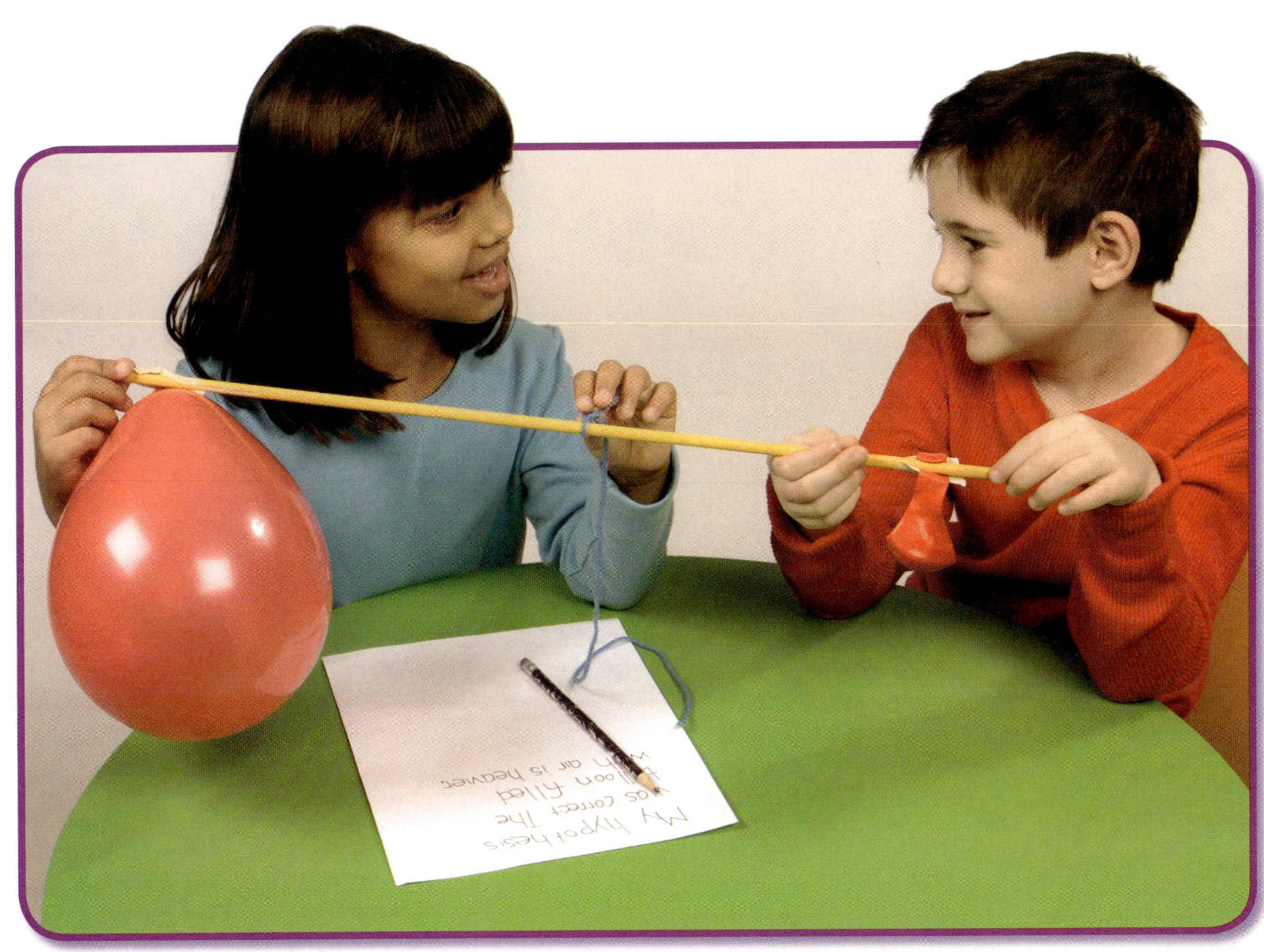

Record What You Observe

Scientists record what they observe. You can also record what you observe. A **pictograph** uses pictures to help you compare numbers of things.

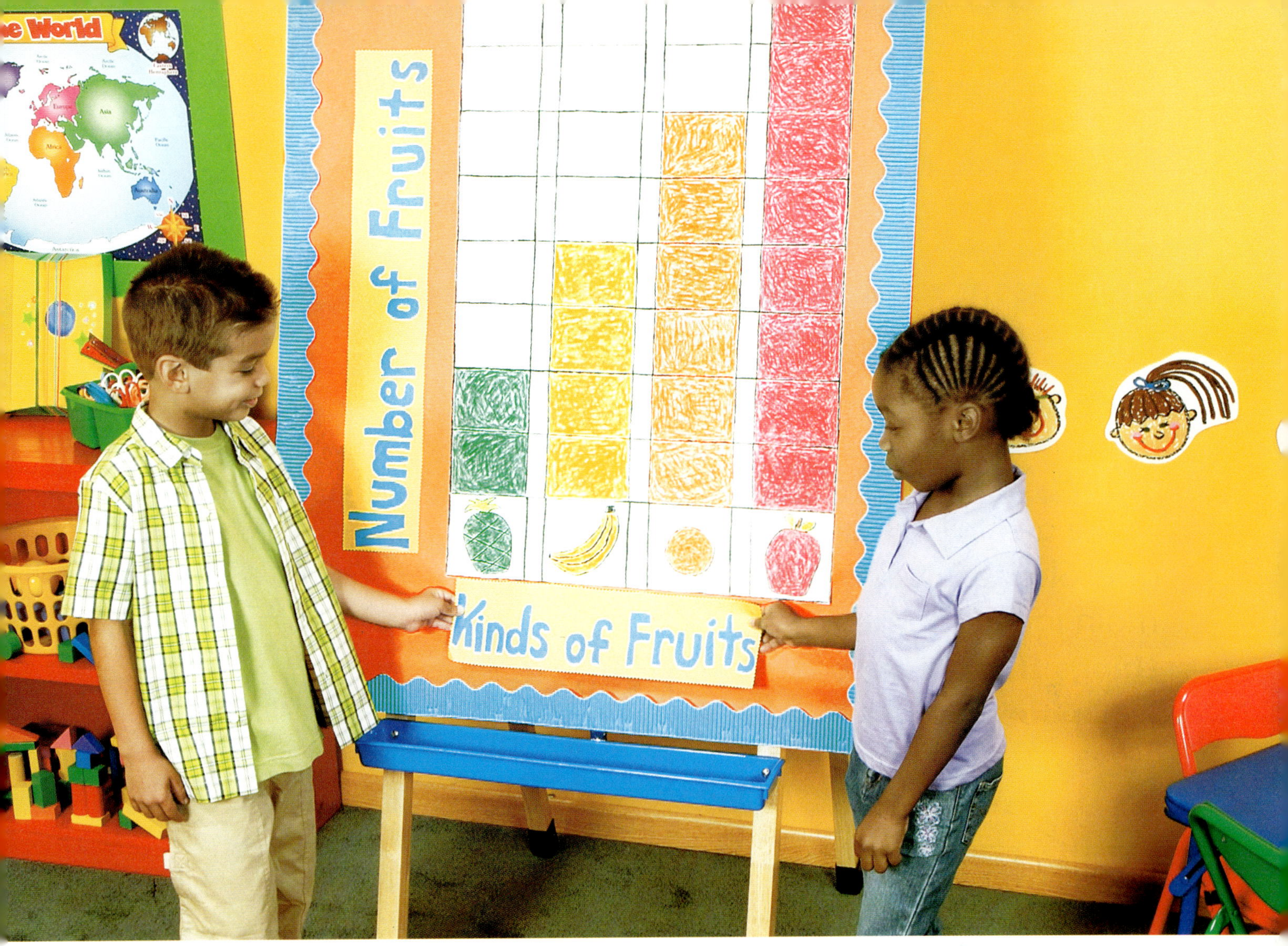

You can use a bar graph to record what you observe. A **bar graph** uses bars to compare things.

MAIN IDEA AND DETAILS

What are some ways you can record what you observe?

Motion Graph

Test some toys. Do they move in a straight path, a curved path, a zigzag path, or a circle? Record. Then make a bar graph to show how many toys move in each way.

GPS Wrap-Up and Lesson Review

Essential Question

How do scientists work?

In this lesson, you learned about the steps that scientists follow in order to test things.

1. Focus Skill **MAIN IDEA AND DETAILS** Make a chart like this one. Show details of this main idea. **Scientists test things they want to learn about.**  S1CS1a

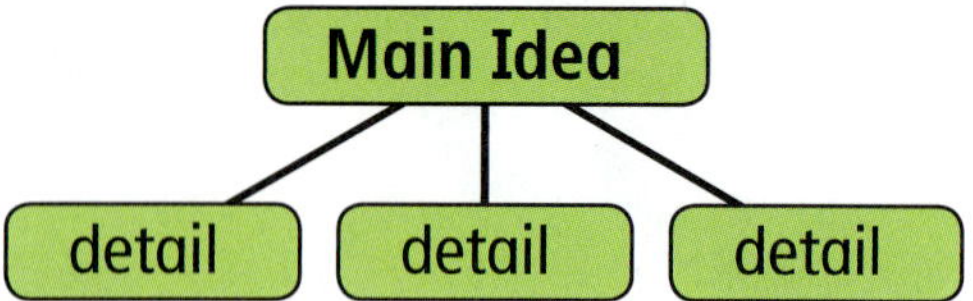

2. **DRAW CONCLUSIONS** How can you work like a scientist to test your ideas? S1CS6c

3. **VOCABULARY** Use the words **bar graph** to tell about this picture. S1CS5c

4. Why do scientists record what they observe? S1CS1a

CRCT Practice

5. What step follows observe and question?

A Do the test.
B Form a hypothesis.
C Plan the test. S1CS6b

The Big Idea

6. What steps do you follow when you test an idea? S1CS1a

Writing

ELA1W1a

Write About How to Make a Plan

1. Write a plan of what you do in the morning to get ready for school.
2. Draw three pictures to show what you do.
3. Put the pictures in order. Label them **first**, **next**, and **last**.

Math

M1D1a

Make a Pictograph

1. Observe children on the playground.
2. Write how many children play on the swings, on the slide, or with a jump rope.
3. Use the data to make a pictograph.

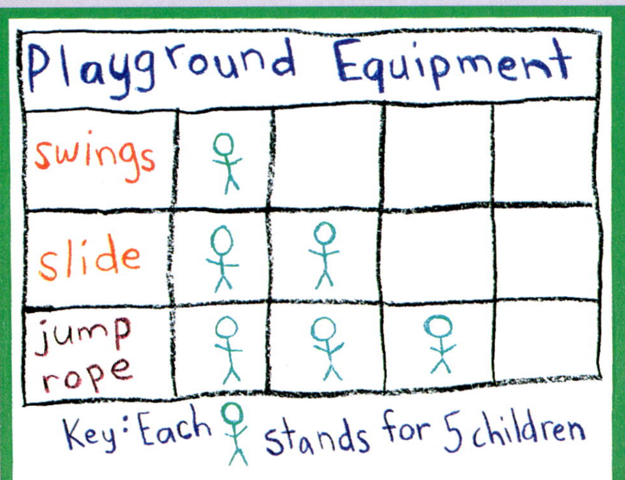

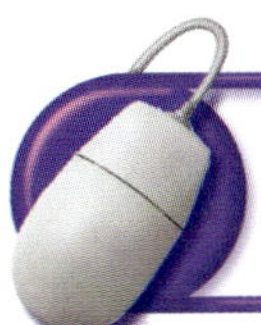

For more links and activities, go to **www.hspscience.com**

Wrap-Up

Visual Summary

Tell how each picture helps explain the **Big Idea**.

Scientists find out about things by asking questions and doing investigations.

Lesson 1 S1CS1a, S1CS4a,c, S1CS5a

Scientists use inquiry skills to find out about things. You can use inquiry skills to find out about things, too.

Lesson 2 S1CS3a,c, S1CS7c

Scientists use tools to find out about things. You can you use science tools to help you observe, compare, and measure things.

Lesson 3 S1CS1a, S1CS5c, S1CS6a,b,c, S1CS7b

You can write a plan to find out things you want to know. Follow your plan. Record what you observe. Compare answers with your classmates. If you get different answers, do your test again.

Show What You Know

Famous Scientists/Write to Inform

Choose a famous scientist. Go to the library. Find out about the scientist you chose. Write a paragraph about who that person is. Tell what he or she is famous for. Dress like your scientist when you read your paragraph to the class. ELA1W1a

Georgia Performance Task

Think Like a Scientist

Work with a partner. Plan an investigation. Do the investigation together. Write down the steps you took to do the investigation. Write down the science tools you used. Then write down your results. Share your results with the class. S1CS1a

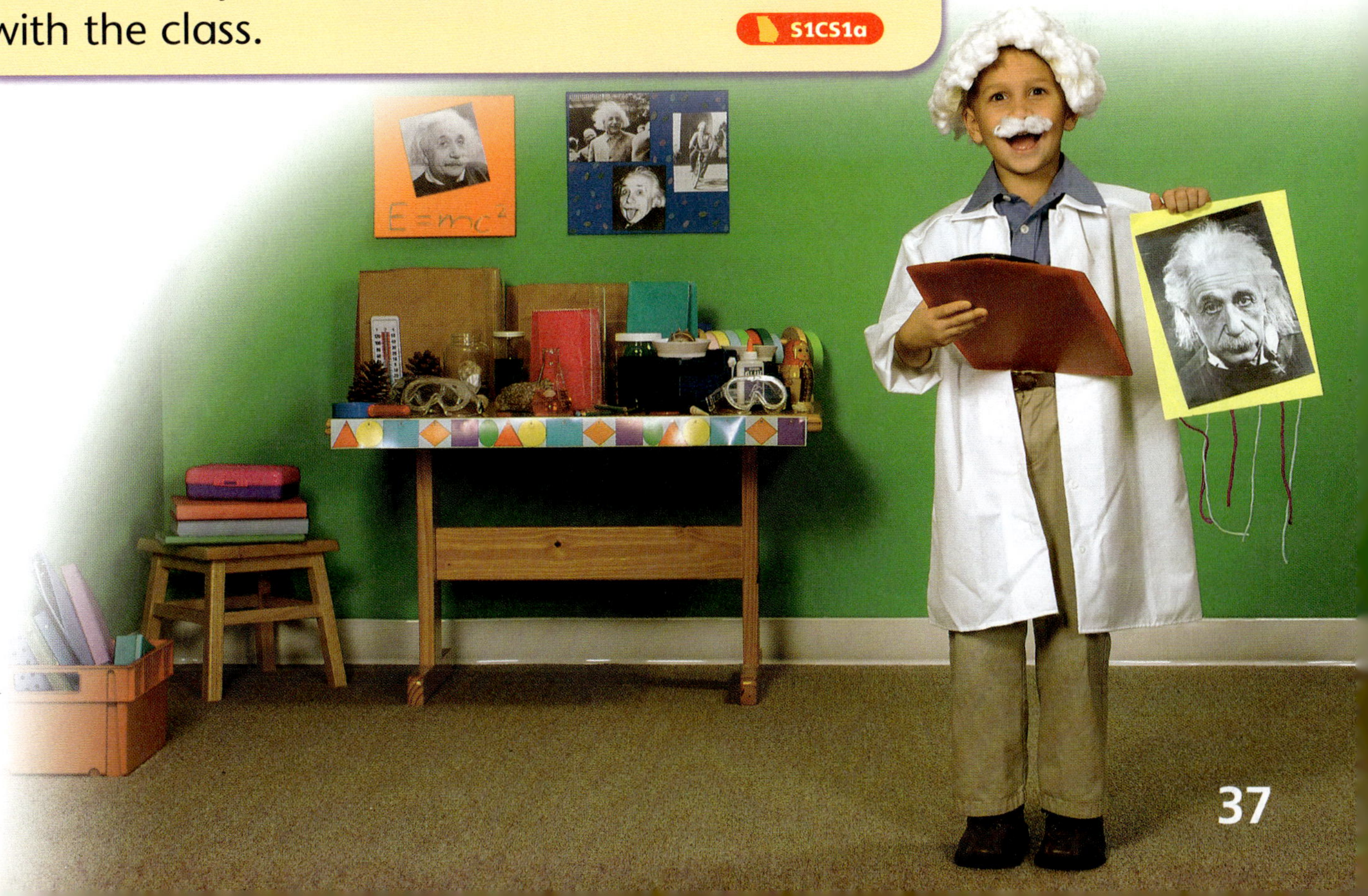

Vocabulary Review

Use the words to complete the sentences. The page numbers tell you where to look if you need help.

inquiry skills p. 6
observe p. 10
science tools p. 18
pictograph p. 32
bar graph p. 33

1. A ______ uses pictures to compare things. S1CS5c
2. Droppers and rulers are ______. S1CS3a
3. A ______ uses bars to compare things. S1CS5c
4. Compare and observe are two ______. S1CS5a
5. When you ______, you use your senses to find out about things. S1CS1a

Check Understanding

6. Which one of these science tools would you use to measure liquid? S1CS3a

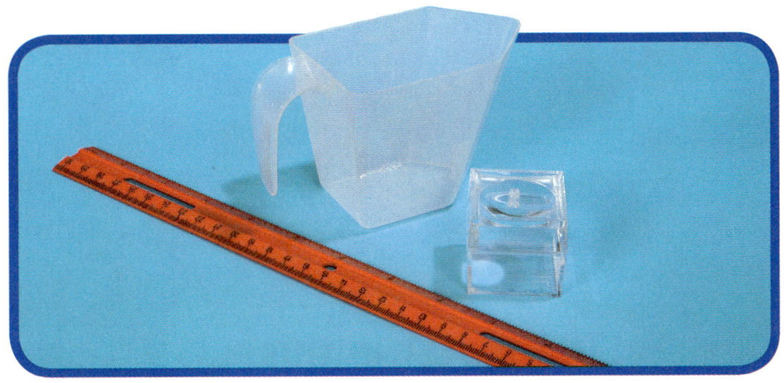

Critical Thinking

7. You did an investigation. You and your classmates got different answers. What should you do? S1CS6a S1CS6c

The Big Idea

8. Tell how doing investigations, observing, and asking questions help you find out what you want to know. S1CS1a

UNIT A

EARTH SCIENCE

The water in this waterfall is a liquid.

GO online for student eBook www.hspscience.com

What do YOU wonder?

This water is liquid. What could make it change to a solid?

Unit Inquiry

Evaporation How does the shape of a puddle affect evaporation? Plan and do a test to find out.

CHAPTER 2

Weather and the Seasons

Georgia Performance Standards in This Chapter

Content

S1E1 Students will observe, measure, and communicate weather data to see patterns in weather and climate.

S1E1a S1E1b S1E1c

This chapter also addresses these co-requisite standards:

Characteristics of Science

S1CS2 Students will have the computation and estimation skills necessary for analyzing data and following scientific explanations.

S1CS2a

S1CS3 Students will use tools and instruments for observing, measuring, and manipulating objects in scientific activities.

S1CS3a

S1CS4 Students will use the ideas of system, model, change, and scale in exploring scientific and technological matters.

S1CS4a S1CS4b

S1CS5 Students will communicate scientific ideas and activities clearly.

S1CS5a

S1CS6 Students will be familiar with the character of scientific knowledge and how it is achieved.

S1CS6a S1CS6c

S1CS7 Students will understand important features of the process of scientific inquiry.

S1CS7c

What's the Big Idea?

Weather patterns help you observe, measure, and communicate about weather.

Essential Questions

for student eBook www.hspscience.com

Science in Georgia

Jekyll Island

Dear Sumi,

My family went to the Georgia Coast Kite Festival. The weather was windy and sunny. We got to make our own kites. Then we got to fly them. Mine won a prize. It flew the highest.

See you soon!

Ana

Read Ana's postcard. What did she learn about weather? How does that help explain the **Big Idea?**

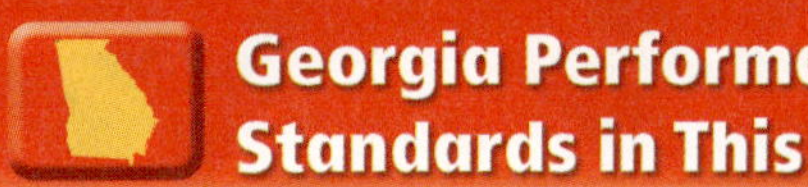

Georgia Performance Standards in This Lesson

LESSON 1

Essential Question

What Is Weather?

Content

S1E1a Identify different types of weather and the characteristics of each type.

Characteristics of Science

S1CS5a

Georgia Fast Fact

The Atlanta Braves

The Braves can play baseball in light rain. They can not play if it is raining too hard or if it is lightning. The game will be rained-out.

Vocabulary Preview
weather p. 48
Atlanta Braves baseball game
JONES
PIAZZA
31

Investigate

Daily Weather

Guided Inquiry

Ask a Question

What is the weather in the photograph like? Investigate to find out. Then read to find out more.

Get Ready

Inquiry Skill Tip

When you compare objects, you see how they are alike and different.

You need

paper

markers

What to Do

Step 1

Observe the weather each day for two weeks.

Step 2

Make a chart. Record what you see.

Step 3

Compare the weather from day to day. Do you see any patterns? Predict next week's weather.

Draw Conclusions

What did you find out about predicting weather?

Independent Inquiry

Blow on your hand. Spray water on your other hand and blow on it. **Compare** how your hands feel.

Understand Science

S1E1a

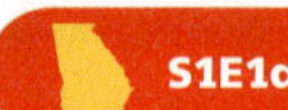

VOCABULARY
weather

Focus Skill COMPARE AND CONTRAST

Look for ways in which weather can be different from day to day.

Weather

Weather is what the air outside is like. You can see and feel the weather. It may be warm or cool. It may be snowy, windy, rainy, cloudy, or sunny.

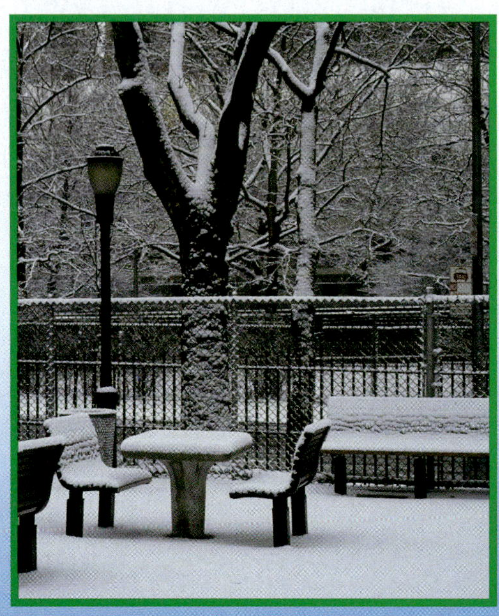

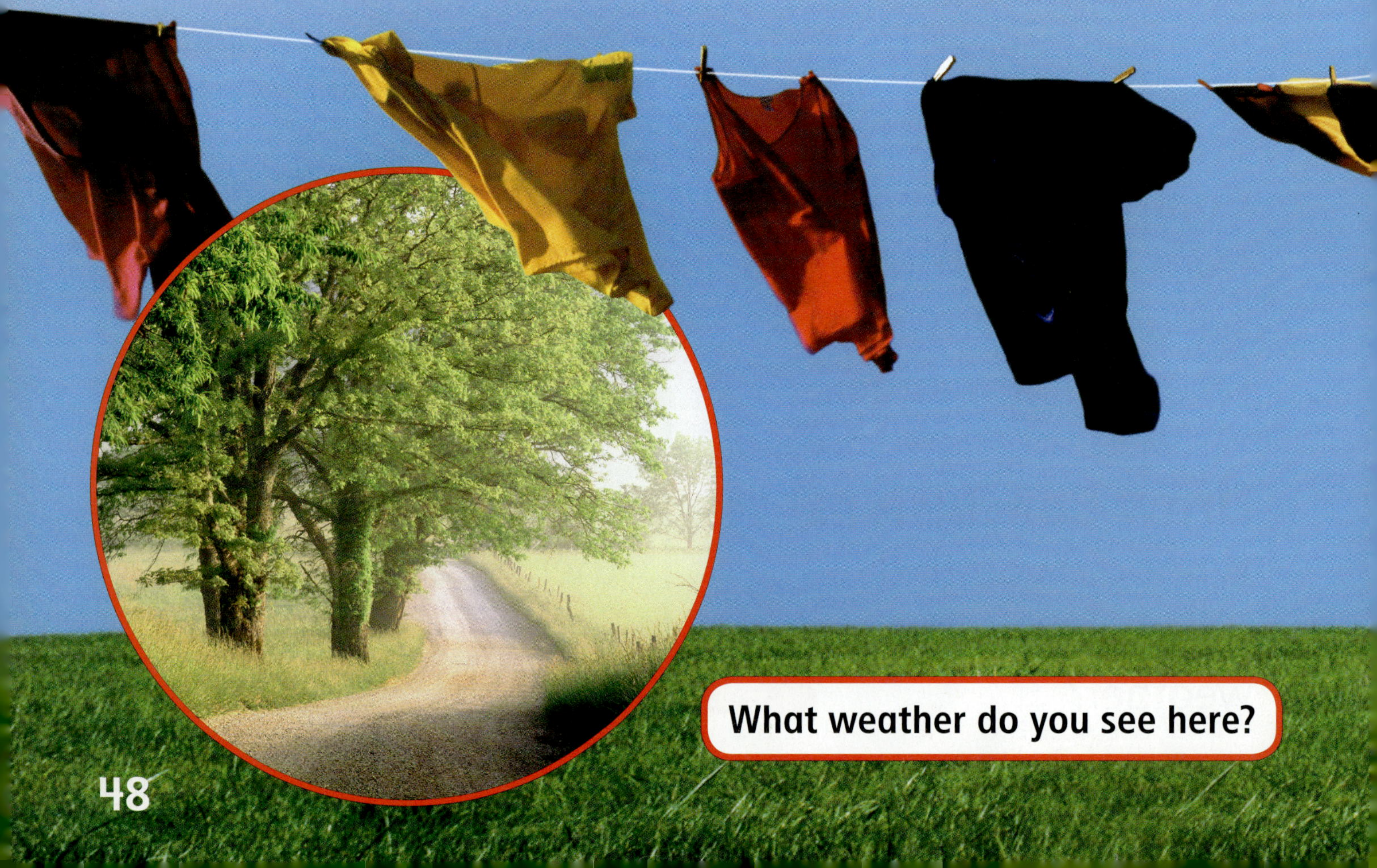

What weather do you see here?

Weather can change. It may be sunny one day. The next day may be cloudy and rainy. It may be cold for many days. Then it may warm up. One day may be windy. Another day may be calm.

Focus Skill **COMPARE AND CONTRAST**

How can weather be different from day to day?

Observing Weather

Look out the window. Observe the sky. Observe what people are wearing. What can you tell about the weather? Repeat each day for a week. Make a chart to show weather data.

Types of Weather

When it is sunny, you can see the sun shining bright in the sky. The sun makes the air warm. If it is cloudy, clouds might cover the sun. The air is cool.

sunny

cloudy

You might see low, gray clouds when it is rainy. When it is snowy, you might also see dark, gray clouds. The air is cold. If it is windy, you might see the leaves on trees blow.

COMPARE AND CONTRAST

How are a sunny day and a rainy day different?

low, gray clouds

leaves blowing in the wind

GPS Wrap-Up and Lesson Review

Essential Question

What is weather?

In this lesson, you learned that weather can be snowy, windy, rainy, cloudy, or sunny.

1. **COMPARE AND CONTRAST** Make a chart like this one. Show how weather can be different from day to day. S1E1a

   alike — different

2. **SUMMARIZE** Write a summary. Tell what you learned about weather. S1E1a

3. **VOCABULARY** Tell about the **weather** in this picture. S1E1a

4. Tell what a rainy day is like. S1E1a

CRCT Practice

5. There are no clouds. What is the weather like?
   - **A** It is cloudy.
   - **B** It is rainy.
   - **C** It is sunny. S1E1a

The Big Idea

6. Draw a picture to show different kinds of weather. S1E1a

Writing

"Sun" Words

1. Make cards. On one side of each card, draw a picture of a "sun" word.
2. On the other side, write the word and a sentence to explain the word.
3. Have a classmate guess your "sun" words by looking at the pictures.

Art

Dressing for the Weather

1. Draw pictures of what to wear during different kinds of weather.
2. Write a sentence to go with each picture.
3. Put your pictures together to make a book.

For more links and activities, go to **www.hspscience.com**

Weather Satellites

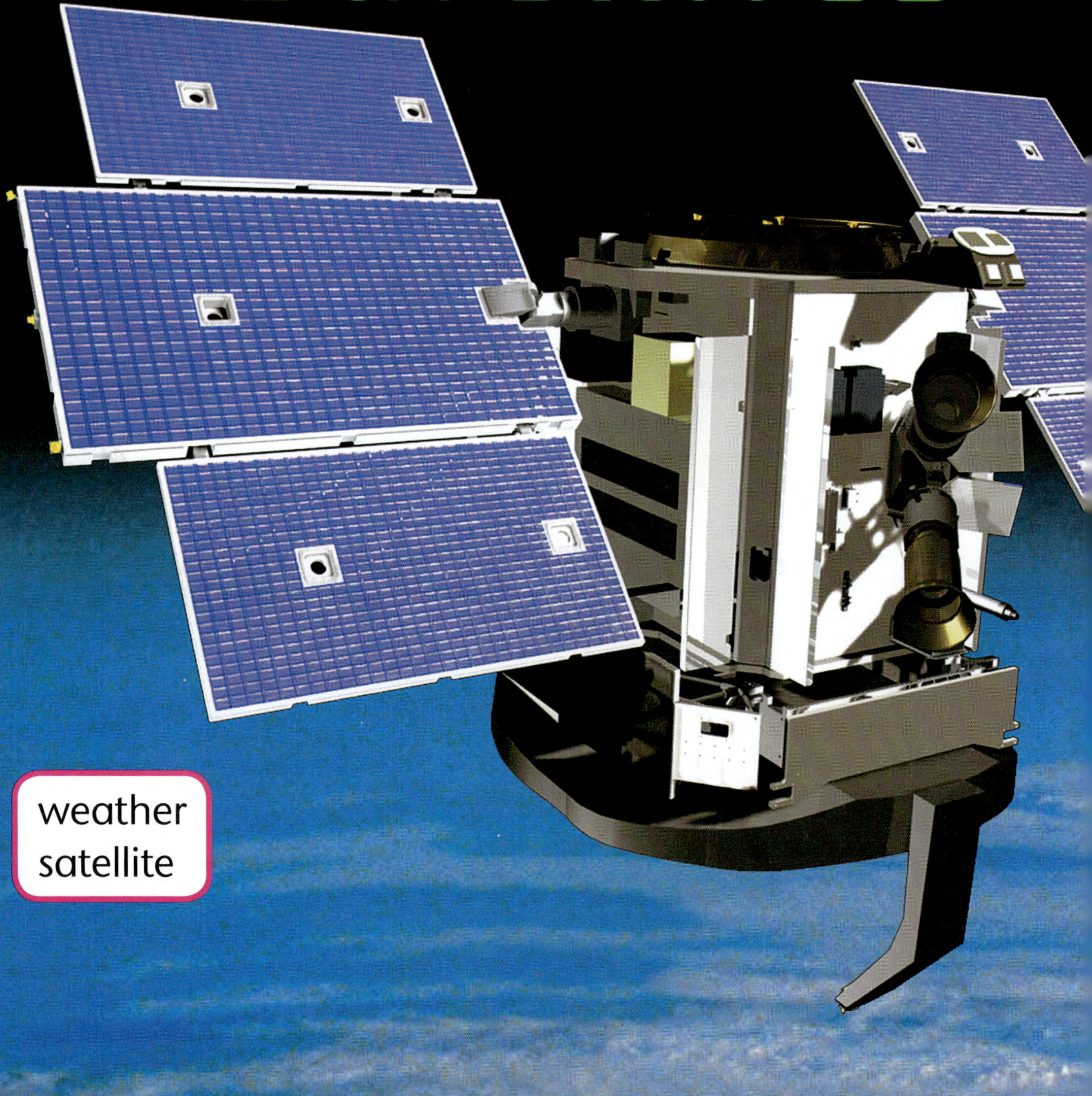

weather satellite

Weather satellites fly very high above Earth. Some weather satellites fly around Earth from the North Pole to the South Pole. Other weather satellites stay above the same place on Earth.

Weather satellites carry cameras that take pictures of Earth. The pictures show clouds in the air. They show snow and ice on the ground. They also show where storms are forming. The satellites send these pictures to Earth. Weather scientists use the pictures to help them predict what the weather will be.

Think and Write

How do weather satellites help scientists predict the weather? S1E1a

picture taken from a weather satellite

Spin-In Find out more. Log on to **www.hspscience.com**

Georgia Performance Standards in This Lesson

Content

S1E1c Correlate weather data (temperature, precipitation, sky conditions, and weather events) to seasonal changes.

Characteristics of Science

S1CS3a S1CS4b S1CS5a S1CS6a S1CS6c S1CS7c

LESSON 2

Essential Question

How Does Weather Change with Each Season?

Georgia Fast Fact

1996 Summer Olympics

The 1996 Summer Olympics were held in Georgia. Savannah was the only place other than Atlanta where the Olympic flame burned.

Vocabulary Preview

season p. 60

sailing on the Savannah River

How to Stay Warm

Guided Inquiry

Ask a Question

People dress for the weather. What weather are these people dressed for? Investigate to find out. Then read to find out more.

Get Ready

Inquiry Skill Tip

To draw a conclusion, use what you observe to decide what something means.

You need

plastic bag

ice water

mitten

What to Do

Step 1

Put your hand in the bag. Dip the bag into the water. How does your hand feel?

Step 2

Put on the mitten. Repeat Step 1. How does your hand feel?

Step 3

Compare your answers with a classmate's answers. If you get different answers, repeat the Investigate.

Draw Conclusions

What is winter weather like? **Draw a conclusion** about what can help keep you warm in winter.

S1E1c

Independent Inquiry

What do people do in summer? Look at the seasons picture cards. **Infer** which cards show summer.

S1CS1a

VOCABULARY
season

Focus Skill SEQUENCE

Look for the order of the seasons and how weather changes from season to season.

Seasons

A **season** is a time of year. A year has four seasons. The seasons are spring, summer, fall, and winter. They form a pattern. After every winter, spring comes.

Focus Skill SEQUENCE

What season comes after summer?

Spring starts in the month of March.

Science Up Close
Seasons
spring
summer
fall
winter
For more links and animations,
go to www.hspscience.com

Spring

The weather changes from season to season. You can predict what the weather will be like in each season. In spring, the air gets warmer. In some places, spring weather is very rainy.

spring

How does the air change in spring?

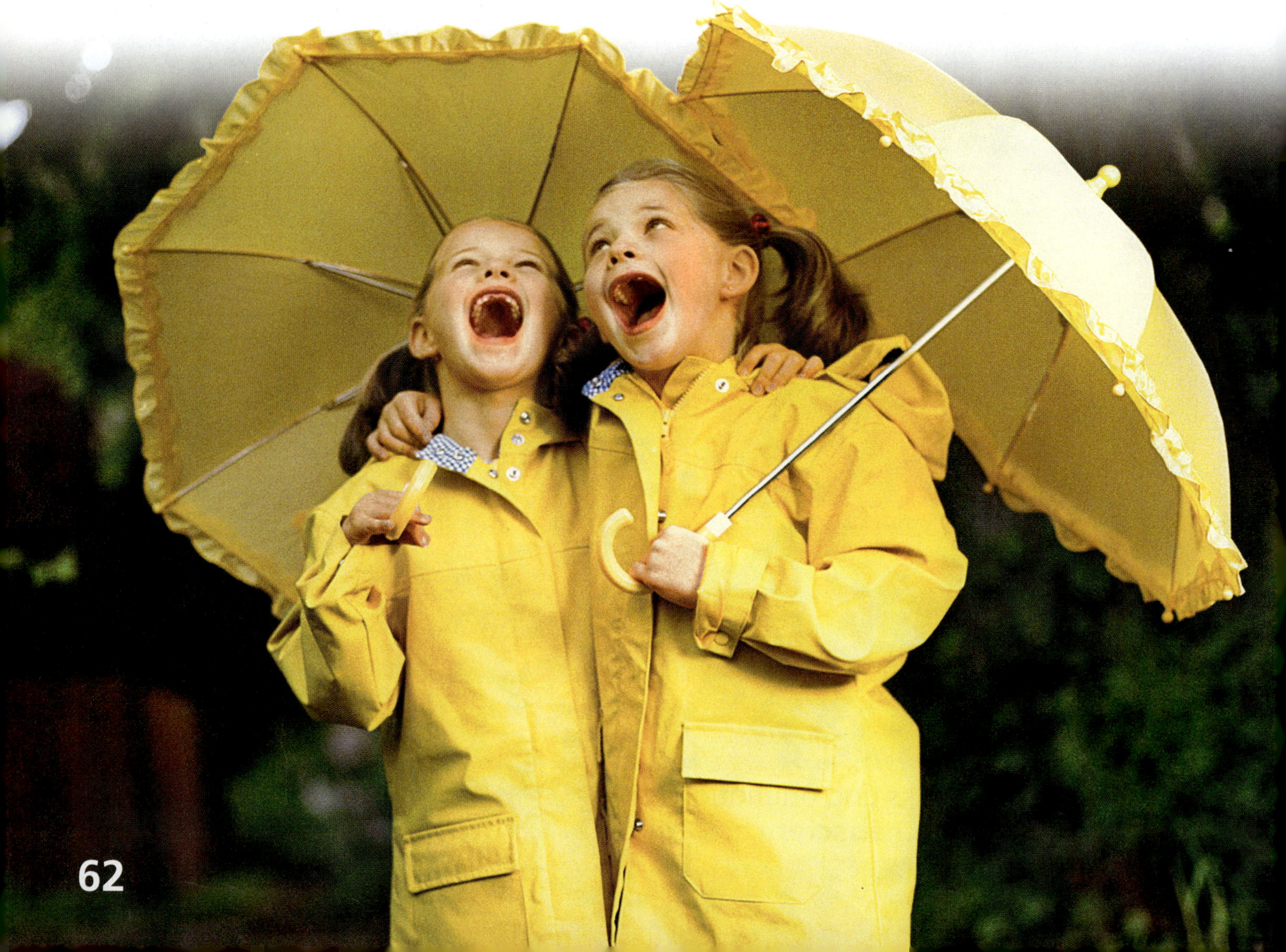

Summer

Summer comes after spring. Summer is usually the warmest time of the year. Summer days are often hot and sunny. In summer, storms can quickly change the weather.

summer

Focus Skill SEQUENCE

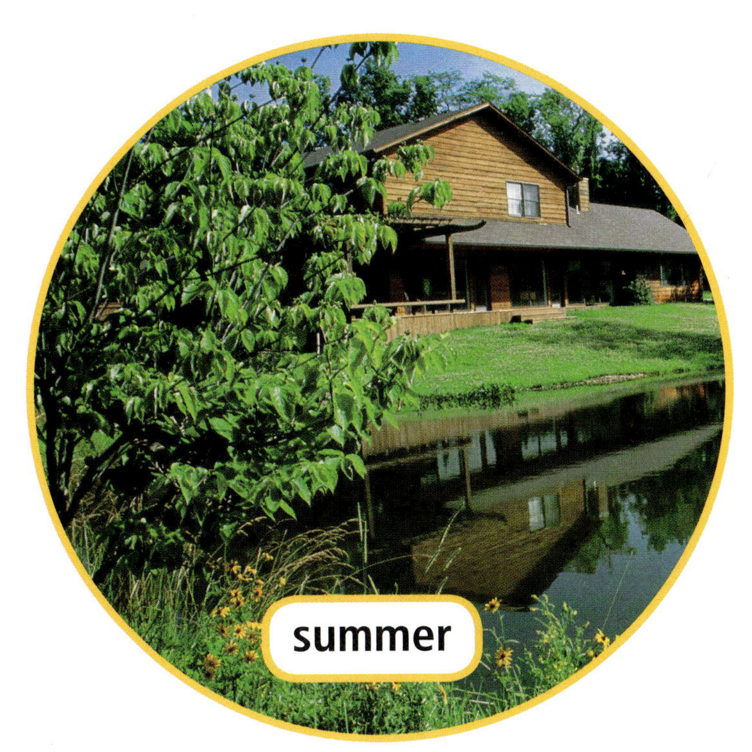

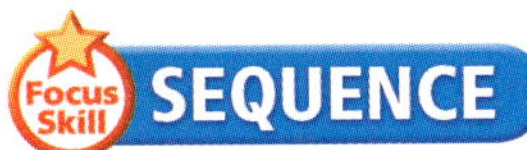

Which season comes after spring?

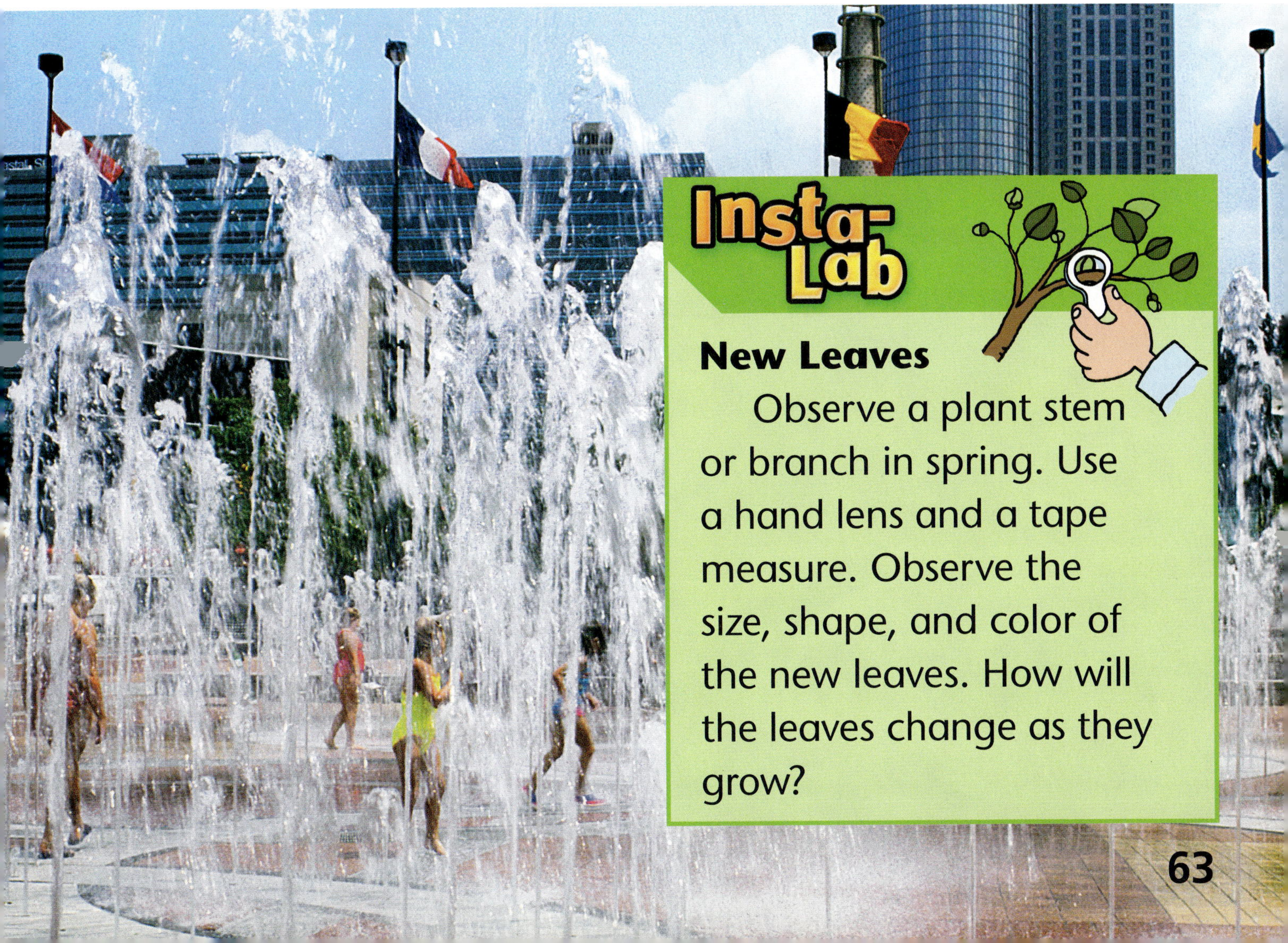

Insta-Lab

New Leaves

Observe a plant stem or branch in spring. Use a hand lens and a tape measure. Observe the size, shape, and color of the new leaves. How will the leaves change as they grow?

Fall

Fall is the next season. In fall, the air gets cooler. Some fall days are sunny. Some other fall days are cloudy.

Focus Skill SEQUENCE

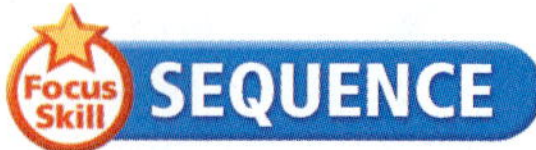

How does weather change from summer to fall?

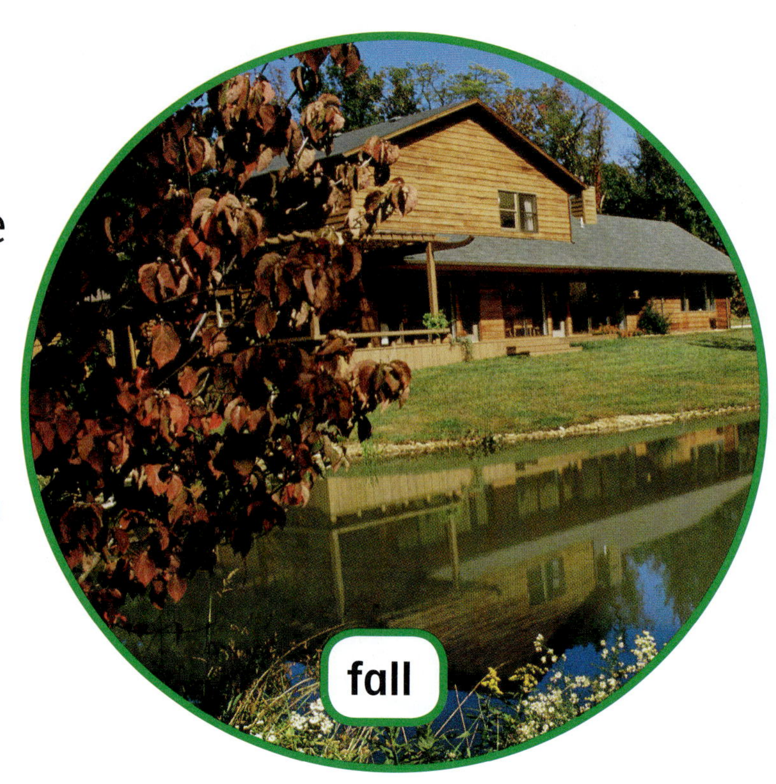

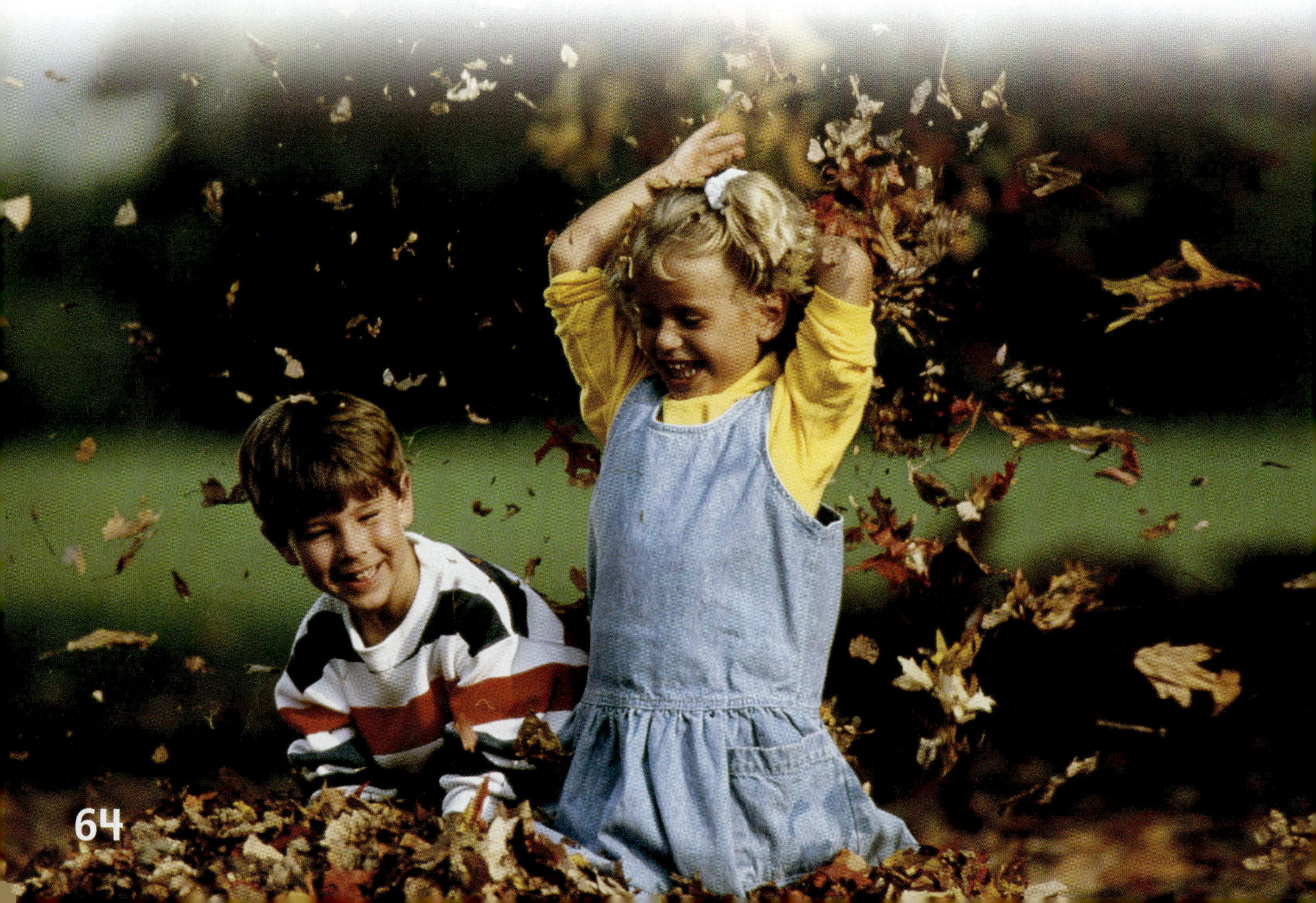

Winter

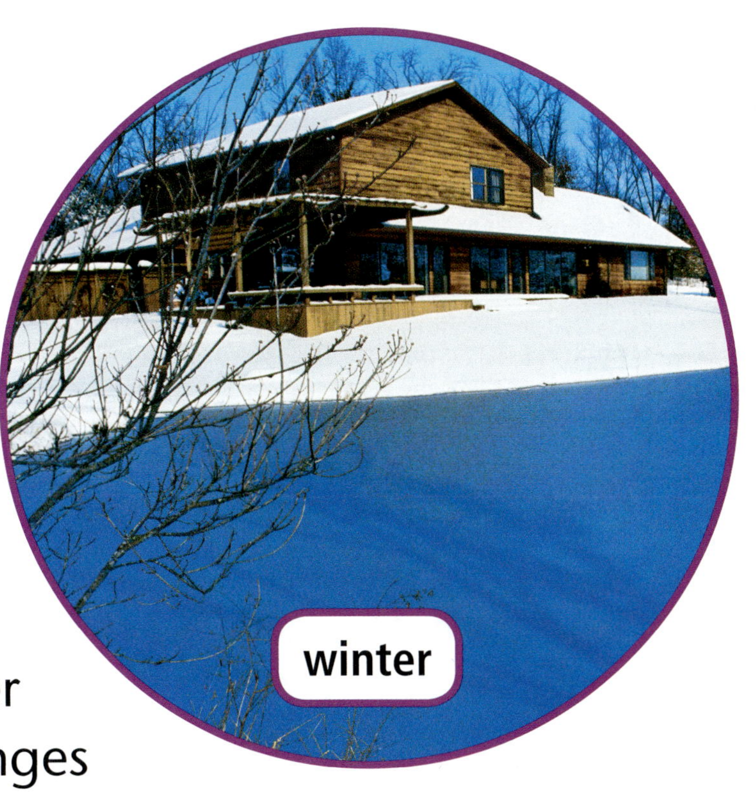

Winter comes after fall. Winter is the coldest season.

In some places, snow falls. In other places, the air cools down just a little. It does not snow there.

Spring comes again after winter. The pattern of changes from season to season repeats.

Focus Skill **SEQUENCE**

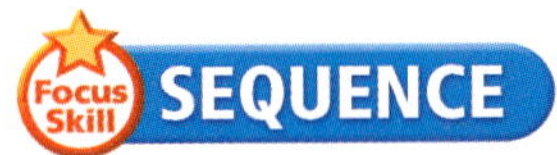

What happens when winter ends?

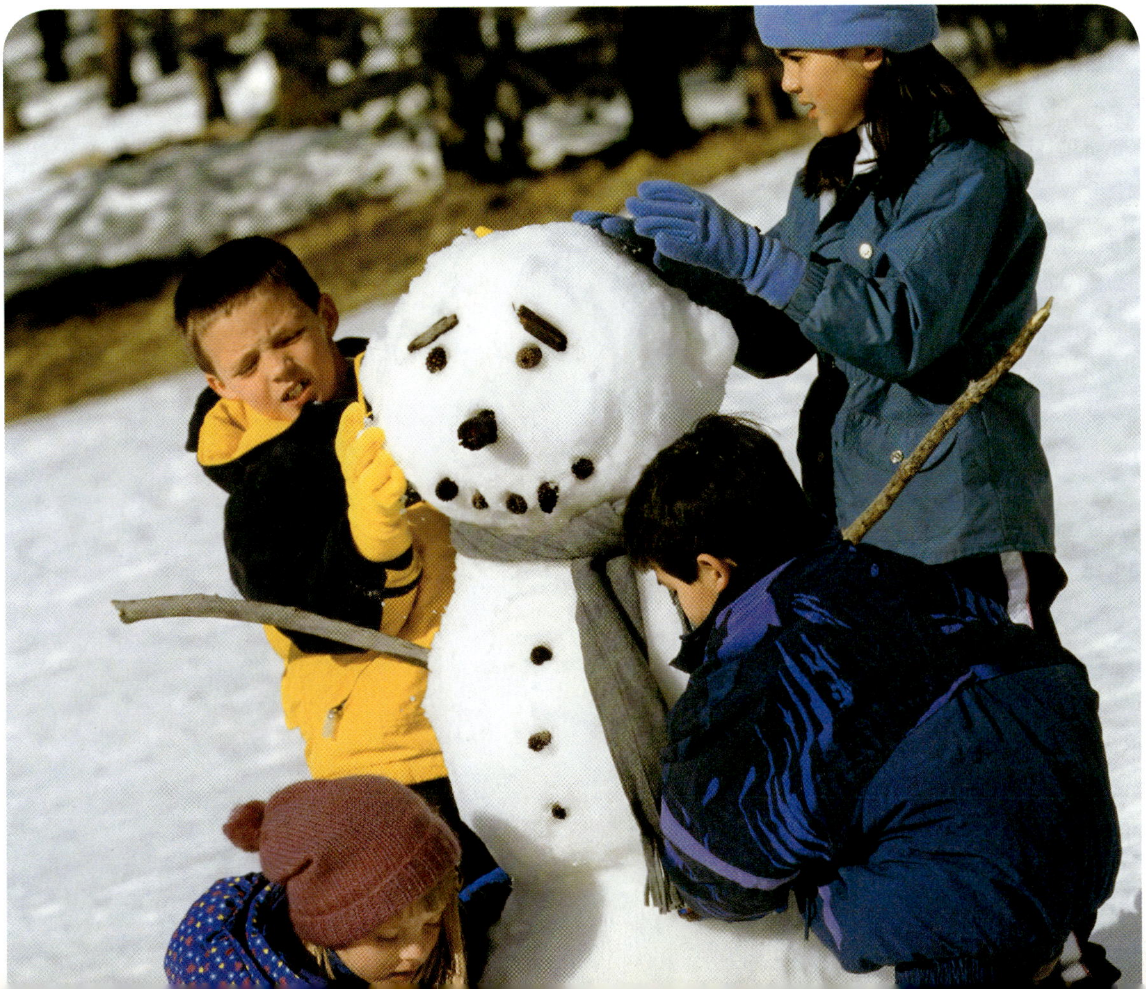

GPS Wrap-Up and Lesson Review

Essential Question

How does weather change with each season?

In this lesson, you learned that the weather for each season can be predicted.

1. **SEQUENCE** Make a chart like this one. Tell how weather changes with the seasons. S1E1c

2. **DRAW CONCLUSIONS** Why can you predict what the weather will be like in each season? S1E1c

3. **VOCABULARY** Use the word **season** to tell about this picture. S1E1c

4. How is winter different in different places? S1E1c

CRCT Practice

5. What season comes after winter?
   A fall
   B spring
   C summer S1E1c

The Big Idea

6. Fold a sheet of paper into four parts. Draw pictures to show the weather for each season. S1E1c

 Writing  ELA1R5a

Write to Inform

1. Think about what one season is like where you live. Write a weather report for one day of that season.
2. Present your weather report to the class. Use a map to point out your city.

 Math  M1M2b

Use a Calendar

1. Use a calendar to answer these questions.
2. How many months are in summer? What are their names?
3. When does summer begin? When does it end?

For more links and activities, go to **www.hspscience.com**

Mary Anderson

Mary Anderson
- Inventor
- Invented windshield wipers

The first cars did not have windshield wipers. Drivers got out of their cars to wipe rain or snow off their windshields.

In the early 1900s, Mary Anderson saw drivers stop to clean their windshields. She thought there had to be a better way. She thought of an idea for a new windshield wiper. A driver could turn it on and off from inside the car. Today all cars have windshield wipers.

Think and Write

What do you think it would be like today if cars did not have windshield wipers? S1E1a

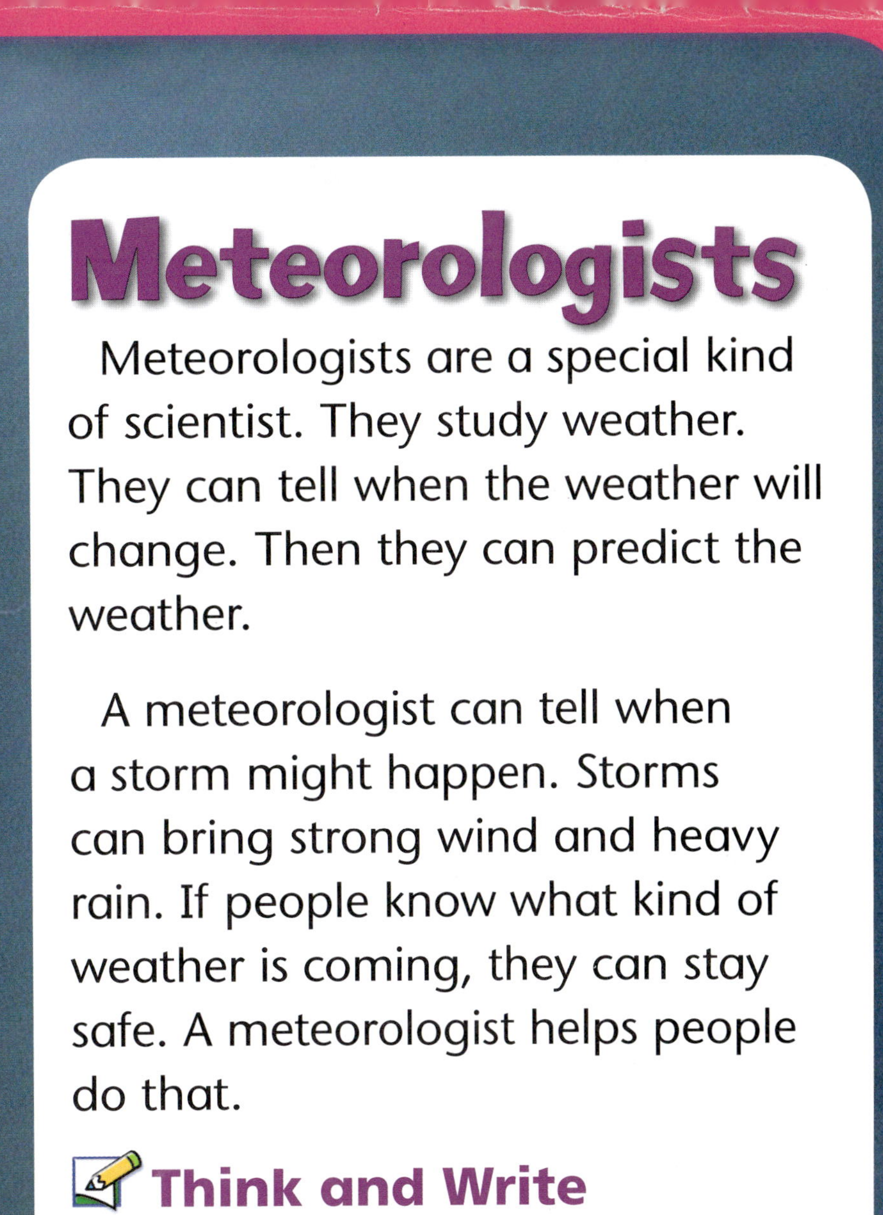

Meteorologists

Meteorologists are a special kind of scientist. They study weather. They can tell when the weather will change. Then they can predict the weather.

A meteorologist can tell when a storm might happen. Storms can bring strong wind and heavy rain. If people know what kind of weather is coming, they can stay safe. A meteorologist helps people do that.

Think and Write

Why is predicting the weather important?

Georgia Performance Standards in This Lesson

LESSON 3

Essential Question

How Can We Measure Weather?

Content

S1E1b Investigate weather by observing, measuring with simple weather instruments (thermometer, wind vane, rain gauge), and recording weather data (temperature, precipitation, sky conditions, and weather events) in a periodic journal or on a calendar seasonally.

Characteristics of Science

S1CS2a S1CS3a

S1CS7c

Georgia Fast Fact

The Weather Channel

The Weather Channel uses tools, such as computers, to track and measure weather.

Vocabulary Preview

temperature p. 75

thermometer p. 75

wind vane p. 76

rain gauge p. 77

Investigate

Measure Weather

Guided Inquiry

Ask a Question

Which thermometer shows what the temperature might be on a cold day? Investigate to find out. Then read to find out more.

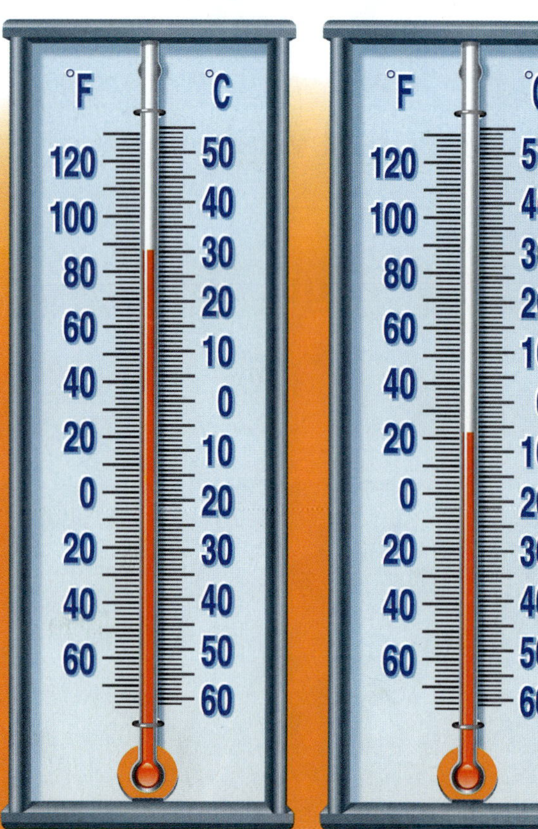

Get Ready

Inquiry Skill Tip

When you measure, you find the size or amount of something.

You need

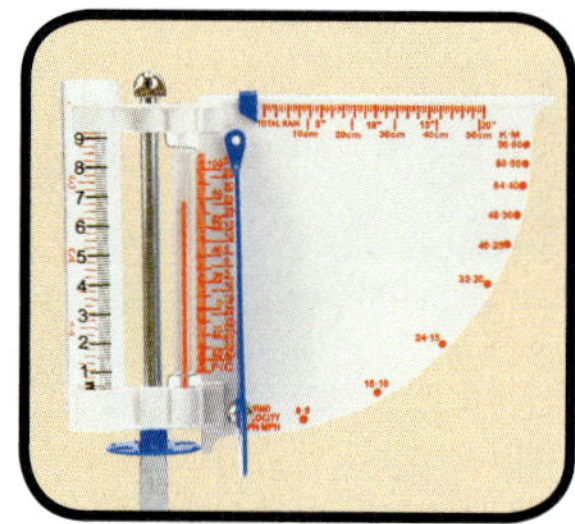

weather station

What to Do

Step 1

Measure the weather each day for five days. Use a thermometer, a wind vane, and a rain gauge or a weather station.

Step 2

Use numbers and words to record your measurements.

Step 3

How did the weather change from day to day? Share your information.

Draw Conclusions

How do tools help you measure weather? S1E1b

Independent Inquiry

Measure the weather in different seasons. Record your measurements. How did the weather change with the seasons? S1CS3a S1CS7c

Understand Science

VOCABULARY
temperature
thermometer
wind vane
rain gauge

Look for the main ideas about measuring weather.

Measuring Weather

You can use tools to measure weather. Measuring weather helps you see patterns. Patterns help you predict the weather.

What does measuring weather help you do?

measuring rainfall

Measuring Temperature

One way to measure weather is to find the temperature. **Temperature** is the measure of how hot or cold something is.

A **thermometer** is a tool for measuring temperature. You look at the numbers to see how hot or cold the air is. Hot air makes the colored liquid go up. Cold air makes the colored liquid go down.

Focus Skill MAIN IDEA AND DETAILS

How can you find out how warm the air outside is?

thermometer

Measuring Wind

You can measure wind, too. Wind is moving air. A **wind vane** shows which way the wind is blowing from. The wind turns the arrow on the wind vane. The arrow points to the direction the wind is coming from.

What tool measures the direction of the wind?

wind vane

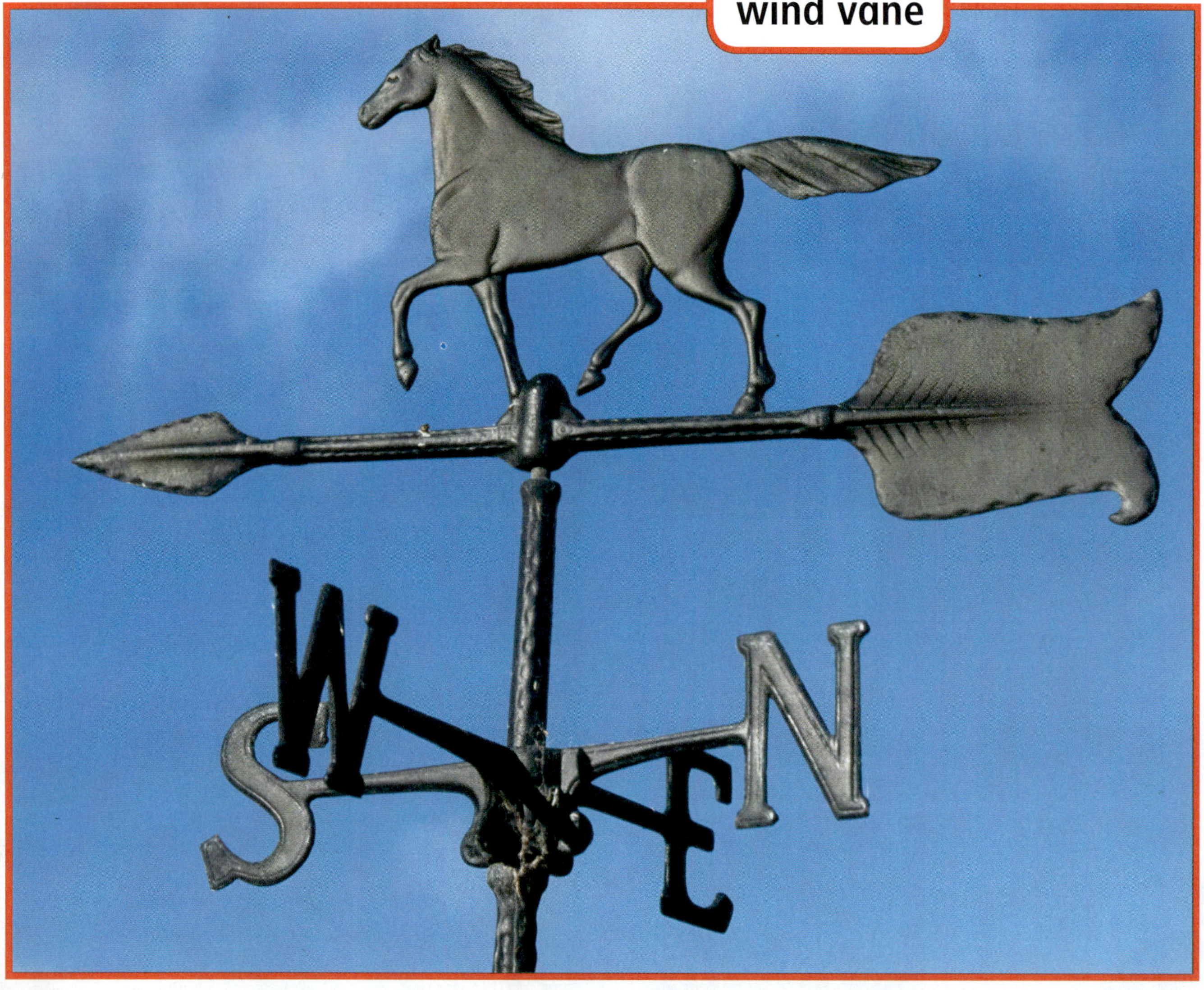

Measuring Rain

You can use a **rain gauge** to measure how much rain falls. A rain gauge catches rain. The numbers show how much rain has fallen.

Focus Skill **MAIN IDEA AND DETAILS**

What tool can you use to measure how much rain has fallen?

rain gauge

Insta-Lab

Observe Wind

Go outside. Use soap bubbles to blow bubbles or hold up a pinwheel. Which way is the wind blowing? How strong is the wind?

GPS Wrap-Up and Lesson Review

Essential Question

How can we measure weather?

In this lesson, you learned how to use a thermometer, a wind vane, and a rain gauge to measure weather.

1. **MAIN IDEA AND DETAILS** Make a chart like this one. Show the details of this main idea. **You can use tools to measure weather.** S1E1b

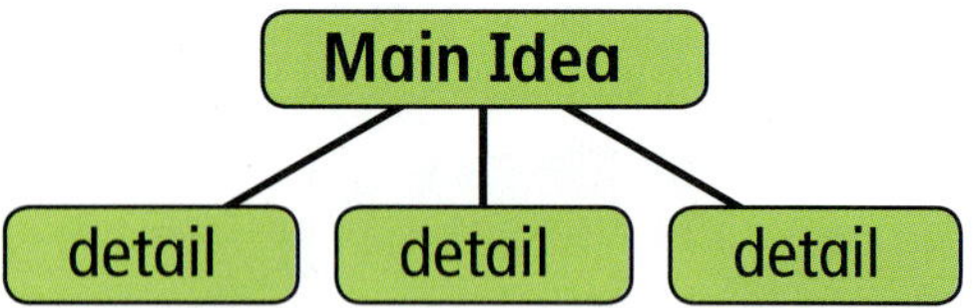

2. **SUMMARIZE** Tell some ways you can measure weather. S1E1b

3. **VOCABULARY** Use the words **thermometer** and **temperature** to tell about this picture. S1E1b

4. How can measuring weather help people? S1E1b

CRCT Practice

5. Which tool would you use to measure how much rain had fallen?
   - **A** a hand lens
   - **B** a rain gauge
   - **C** a thermometer S1E1b

The Big Idea

6. What are three tools you can use to measure weather? S1E1b

Writing

Keep a Weather Journal

1. Keep a weather journal.
2. How does the weather change with each season? What tools can you use to find out?
3. Write sentences to describe the weather. Draw pictures to show the changes.

Math

Make a Bar Graph

1. This chart shows the temperature for a city in some months.
2. Use the data to make a bar graph.
3. Share your graph with the class.

Augusta, Georgia Data	
month	temperature
January	44°F
February	47°F
October	64°F
November	55°F

For more links and activities, go to **www.hspscience.com**

Wrap-Up

Visual Summary

Tell how each picture helps explain the **Big Idea**.

The Big Idea **Weather patterns help you observe, measure, and communicate about weather.**

Lesson 1 S1E1a

Weather changes from day to day. Weather may be sunny or cloudy. It may be windy, rainy, or snowy.

Lesson 2 S1E1c

Weather changes from season to season. You can predict what the weather will be like in each season. The weather in each season is the same year after year.

Lesson 3 S1E1b

You can use weather tools to observe and measure things about the weather. A rain gauge measures how much rain has fallen.

Show What You Know

Chapter Writing Activity

Weather Sayings/Write to Describe

Long ago, sailors looked for patterns to predict the weather. Observe the weather for a week. Look for patterns. Make up a weather saying about a pattern you observe. ELA1W1b

Georgia Performance Task

Record Data for a Week of Weather

Make a weather chart for one week. Check the temperature and the wind. Is it cloudy or sunny? Is it raining or snowing? Give a weather report to the class. Repeat in three months. Then compare your two charts. Predict what the weather will be like in another three months. S1E1a, b, c

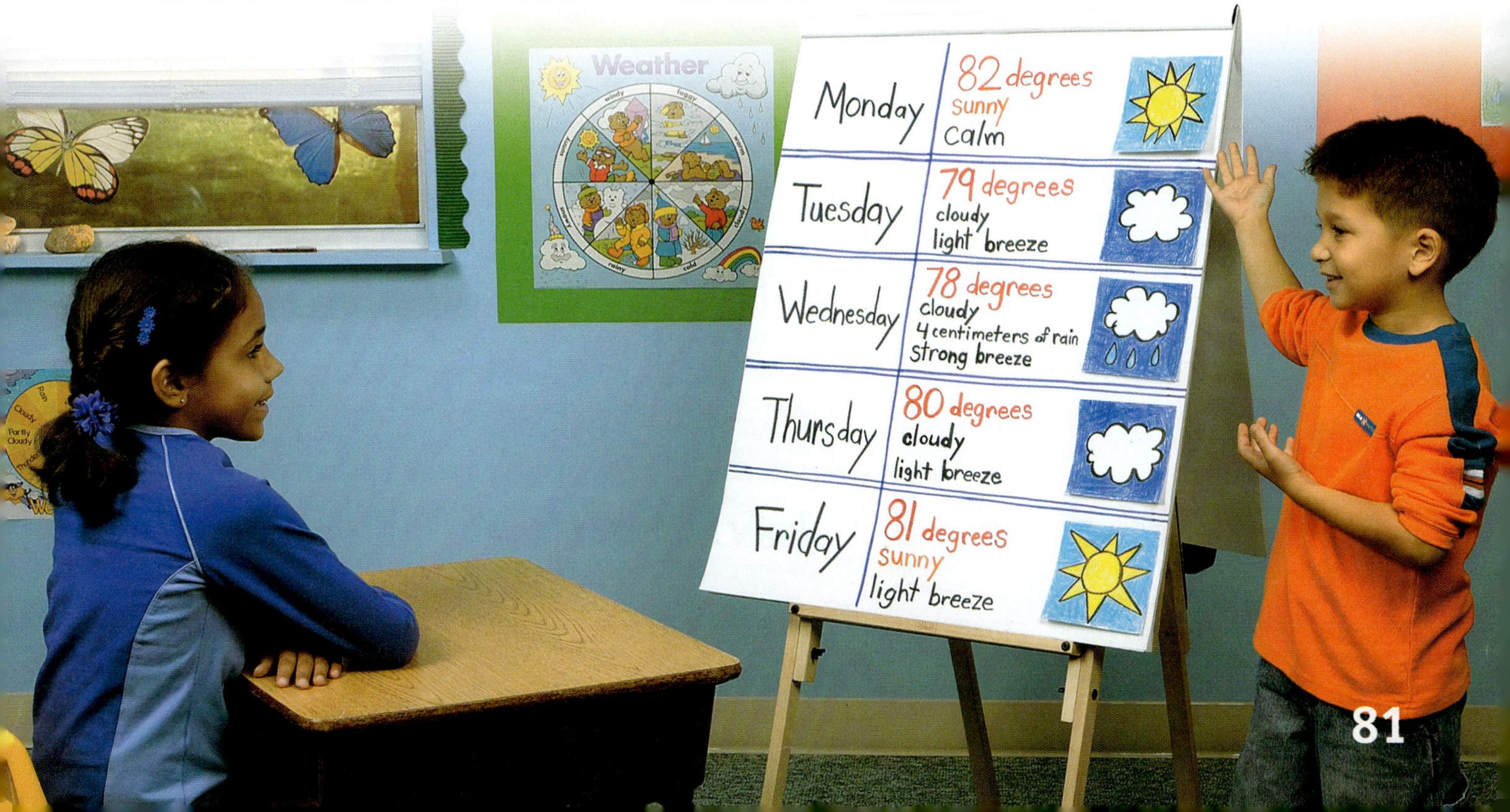

Vocabulary Review

Use the words to complete the sentences. The page numbers tell you where to look if you need help.

weather p. 48	**thermometer** p. 75
season p. 60	**wind vane** p. 76
temperature p. 75	**rain gauge** p. 77

1. A _______ is a tool for measuring temperature. S1E1b
2. A _______ is a time of year. S1E1c
3. The _______ is what the air outside is like. S1E1a
4. A _______ is a tool that shows which way the wind blows from. S1E1b
5. The _______ of something is the measure of how hot or cold it is. S1E1b
6. A _______ is a tool that measures how much rain falls. S1E1b

Check Understanding

7. How does weather change between summer and fall? S1E1c

A It gets cold enough to snow in fall.

B It gets cooler in the fall.

C It gets warmer in the fall.

8. Tell what each of these tools does. S1E1b

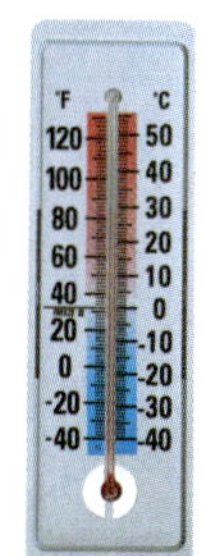

Critical Thinking

9. In what ways can weather change from day to day? S1E1a

The Big Idea

10. Tell how you can observe, measure, and communicate weather data.

Changes in Water

Georgia Performance Standards in This Chapter

Content

S1E2 Students will observe and record changes in water as it relates to weather.

S1E2a S1E2b

S1E2c S1E2d

This chapter also includes these co-requisite standards:

Characteristics of Science

S1CS2 Students will have the computation and estimation skills necessary for analyzing data and following scientific explanations.

S1CS2b S1CS2c S1CS2d

S1CS3 Students will use tools and instruments for observing, measuring, and manipulating objects in scientific activities.

S1CS3a S1CS3b

S1CS4 Students will use the ideas of system, model, change, and scale in exploring scientific and technological matters.

S1CS4a

S1CS5 Students will communicate scientific ideas and activities clearly.

S1CS5a

What's the Big Idea?

You can observe and record changes in water with the weather.

Essential Questions

for student eBook www.hspscience.com

Science in Georgia

Appalachian Trail

Dear Cindy,

I went hiking on the Appalachian Trail with Uncle Joey. There was snow and ice everywhere. Uncle Joey said it would melt in spring. We want to go back then.

Your pal,

Trey

Read Trey's postcard. What did he learn about precipitation? How do you think that helps explain the **Big Idea?**

Georgia Performance Standards in This Lesson

LESSON 1

Essential Question

What Are Some Forms of Precipitation?

Content

S1E1b Investigate weather by observing, measuring with simple weather instruments (thermometer, wind vane, rain gauge), and recording weather data (temperature, precipitation, sky conditions, and weather events) in a periodic journal or on a calendar seasonally.

S1E2b Identify forms of precipitation such as rain, snow, sleet, and hailstones as either solid (ice) or liquid (water).

Characteristics of Science

S1CS2b S1CS3b S1CS4a

Georgia Fast Fact

Brasstown Bald

Brasstown Bald is Georgia's highest mountain peak. From 55 to 65 inches of rain and snow fall there each year.

Vocabulary Preview

precipitation p. 90

sleet p. 91

hail p. 91

Snow in Georgia.

Investigate

Make a Rain Gauge

Guided Inquiry

Ask a Question

What form of precipitation is in this rain gauge? Investigate to find out. Then read to find out more.

rain gauge

Get Ready

Inquiry Skill Tip

When you make a model, you make an object to show how something works.

You need

2 rulers

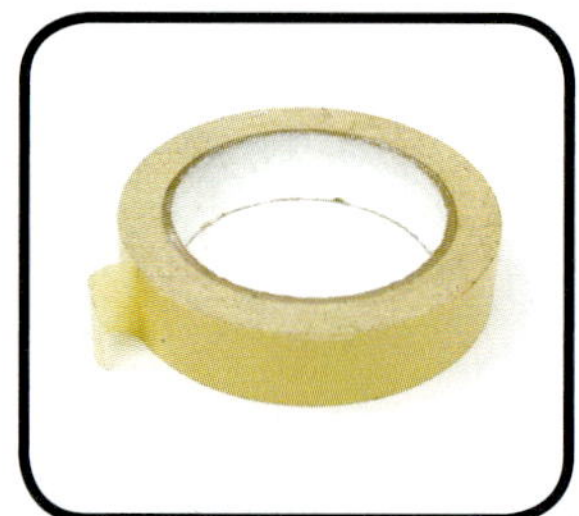
tape

2 clear jars

What to Do

Step 1

Make a model of a rain gauge. Tape the rulers to the outside of the jars.

Step 2

Put the jars outside before it rains. Put one under a tree. Put one in an open place.

Step 3

After it rains, use the rulers to measure how much rain fell into the jars.

Draw Conclusions

How is the model you made like a rain gauge?  S1E1b

Independent Inquiry

Use your **model** rain gauge to measure how much rain falls each day for one week. S1CS3b S1CS4a

S1E2b

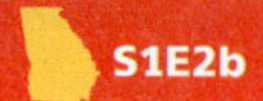

VOCABULARY
precipitation
sleet
hail

Focus Skill **COMPARE AND CONTRAST**

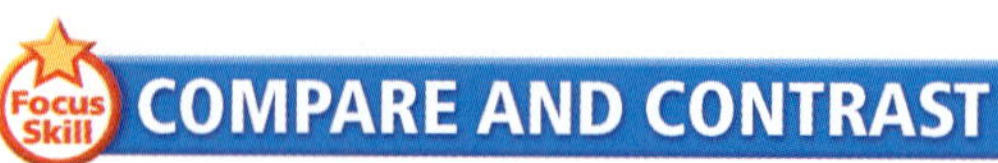

Look for ways in which forms of precipitation are alike and different.

Solid Precipitation

Water that falls from the sky is called **precipitation**. It falls in different forms. Some precipitation falls as a solid. A solid has its own shape.

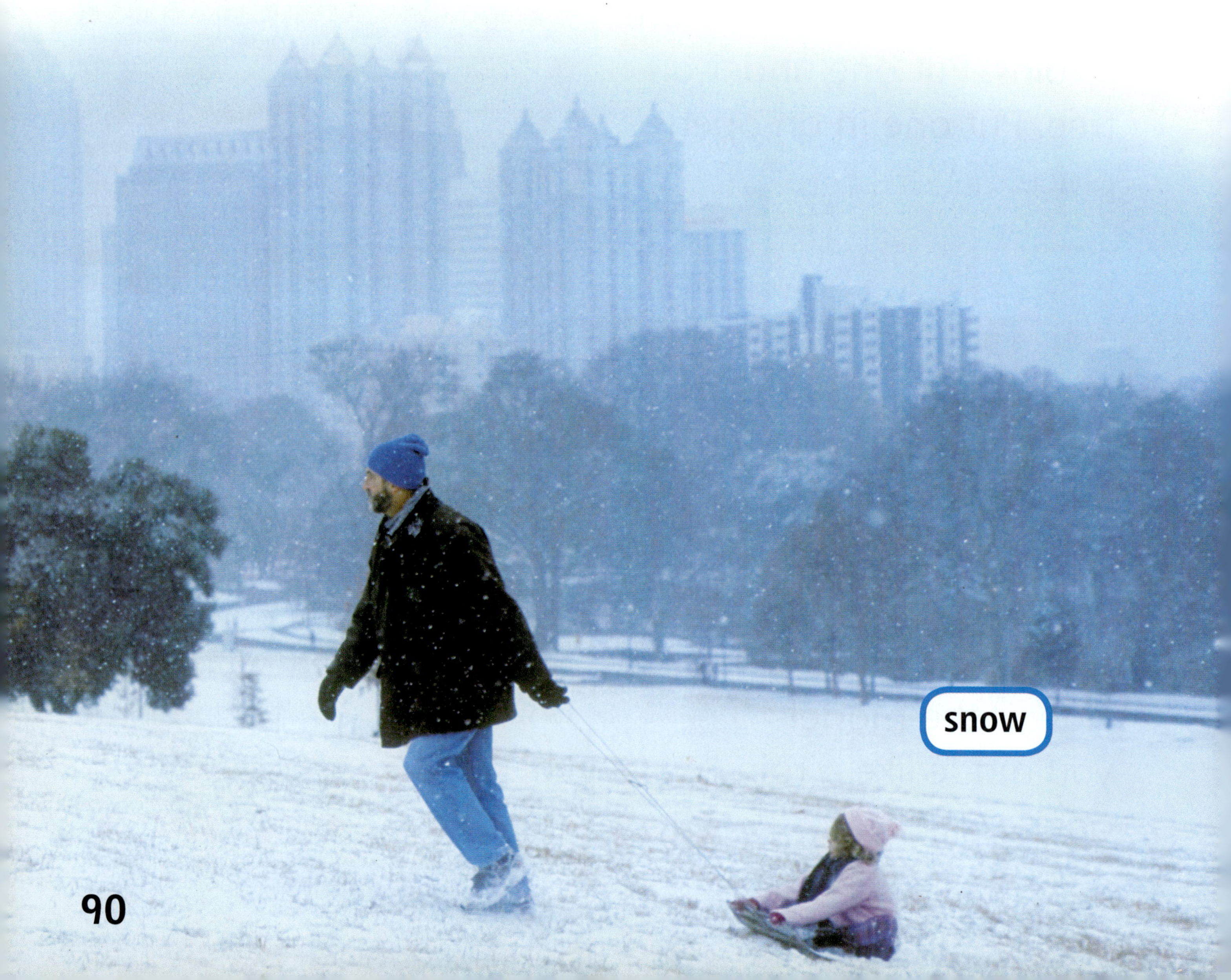

snow

Drops of rain can turn to ice. These tiny drops of ice are called **sleet**. Sleet is a solid form of precipitation.

Sometimes ice builds up into bigger balls. These big balls of ice are called **hail**. Hail is also a solid form of precipitation.

How are snow, sleet, and hail alike?

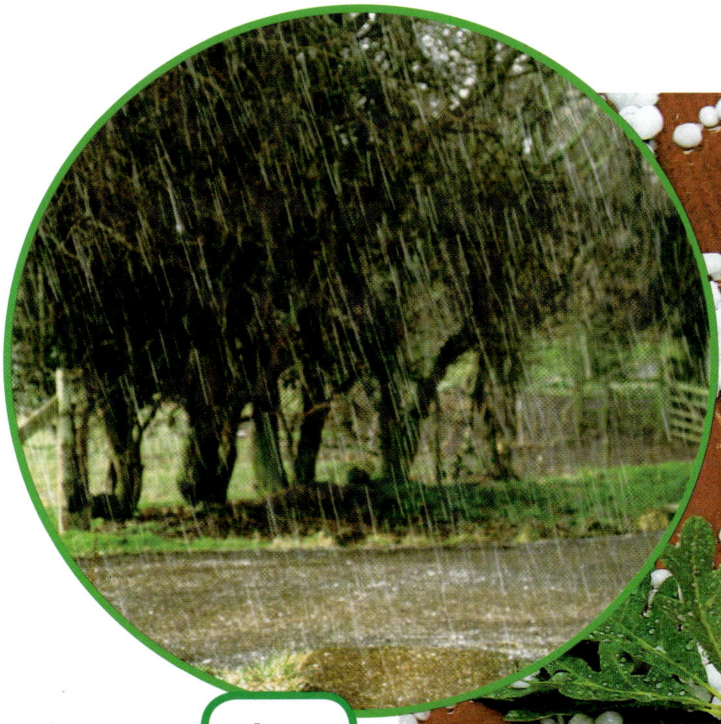

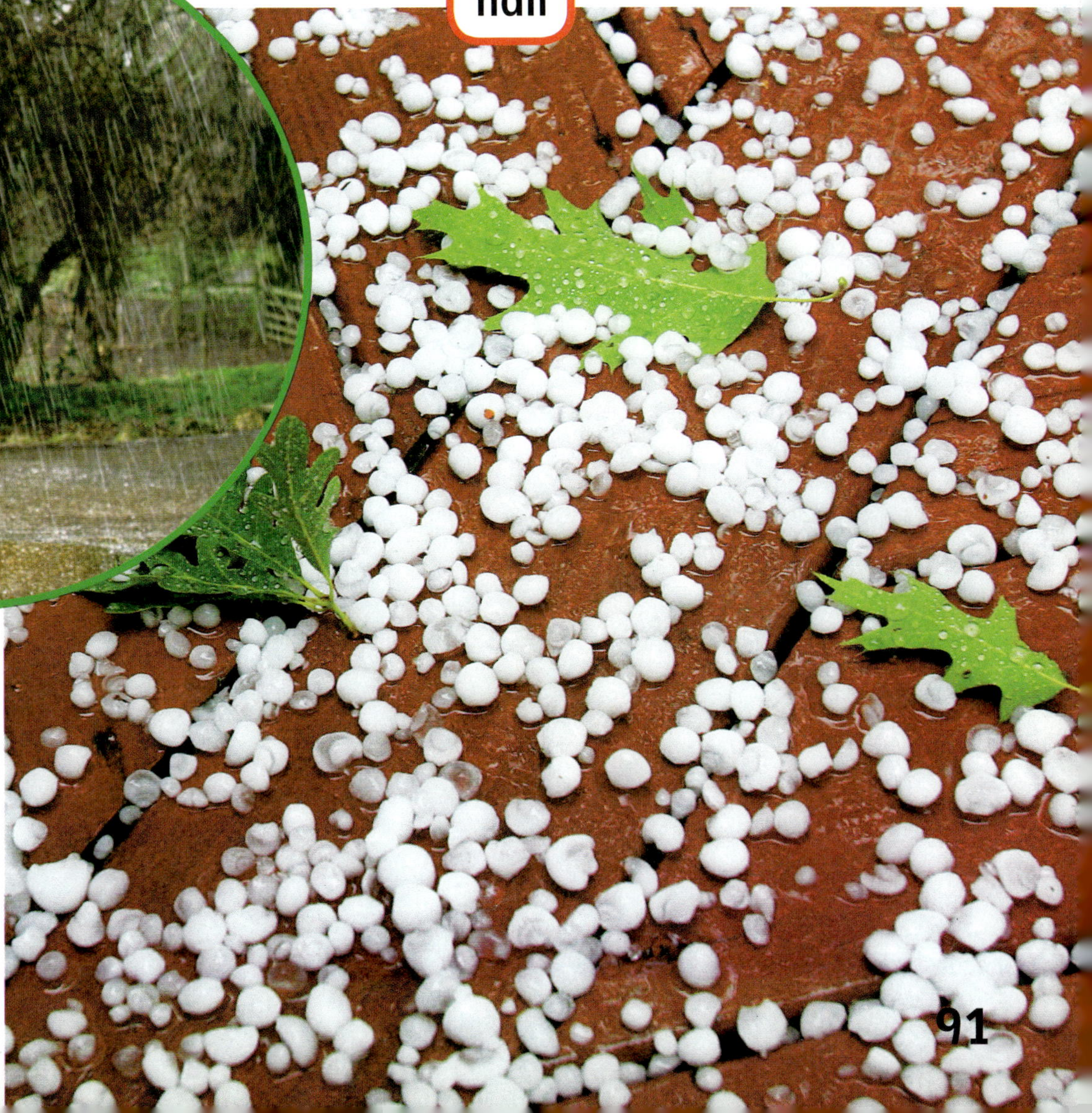

hail

sleet

Liquid Precipitation

Water that falls from the sky as a liquid is called rain. A liquid flows. It does not have its own shape. It takes the shape of its container, such as a rain gauge. It flows on the ground.

rain

Most rainy days are dark and cloudy. Rain falls from the dark clouds. Sometimes the sun shines between the clouds when it rains. You can see a rainbow when sun shines through rain.

How is rain different from snow, sleet, and hail?

rainbow

Insta-Lab

Make a Rainbow

Place a mirror in a jar of water. Turn off the light. Shine a flashlight on the mirror. Move the light around. Look for the rainbow colors.

GPS Wrap-Up and Lesson Review

Essential Question

What are some forms of precipitation?

In this lesson, you learned that rain is a liquid form of precipitation. You also learned that snow, sleet, and hail are solid forms of precipitation.

1. Focus Skill **COMPARE AND CONTRAST** Make a chart like this one. Compare and contrast forms of precipitation. S1E2b

alike	different

2. **SUMMARIZE** What is this lesson about? Write a summary. S1E2b

3. **VOCABULARY** Use the word **precipitation** to tell about this picture. S1E2b

4. Tell about a change that can happen to water. S1E2b

CRCT Practice

5. What is sleet?
   A big balls of ice
   B a liquid
   C rain that turned to ice S1E2b

The Big Idea

6. Name a solid form of precipitation. Name a liquid form of precipitation. S1E2b

Writing

Write a Poem

1. Think about your favorite kind of weather.

2. Write about it. Start each line with a letter of a word for that weather.

3. Tell why you like this kind of weather.

Math

Solve Problems

1. Read the problem.

2. Juan checked his rain gauge. He saw 3 centimeters of rain on Monday. He saw 2 more centimeters on Tuesday.

3. How much rain fell in all?

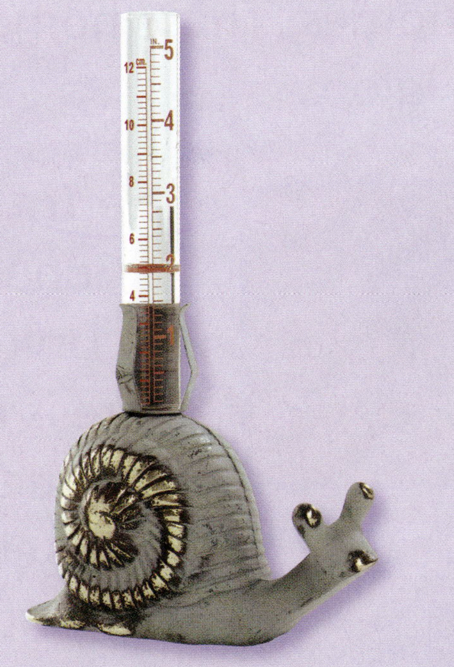

For more links and activities, go to **www.hspscience.com**

Snow Is Useful

When snow falls, it is soft and fluffy. Over time, it gets packed down.

Snow is strong and holds heat well. Some people use it to build homes. These homes are called igloos.

The Inuit

Canada is a country north of the United States. In Canada, there is a group of people called the Inuit. Sometimes they have to travel during the winter. They move across large areas of snow and ice.

To use a tent on the snow and ice would be too cold. So the Inuit use snow to build an igloo.

The Inuit cut snow into blocks. Then they stack the blocks into a curved shape. It looks sort of like the top of your head. A narrow tunnel is built. It is used to get into the igloo. The tunnel stops the wind from blowing in.

- The largest snowflake was more than a foot across.
- No two snowflakes are alike.
- All snowflakes have six sides.
- Stampede Pass, Washington, is the snow capital of the United States!

Think and Write

Why do you think igloos are built only during the winter? S1E2b

Georgia Performance Standards in This Lesson

Content

S1E2a Recognize changes in water when it freezes (ice) and when it melts (water).

S1E2c Determine that the weight of water before freezing, after freezing, and after melting stays the same.

S1E2d Determine that water in an open container disappears into the air over time, but water in a closed container does not.

Characteristics of Science

S1CS2c S1CS2d S1CS3a S1CS4b S1CS5a

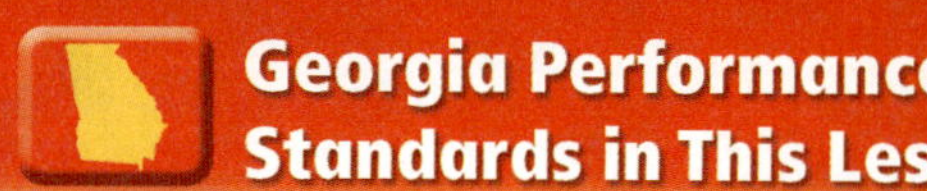

LESSON 2

Essential Question

How Can Water Change?

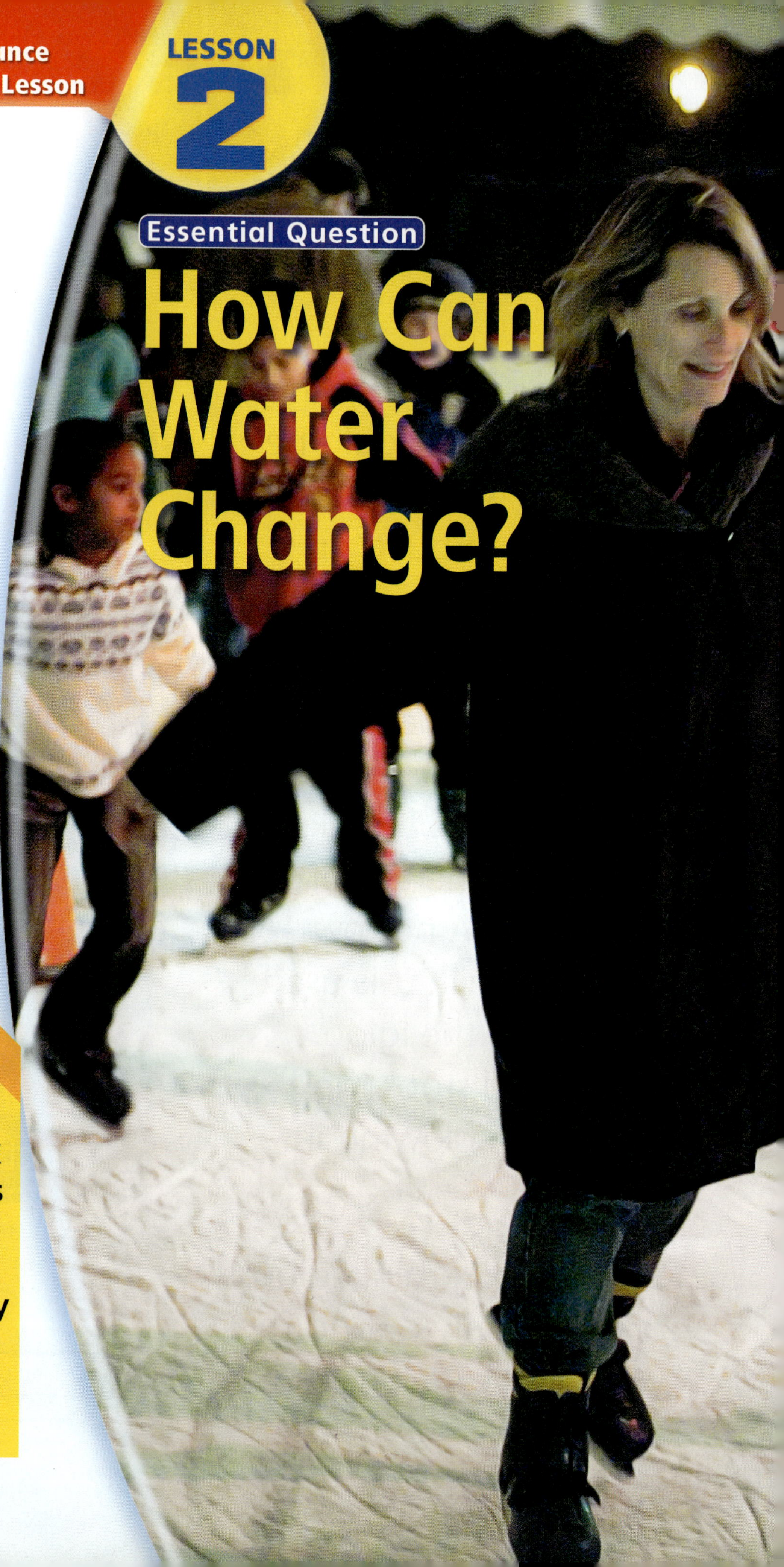

Georgia Fast Fact

Ice-Skating Rink
The pipes under this rink are filled with an icy cold liquid. It makes the floor very cold. When water is poured on the floor, the water freezes.

Vocabulary Preview

freeze p. 102

melt p. 102

evaporate p. 103

condense p. 103

water cycle p. 104

Centennial Olympic Park ice-skating rink

Weight of Water

Guided Inquiry

Ask a Question

Which tray of juice do you think weighs more? Investigate to find out. Then read to find out more.

melted

frozen

Get Ready

Inquiry Skill Tip

When you measure, you find the size or amount of something.

You need

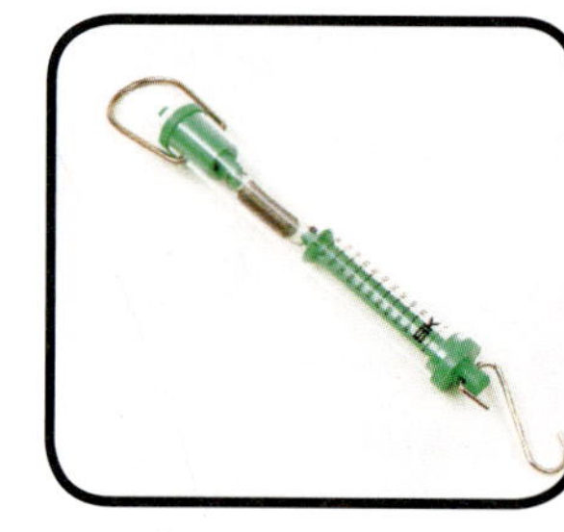

spring scale

water

zip-top bag

freezer

What to Do

Step 1

Put some water in a zip-top bag. Do not fill the bag completely.

Step 2

Estimate the weight of the water in the bag before freezing, after freezing, and after melting.

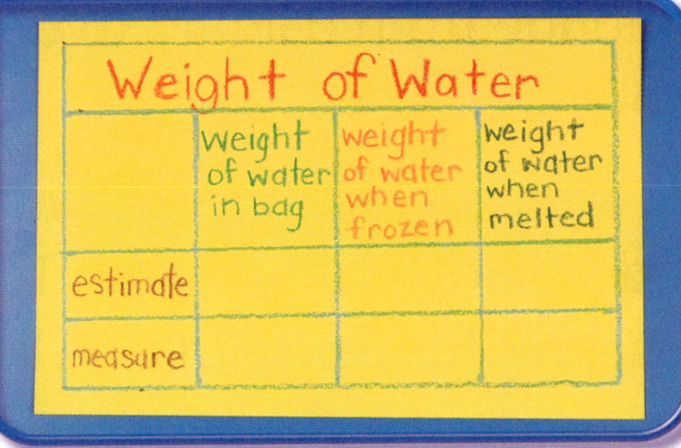

Weight of Water

	weight of water in bag	weight of water when frozen	weight of water when melted
estimate			
measure			

Step 3

Measure the water in the bag before freezing, after freezing, and after melting. Compare the measurements.

Draw Conclusions

Were your estimates correct? What did you find out about water? S1E2c

Independent Inquiry

Estimate and then **measure** the weight of a different liquid before freezing, after freezing, and after melting. S1CS2c S1CS2d S1CS4b S1CS5b

VOCABULARY
freeze
melt
evaporate
condense
water cycle

Focus Skill **CAUSE AND EFFECT**

Look for ways water changes.

How Water Changes

Water changes to ice when it gets cold enough. It freezes. To **freeze** is to change from a liquid to a solid. Ice is a solid.

Ice changes to water when warm air adds heat to it. It melts. To **melt** is to change from a solid to a liquid. Water is a liquid.

ice

water

Water evaporates when it is heated. To **evaporate** is to change from a liquid to a gas. Water changes to water vapor, which is a gas. You can not see it.

Water vapor condenses when it meets something cold. To **condense** is to change from a gas to tiny drops of liquid.

Focus Skill CAUSE AND EFFECT
What causes water drops to form on the outside of a glass?

The sun warms the water.

The water evaporates.

condensation

Insta-Lab

Evaporation

Put the same amount of water in two jars. Mark the water line on each jar with a piece of tape. Cover one jar with a lid. Put the jars in a warm, sunny place. Watch for several days. Compare the water in the jars. What happened? Why?

The Water Cycle

Water moves from Earth to the air. Then it moves back again. This movement of water is called the **water cycle**.

What causes water to evaporate?

The Water Cycle

1 The sun makes water warm. This causes the water to evaporate, or change to water vapor.

2 Water vapor meets cool air. The cool air causes the water vapor to condense, or change into tiny drops of water. The drops form clouds.

For more links and animations, go to **www.hspscience.com**

3 Water drops come together and get bigger and heavier. Then they fall as rain or snow.
4 Some rain and snow falls into rivers, lakes, and oceans. Some falls on land and then flows into rivers, lakes, and oceans.
5 The water cycle begins again.

GPS Wrap-Up and Lesson Review

Essential Question

How can water change?

In this lesson, you learned that water can change from a liquid to a solid. It also changes from a solid to a liquid. You also learned that water can change from a liquid to a gas. It also changes from a gas to a liquid.

1. **CAUSE AND EFFECT** Make a chart like this one. When the sun shines on Earth, what are the effects? S1E2d

2. **DRAW CONCLUSIONS** What happens to water after it falls on land and flows into rivers, lakes, and oceans? S1E2d

3. **VOCABULARY** Explain what happens during the **water cycle**. S1E2d

4. Does the weight of water change when it is frozen? S1E2c

CRCT Practice

5. Which word means "to change from a solid to a liquid"?
   A freeze
   B gas
   C melt S1E2a

The Big Idea

6. Can ice that becomes a liquid change back to a solid? Explain. S1E2a

Writing

The Water Cycle

1. Work with a partner to draw the steps of the water cycle.
2. Write about each step.
3. Use the words **first**, **second**, **third**, **fourth**, and **fifth** to tell about the steps.

Math

Measuring Water

1. Put water in a cup. Mark the water line. Measure and record its height.
2. Put the cup in a freezer.
3. Mark the ice line. Measure and record its height.
4. What does this show you about how water changes?

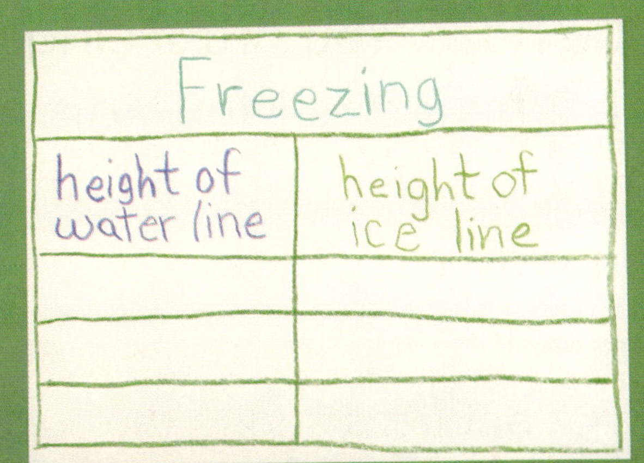

For more links and activities, go to **www.hspscience.com**

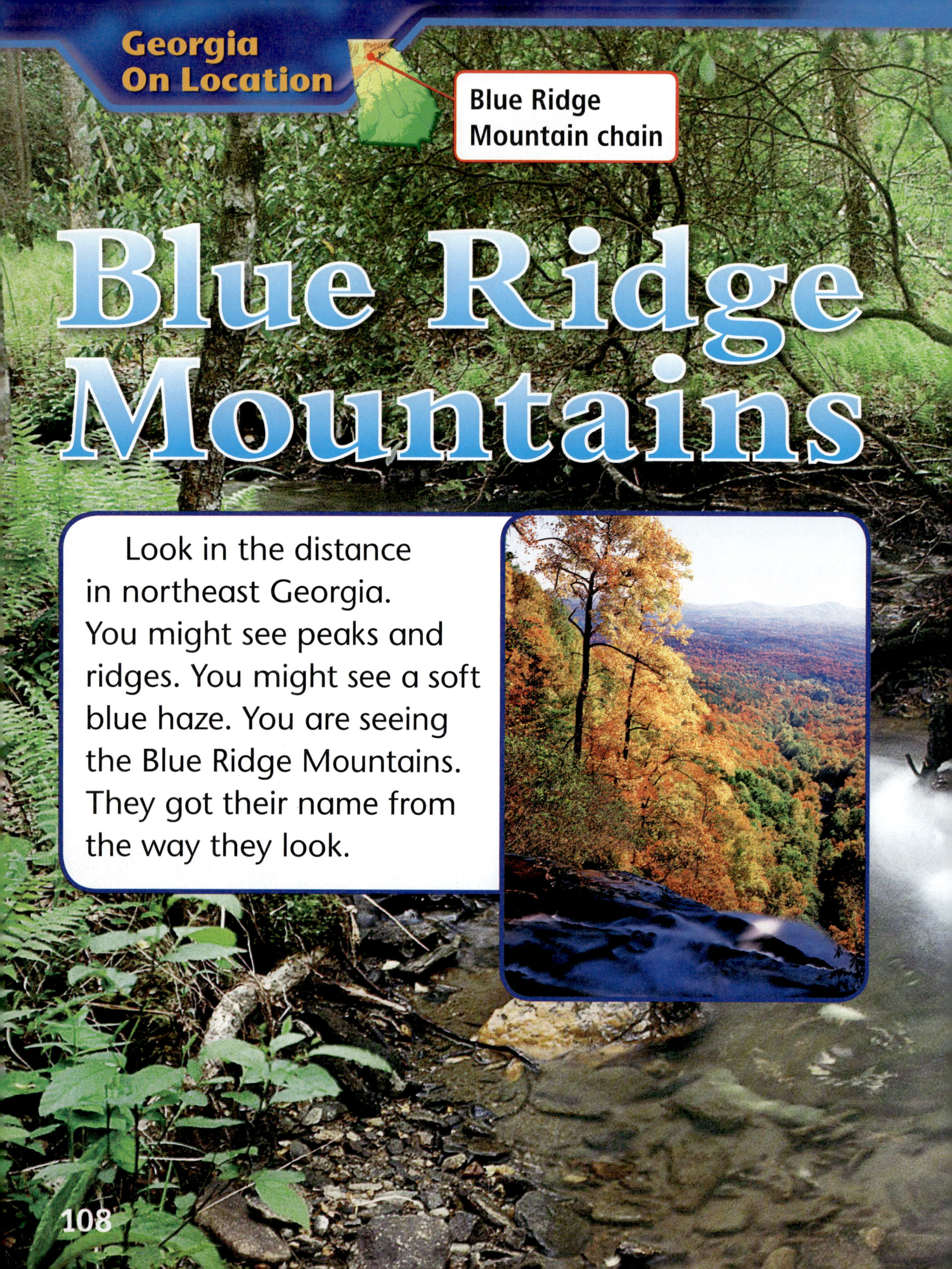

Blue Ridge Mountains

Look in the distance in northeast Georgia. You might see peaks and ridges. You might see a soft blue haze. You are seeing the Blue Ridge Mountains. They got their name from the way they look.

The Water Cycle in the Mountains

The Blue Ridge Mountains stretch for almost 100 miles across Georgia. The mountains get more rainfall than any other place in Georgia. Some parts of the Blue Ridge Mountains get over 80 inches of rain each year.

This rain fills creeks and rivers. As the water rushes along, tiny drops evaporate. The drops gather in the clouds. In time the drops fall back over the mountains as rain. Sometimes, they fall back to Earth as snow!

Think and Write

How do you think a large amount of rainfall affects the plants and animals in the Blue Ridge Mountains? S1E2b

Wrap-Up

Visual Summary

Tell how each picture helps explain the **Big Idea**.

You can observe and record changes in water with the weather.

Lesson 1 S1E2b

Precipitation can be either a solid or a liquid. Hail, sleet, and snow are solid forms of precipitation. Rain is a liquid form of precipitation.

Lesson 2 S1E2a; S1E2c; S1E2d

The weather causes water to change form. When water gets cold enough, it freezes. When enough heat is added to frozen water, it melts. When enough heat is added to liquid water, it evaporates.

Show What You Know

Chapter Writing Activity

Where Does a Raindrop Go?/Write a Story

Think about a raindrop. What does its cloud look like? Where does the raindrop land when it falls to Earth? Where does it go on Earth? Draw pictures. Show the raindrop in each part of the water cycle.

ELA1W1a

Georgia Performance Task

Which Paper Towel Dries First?

With a classmate, wet three paper towels. Put each towel in a different place. Predict which towel will dry first. Check the towels every 15 minutes. Which one dries first? Which one dries last? Why?

S1E2d

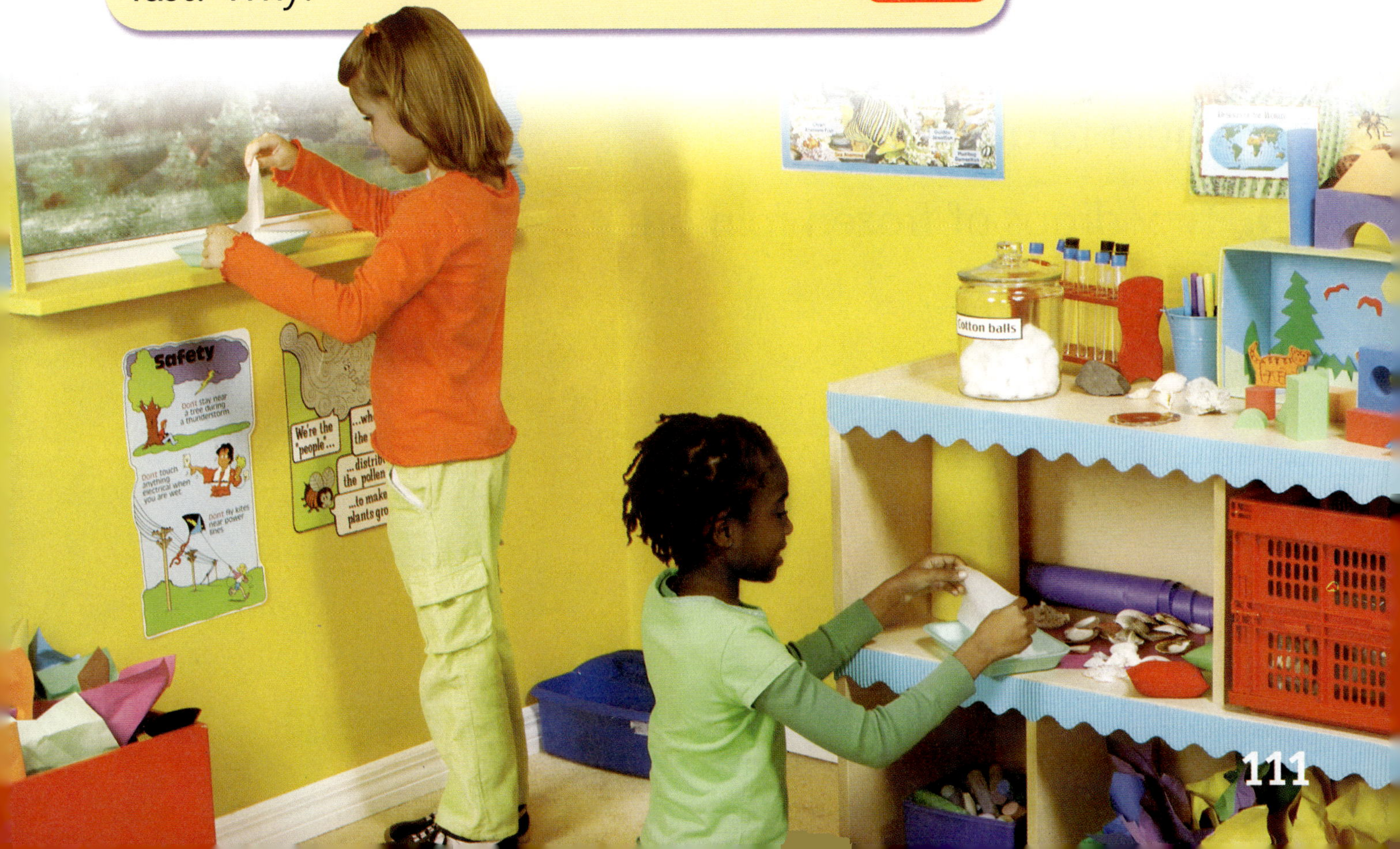

Vocabulary Review

Use the words to complete the sentences. The page numbers tell you where to look if you need help.

precipitation p. 90 **melt** p. 102

sleet p. 91 **freeze** p. 102

1. Rain, snow, sleet, and hail are forms of ______. S1E2b
2. To ______ is to change from a solid to a liquid. S1E2a
3. To ______ is to change from a liquid to a solid. S1E2a
4. Tiny drops of frozen rain are called ______. S1E2b

Check Understanding

5. Look at the picture. Tell what happens in the water cycle. S1E2d

6. Which tool measures how much liquid precipitation has fallen? S1E2b

A balance

B rain gauge

C thermometer

Critical Thinking

7. An ice cube melts. What do you know about its weight? S1E2c

The Big Idea

8. How does the weather cause water to change forms? S1E2a S1E2d

CRCT Practice Earth Science

1. What are rainy, snowy, and windy?

A. kinds of rocks

B. kinds of weather

C. kinds of clouds

S1E1a

2. Over time, what happens to water in an open container?

A. It evaporates.

B. It condenses.

C. It freezes.

S1E2d

3. Look at the picture. What season is it?

A. fall

B. winter

C. summer

S1E1c

4. Which tool can help you measure temperature?

A. 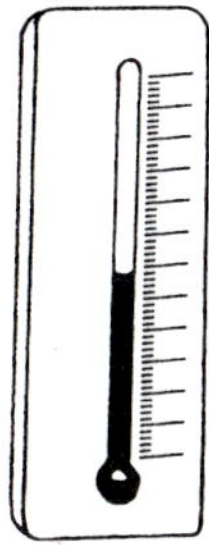

C. 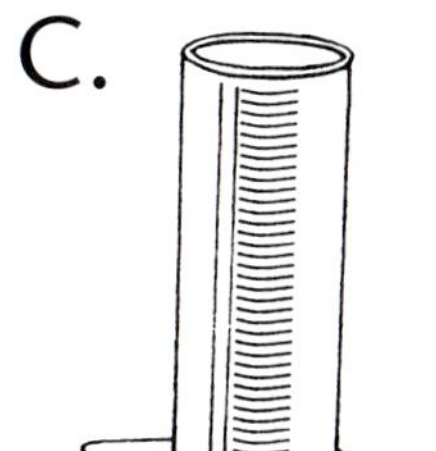

B. 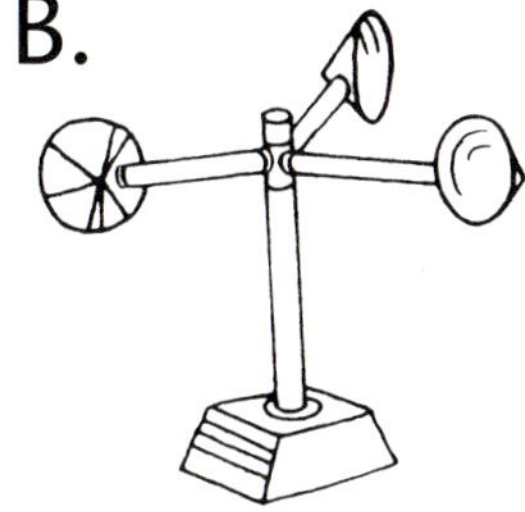

S1E1b

5. What are snow, sleet, and hail?

A. kinds of liquid precipitation

B. kinds of liquid evaporation

C. kinds of solid precipitation

S1E2b

6. What happens when water changes from a liquid to a solid?

A. It freezes.

B. It melts.

C. It evaporates.

S1E2a

UNIT B

PHYSICAL SCIENCE

GO online for student eBook www.hspscience.com

What do YOU wonder?

These children are making music. Why do different musical instruments make different sounds?

children making music

Unit Inquiry

Sound and Vibration How does a drum make sound? Plan and do a test to find out.

Light and Sound

Georgia Performance Standards in This Chapter

Content

S1P1 Students will investigate light and sound.

S1P1a S1P1b S1P1c S1P1d S1P1e

This chapter also addresses these co-requisite standards:

Characteristics of Science

S1CS2 Students will have the computation and estimation skills necessary for analyzing data and following scientific explanations.

S1CS2a

S1CS3 Students will use tools and instruments for observing, measuring, and manipulating objects in scientific activities.

S1CS3a

S1CS4 Students will use the ideas of system, model, change, and scale in exploring scientific and technological matters.

S1CS4b S1CS4c

S1CS5 Students will communicate scientific ideas and activities clearly.

S1CS5a S1CS5b

What's the Big Idea?

Light can make shadows. Vibrations make sound.

Essential Questions

for student eBook www.hspscience.com

Science in Georgia

Macon

Dear Hayden,

I went to the Georgia Music Hall of Fame in Macon. I saw old instruments. I learned how the strings vibrate to make sound. I hope you can visit there, too!

Your friend,

Leah

Read Leah's postcard. What did Leah learn about sound? How do you think that helps explain the **Big Idea?**

Georgia Performance Standards in This Lesson

Content

S1P1a Recognize sources of light.

S1P1b Explain how shadows are made.

Characteristics of Science

S1CS2a S1CS4b S1CS4c S1CS5a S1CS5b

LESSON 1

Essential Question

What Is Light?

Georgia Fast Fact

Atlanta Skyline
The tallest buildings in Atlanta are in Downtown Atlanta. At night, you can see millions of lights in the city.

Atlanta at night

Vocabulary Preview

light p. 124

shadow p. 127

Investigate

Look at Shadows

Guided Inquiry

Ask a Question

How are shadows made? Investigate to find out. Then read to find out more.

Get Ready

Inquiry Skill Tip

To draw a conclusion, use what you observed and what you already know.

You need

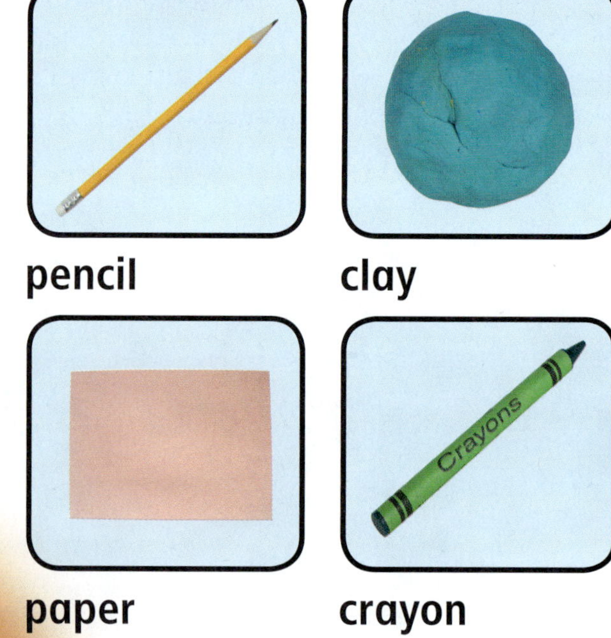

pencil

clay

paper

crayon

What to Do

Step 1

Put a pencil in clay. Put it on the paper. Put it in a sunny place.

Step 2

Trace the shadow you see on the paper. Then trace it at two other times of the day.

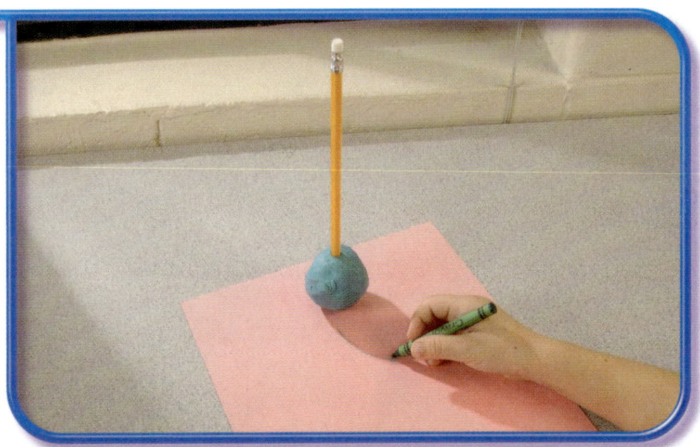

Step 3

Draw a conclusion about why the shadow changed.

Draw Conclusions

What did you find out about shadows? S1P1b

Independent Inquiry

Put a pencil in clay and trace the shadow. Repeat during the year. **Draw a conclusion** about why the shadow changed. S1CS5a

VOCABULARY
light
shadow

Focus Skill MAIN IDEA AND DETAILS

Look for the main ideas about light and what it does.

Light

Light is a kind of energy. Light lets us see. Light from the sun lights up the world around us.

sunlight

Fire and lamps give off light. Candles give off light, too. Lightning lights up the night sky.

What is the main thing light does for us?

fire

lightning

lamp

candle

Shadows

Light can move. It can pass through clear objects. It passes through glass. Light can not pass through all objects. Objects that are not clear block light.

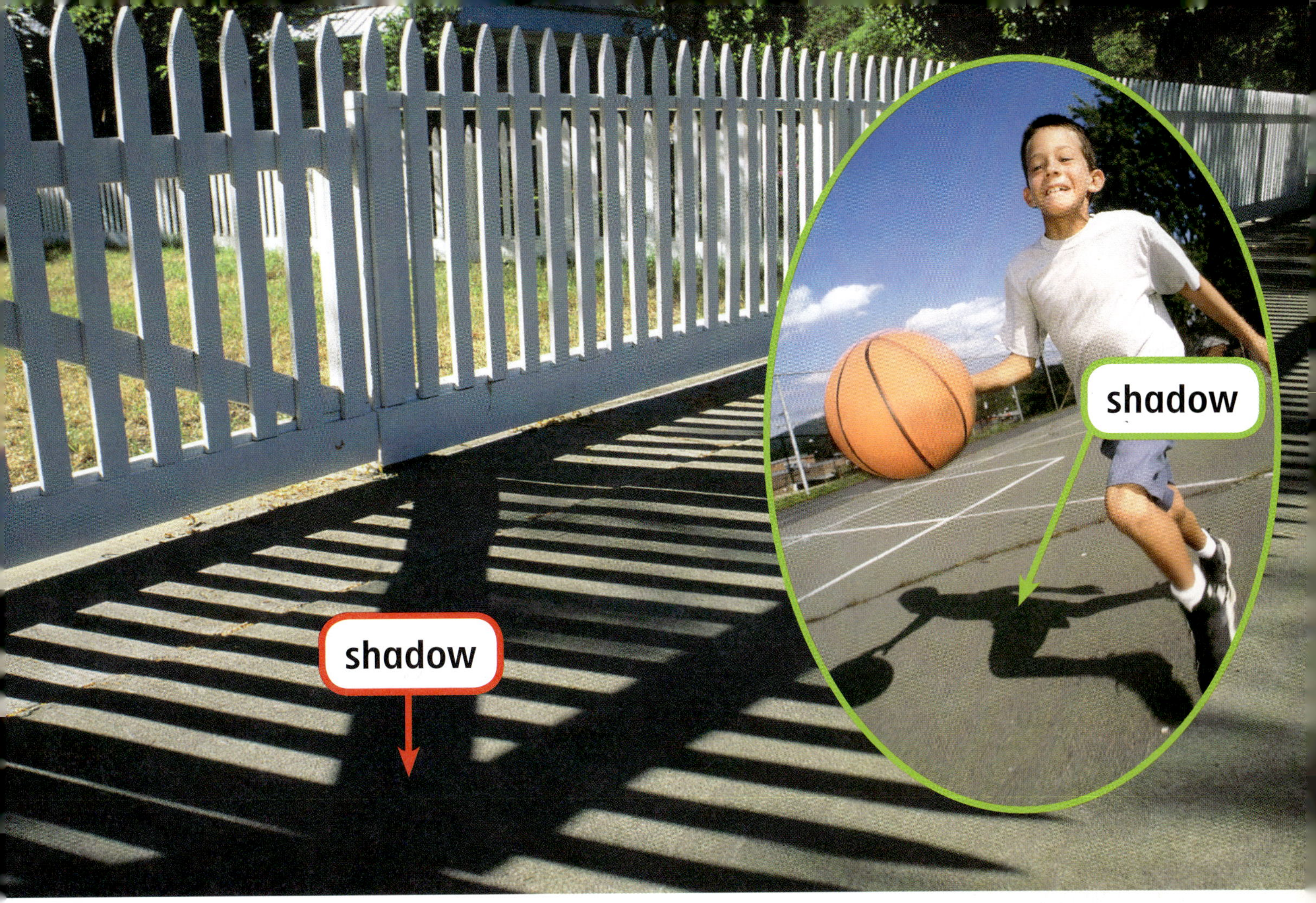

A **shadow** is a dark place made when an object blocks light. You can see many shadows on a sunny day.

Focus Skill MAIN IDEA AND DETAILS

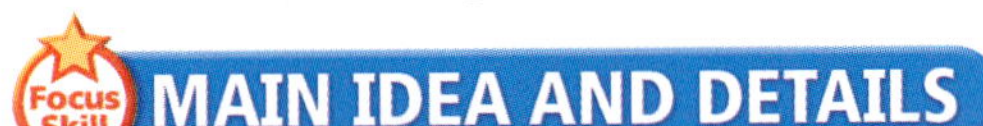

What makes shadows?

Insta-Lab

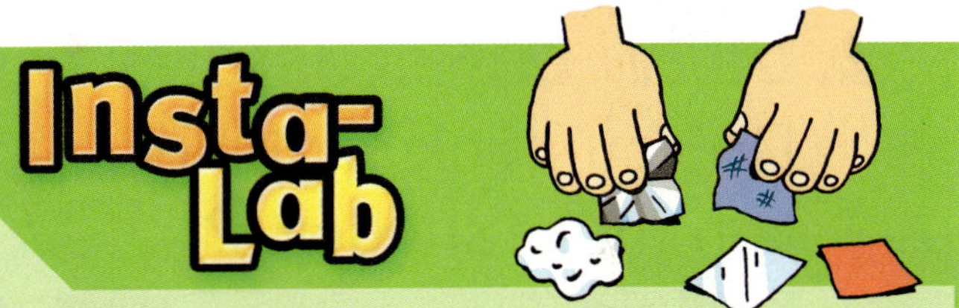

What Can Light Pass Through?

Get some art materials. Predict which ones light will pass through. Which ones will block light? Test your ideas in a sunny place or next to a lamp. **CAUTION:** A lamp may get hot.

GPS Wrap-Up and Lesson Review

Essential Question

What is light?

In this lesson, you learned about some things that give off light. You also learned how shadows are made.

1. MAIN IDEA AND DETAILS Make a chart like this one. Show the details of this main idea. **Light lets us see.** 

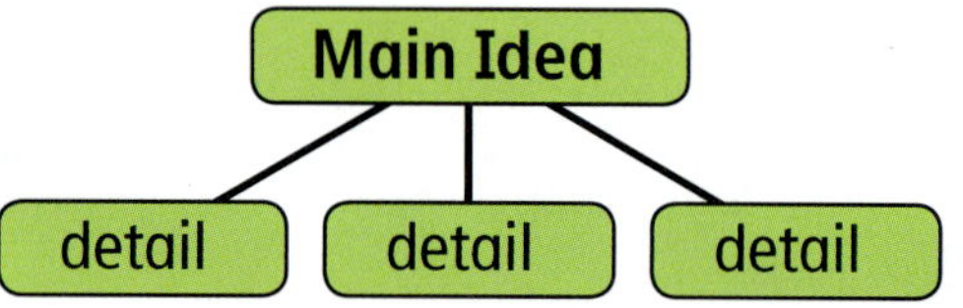

2. DRAW CONCLUSIONS Do you think all things can make shadows? Explain. S1P1b

3. VOCABULARY Use the words **light** and **shadow** to tell about this picture. S1P1a S1P1b

4. Name something that light can pass through. Tell why you think it can. S1P1b

CRCT Practice

5. What is one thing that gives off light?

A a candle

B an oven

C a stove

S1P1a

The Big Idea

6. Explain how shadows are made. S1P1a

Writing

Write a Report

1. Read about the sun.
2. Write a short report about what you read. Tell what the sun is and where it is. Tell what it is made of and what it does.
3. Draw pictures to go with your report.

Math

Measure a Shadow

1. Measure how tall you are. Record the number.
2. Then go outside. Have a partner measure the shadow of you that the sun makes. Record the number.
3. Compare the numbers. Are they the same?

For more links and activities, go to **www.hspscience.com**

Tybee Island

Tybee Lighthouse

The Tybee Lighthouse is on Tybee Island. It has lit up the entrance to the Savannah River since 1736.

It is one of the oldest lighthouses in the United States. It is still hard at work guiding boats safely in storms.

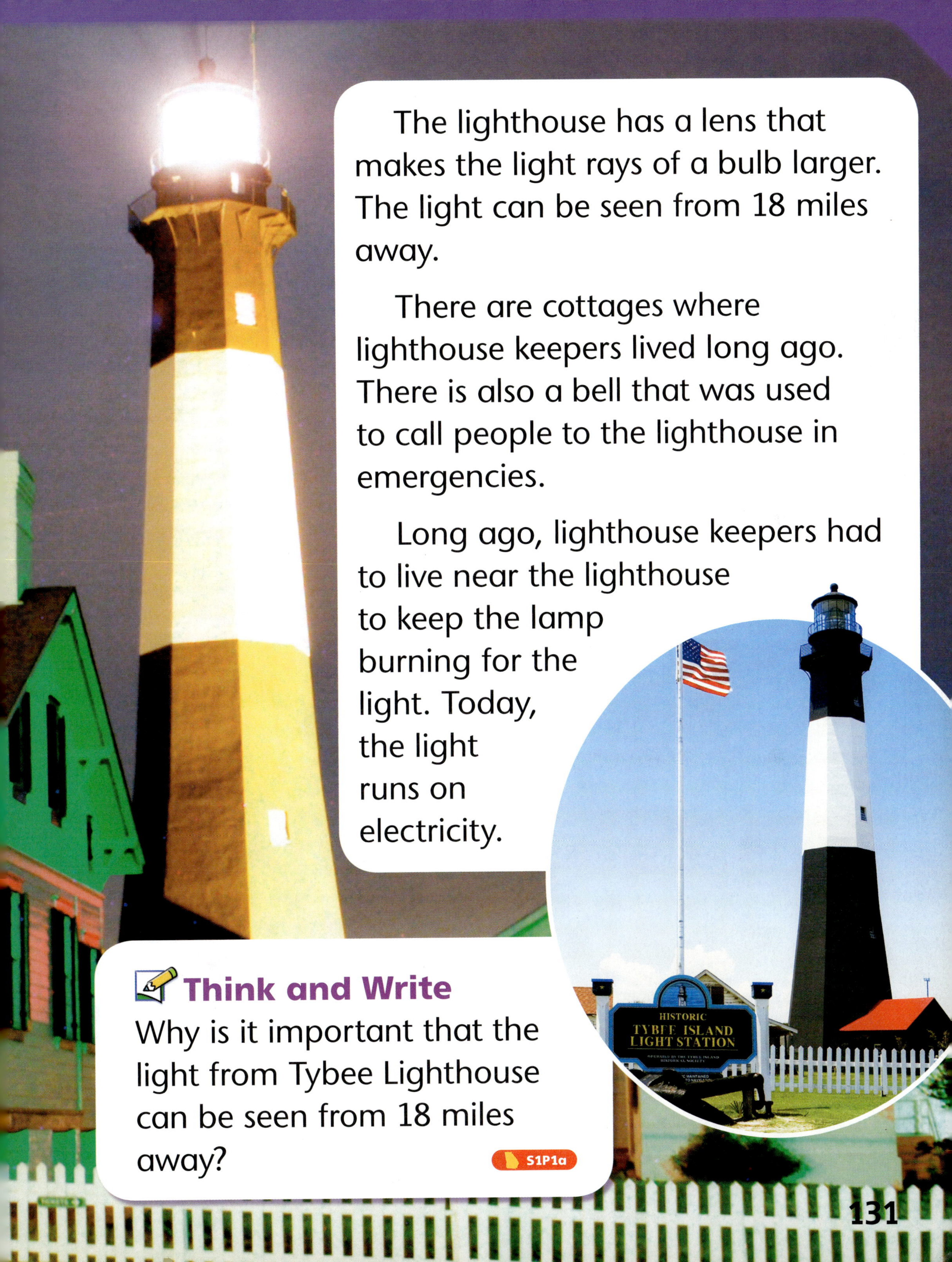

The lighthouse has a lens that makes the light rays of a bulb larger. The light can be seen from 18 miles away.

There are cottages where lighthouse keepers lived long ago. There is also a bell that was used to call people to the lighthouse in emergencies.

Long ago, lighthouse keepers had to live near the lighthouse to keep the lamp burning for the light. Today, the light runs on electricity.

Think and Write

Why is it important that the light from Tybee Lighthouse can be seen from 18 miles away? S1P1a

Georgia Performance Standards in This Lesson

Content

S1P1c Investigate how vibrations produce sound.

S1P1d Differentiate between various sounds in terms of (pitch) high or low and (volume) loud or soft.

S1P1e Identify emergency sounds and sounds that help us stay safe.

Characteristics of Science

S1CS3b

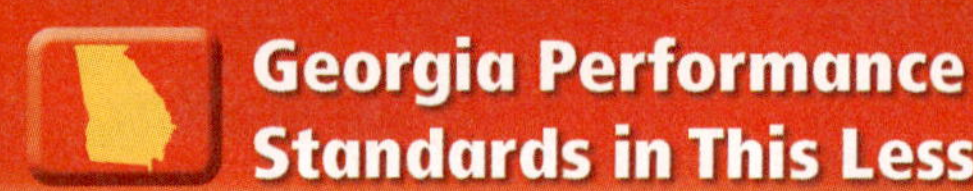

LESSON 2

Essential Question

What Is Sound?

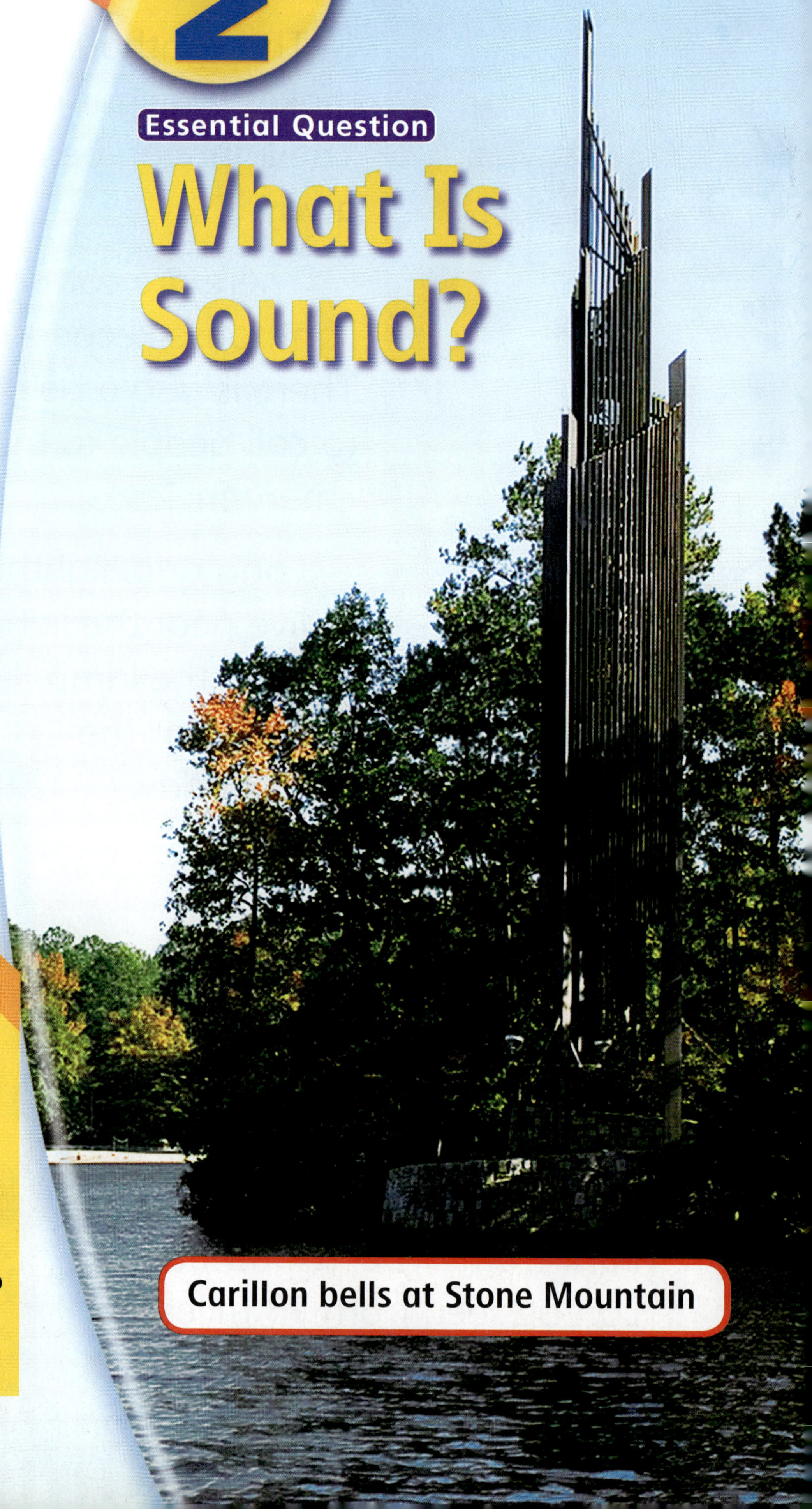

Carillon bells at Stone Mountain

Georgia Fast Fact

Carillon Bells

These bells were made for the New York World's Fair. In 1965, the 732 bells were moved to Stone Mountain in Georgia.

Vocabulary Preview

sound p. 136

vibration p. 137

volume p. 138

pitch p. 140

Investigate

How Sound Is Made

Guided Inquiry

Ask a Question

How are these people making sound? Investigate to find out. Then read to find out more.

Get Ready

Inquiry Skill Tip

When you observe, you use your senses to find out about things.

You need

tissue box

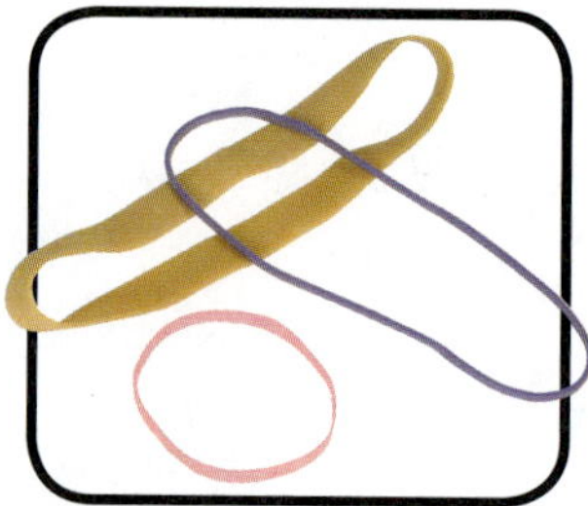

rubber bands

What to Do

Step 1

Stretch rubber bands over the box. Pluck the rubber bands. Touch them gently. What do you feel?

Step 2

Pluck the rubber bands more gently. Touch them. Listen to the sound. Then pluck them harder. Touch them. Listen to the sound.

Step 3

Draw pictures or write sentences to record what you **observe**.

Draw Conclusions

Why did changing the way you plucked the rubber bands change the sound? S1P1d

Independent Inquiry

Use other materials to make a different musical instrument. Find ways to make sounds with it. Record what you **observe** about how sound is made. S1CS3b

S1P1c, 1d, 1e

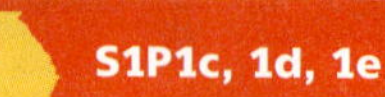

VOCABULARY
sound
vibration
volume
pitch

Focus Skill CAUSE AND EFFECT

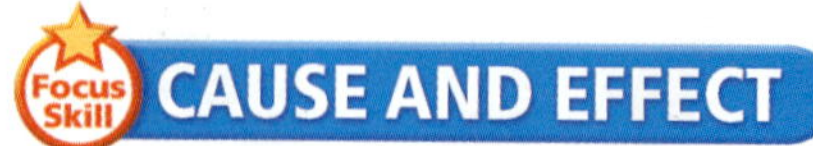

Look for what causes sound.

Vibrations Make Sound

Sound is what you hear. You may hear a dog barking or someone blowing a whistle. You may hear music playing or people talking.

What sounds might you hear on this street?

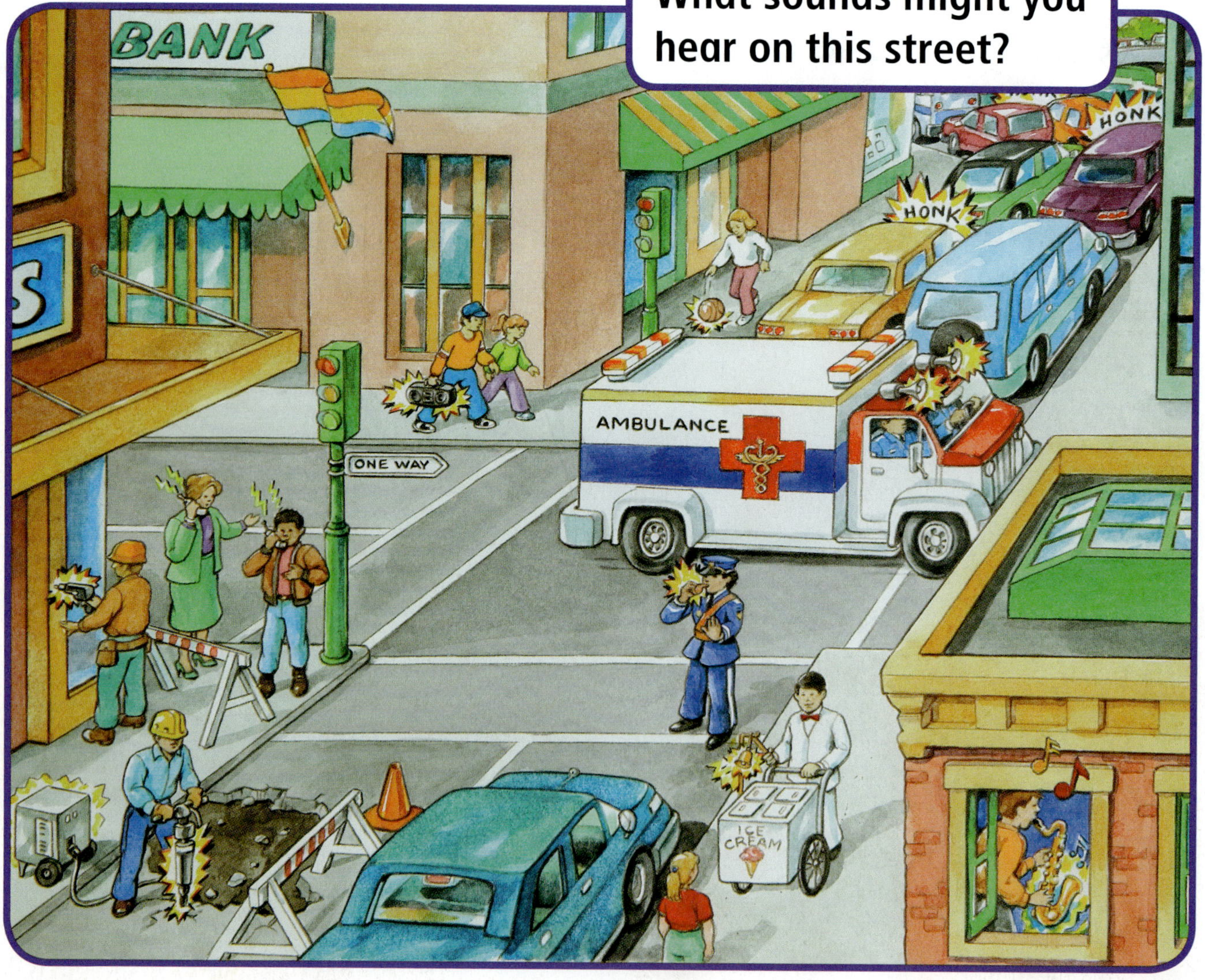

All sound is made when something moves back and forth. This back and forth motion is **vibration**. The sound stops when the vibration stops.

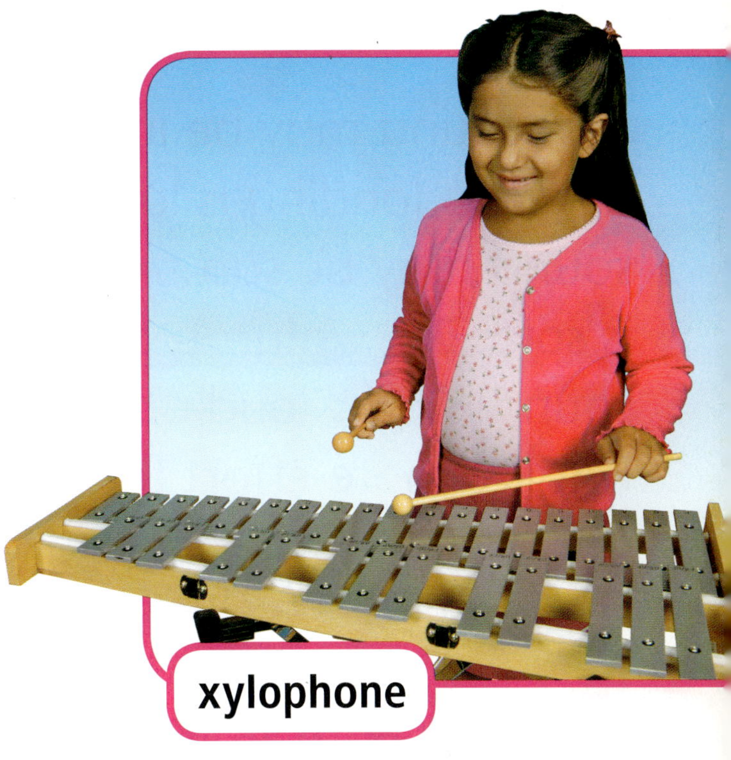

The boy plucks the guitar strings. This makes the guitar strings vibrate. You can touch the strings to feel the vibration.

xylophone

Focus Skill **CAUSE AND EFFECT**

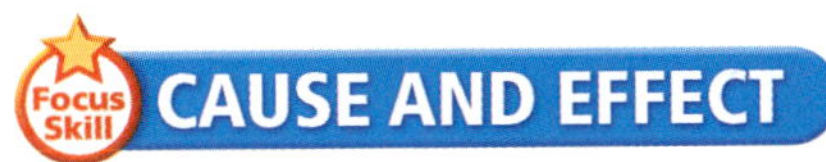

What causes sound?

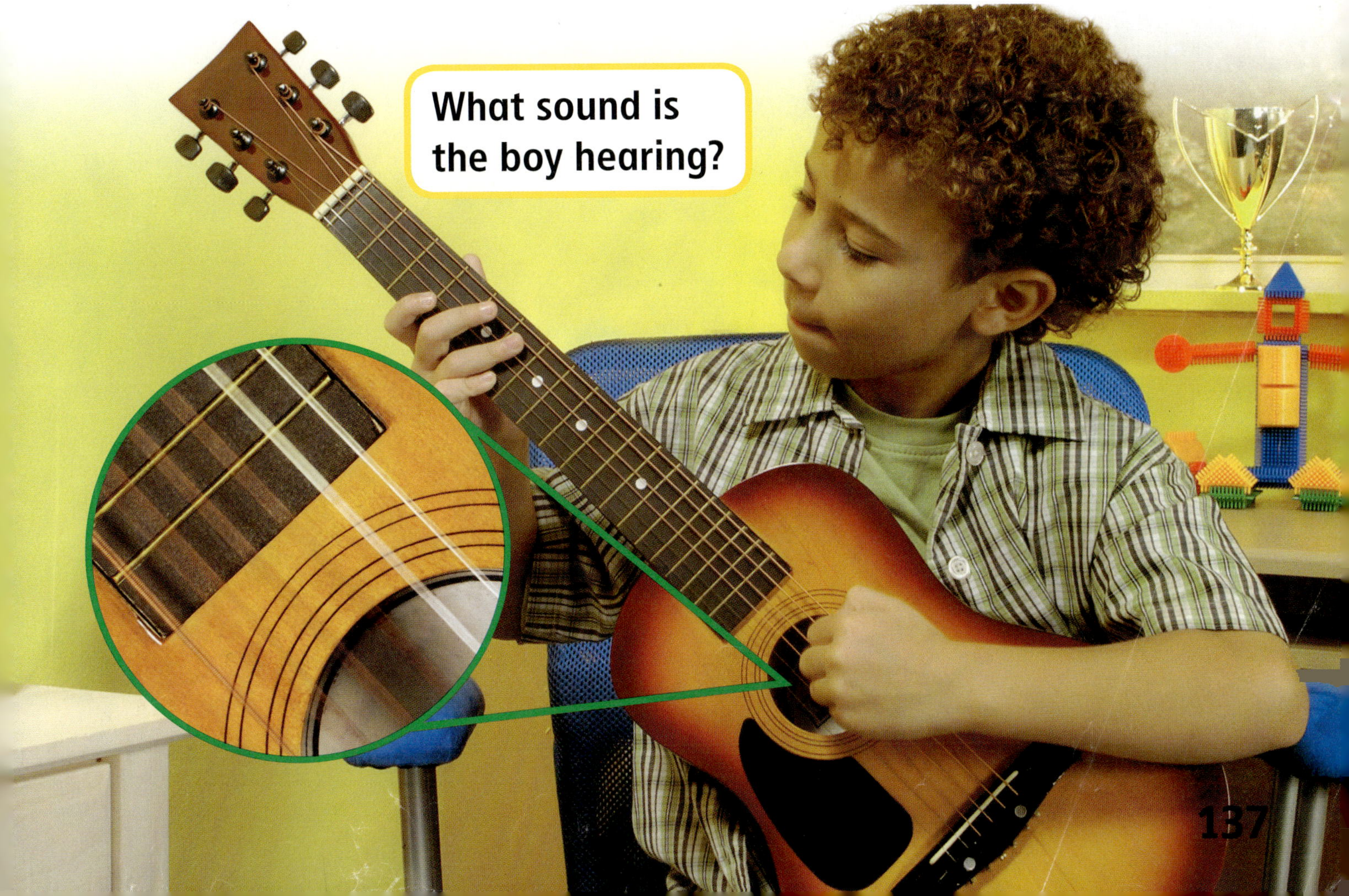
What sound is the boy hearing?

Loud and Soft

A sound may be loud. An airplane landing is loud. A sound may be soft. A whisper is soft. The **volume** of a sound is how loud or soft it is. It takes more effort to make a loud sound than to make a soft sound.

whispering

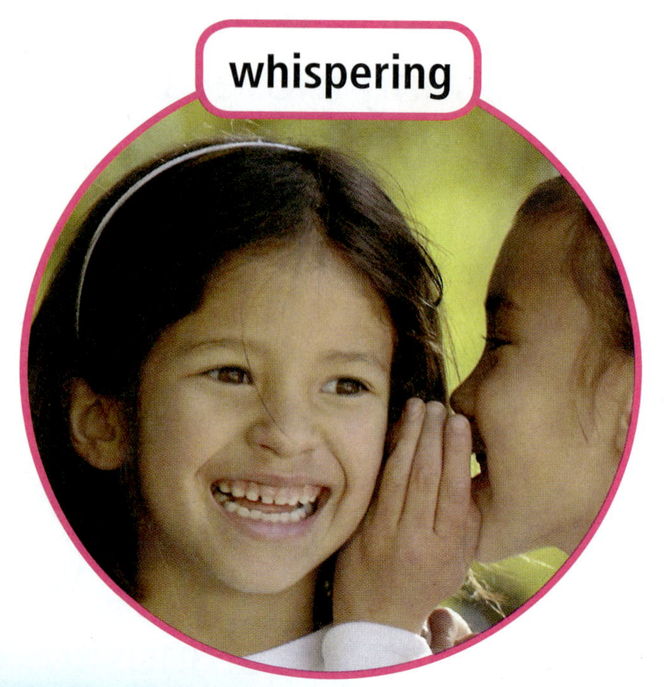

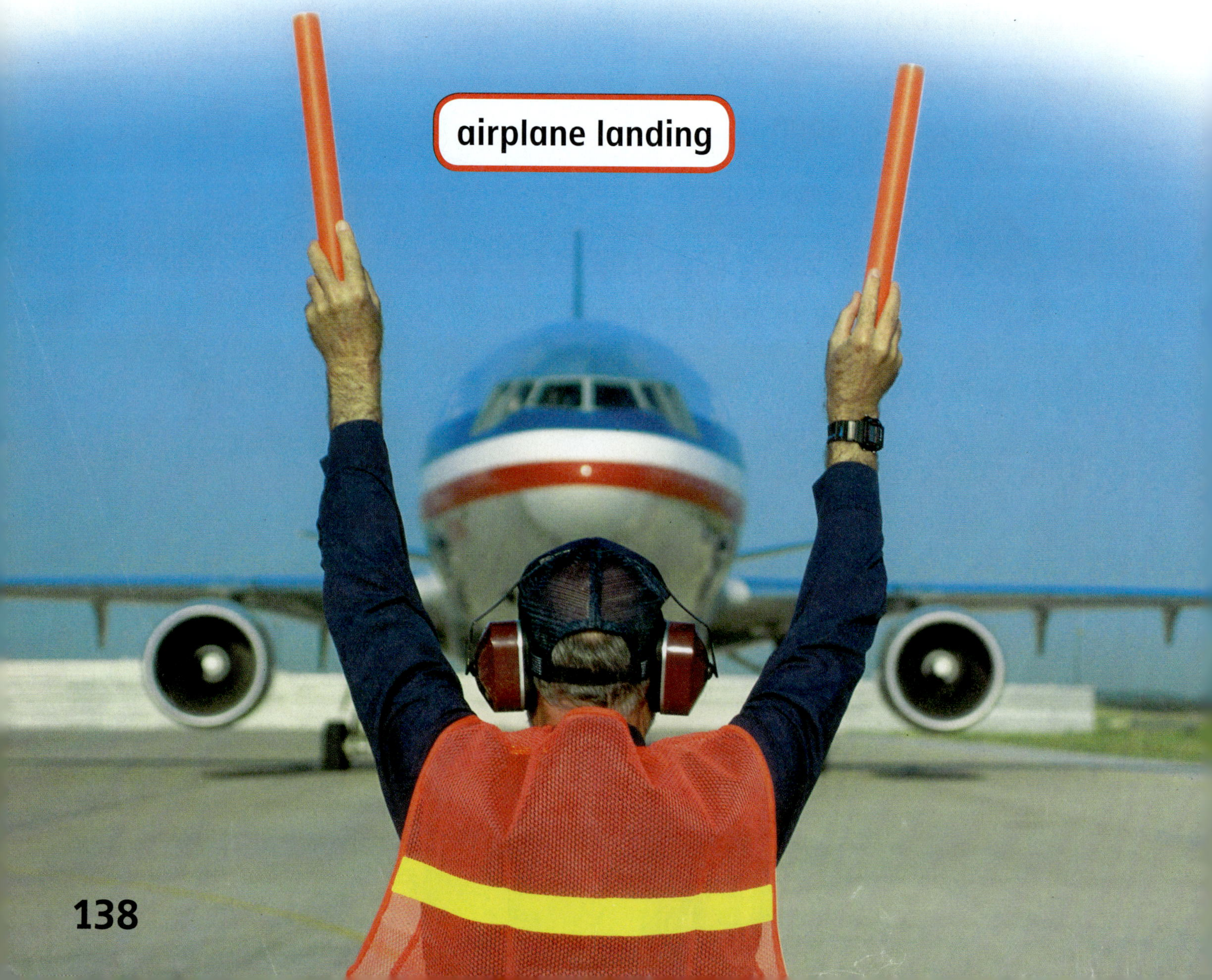
airplane landing

Stand near some people. You can hear them talk. Hearing them talk gets harder as you move farther away from them.

As an ambulance moves closer, the sound gets louder. As the ambulance moves away, the sound gets fainter. Then you can not hear it at all.

Focus Skill **CAUSE AND EFFECT**

What can cause the same sound to sometimes seem louder and sometimes softer?

ambulance

High and Low

Some sounds are high. Others are low. **Pitch** is how high or low a sound is. Small chimes have a high pitch. A big bell has a low pitch.

Fast vibrations make a sound with a high pitch. Slow vibrations make a sound with a low pitch.

chimes

bell

Hit a tuning fork against an object. It will vibrate and make a sound. The sound has the same pitch every time. People use a tuning fork to help them start playing or singing on the correct pitch.

CAUSE AND EFFECT

What makes a sound's pitch high or low?

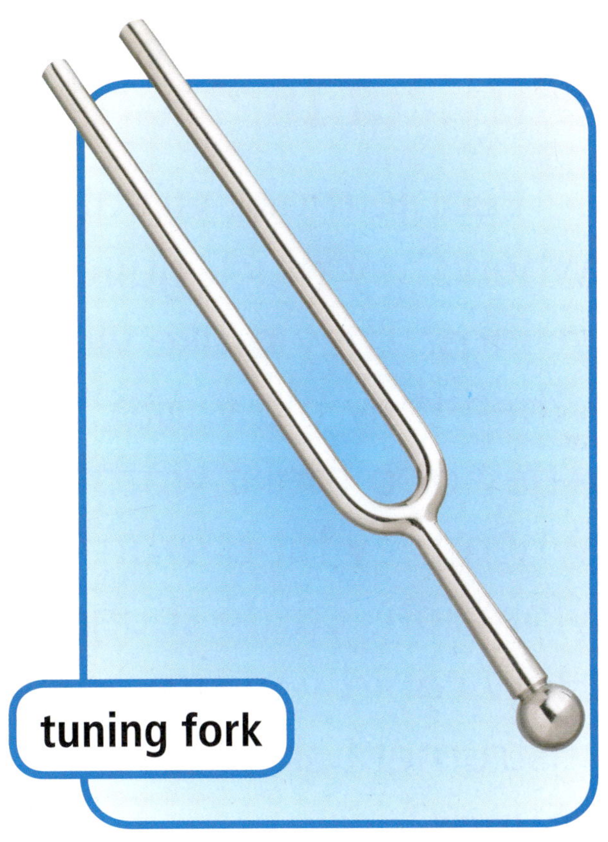

chorus

Musical Instruments

People make vibrations when they pluck guitar strings. They make vibrations when they blow into horns. They also make vibrations when they hit a drum. The vibrations cause sounds. How could you use each instrument shown to make sounds?

What causes musical instruments to make sounds?

Straw Instrument

Cut a straw so the top forms a V. Pinch the top with your lips. Blow very hard. Listen. Then cut off some of the straw at the bottom. Blow again. How does the sound change?

Science Up Close

Musical Instruments

For more links and animations, go to **www.hspscience.com**

Safety Sounds

Some sounds help us stay safe. A fire alarm tells us that there is a fire. A car horn lets us know to get out of the way.

How does a police siren keep us safe?

How do smoke detectors and fire alarms keep us safe?

People's voices help keep us safe, too. A scream tells us that someone is in danger. Your teacher and parents can tell you what you need to do to stay safe.

Focus Skill CAUSE AND EFFECT

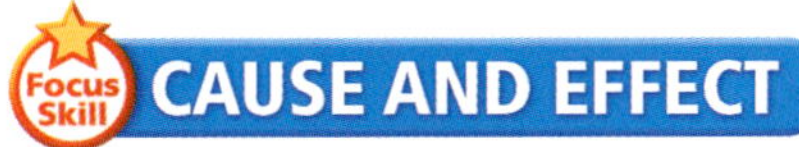

What helps us stay safe?

How is this teacher keeping her students safe?

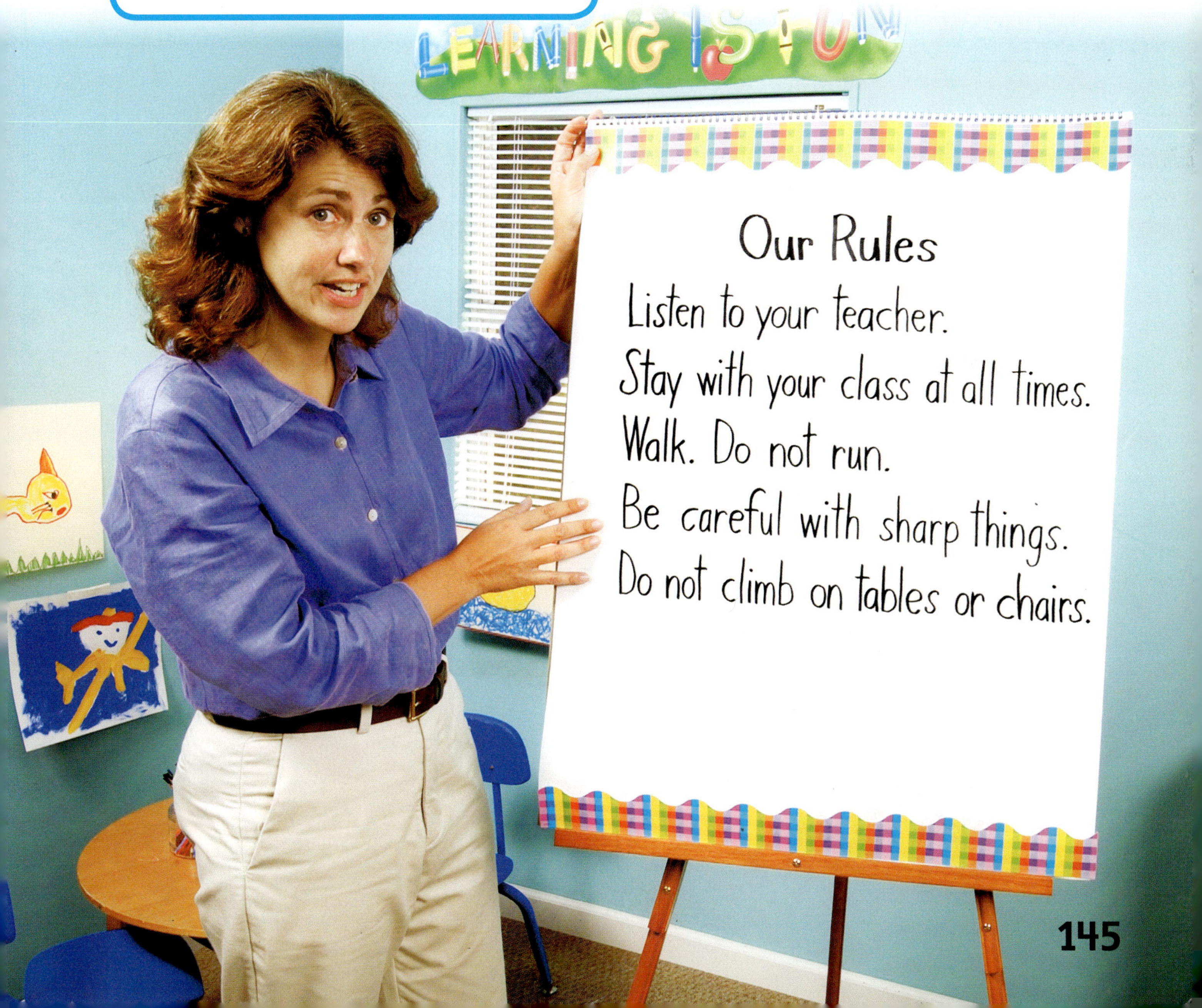

GPS Wrap-Up and Lesson Review

Essential Question

What causes sound?

In this lesson, you learned that sound is caused by the vibrations of objects. You can describe a sound by its pitch, or how high or low it is, and its volume, or how loud or soft it is.

1. Focus Skill **CAUSE AND EFFECT** Make a chart like this one. Show what causes different sounds. S1P1d

cause → effect

2. **DRAW CONCLUSIONS** Why do different musical instruments make different sounds? S1P1d

3. **VOCABULARY** Use the words **sound** and **vibration** in a sentence about this picture. S1P1c

4. What sounds do you hear at school that help keep you safe? S1P1e

CRCT Practice

5. What happens when a guitar string vibrates more quickly?

A It makes a higher sound.
B It makes a lower sound.
C It makes no sound.

S1P1c S1P1d

The Big Idea

6. What parts of a guitar vibrate to make sounds? How do you know? S1P1c

Writing

ELA1W1b

Write to Describe

1. Sit quietly and listen to the sounds around you.
2. Write about the sounds you hear. Describe them.
3. Compare descriptions with a classmate.

I hear a door squeak.

A dog barks outside.

Math

M1D1a

How Long a Sound Lasts

1. Hold a triangle by its string. Tap the triangle gently. Record how many seconds the sound lasts.
2. Tap a bit harder. Record the number of seconds.
3. Hit the triangle very hard. Record the number of seconds.
4. Look at the data in your chart. Which sound lasted the longest? Why?

How Long Sounds Last

tap	seconds
gentle tap	
medium tap	
hard tap	

For more links and activities, go to **www.hspscience.com**

Alexander Graham Bell

- Inventor
- Invented many things

Alexander Graham Bell

Alexander Graham Bell was an inventor. He worked on machines that used sound. He wanted to help people who could not hear.

Alexander Graham Bell made a discovery. He found that he could send speech sounds over an electric wire. He and other scientists worked to make something that is still very important today—the telephone!

Think and Write

How has Alexander Graham Bell's work with the telephone helped keep us safe?

model of a telephone

Ray Charles

Ray Charles was a singer and pianist. He was born in Albany, Georgia. Ray Charles started playing music when he was three years old. He listened to many kinds of music. He used sounds from different kinds of music in his own music. He came up with his own style of music called "soul."

- **Ray Charles**
- **Georgia Musician**
- **Wrote and sang songs and played the piano**

One of Ray Charles's best-known songs is "Georgia On My Mind." This is the state song of Georgia.

Think and Write

How did Ray Charles make sound with his piano? S1P1c

Wrap-Up

Visual Summary

Tell how each picture helps explain the **Big Idea**.

Light can make shadows.
Vibrations make sound.

Lesson 1 S1P1a, S1P1b

The sun, lamps, candles, fire, and lightning are some things that give off light. Shadows are made when an object blocks light.

Lesson 2 S1P1c, S1P1d, S1P1e

Sound is made by vibrations, or back and forth movements. Sound has pitch and volume. Some sounds help keep us safe.

Show What You Know

Chapter Writing Activity

Musical Instruments/Write Sentences

Choose a musical instrument you like. Read about it. Then write sentences to explain how the instrument makes sound. Tell who invented the instrument and what it is made of. Draw a picture of the instrument. Share your writing with the class. ELA1W1e

Georgia Performance Task

Shadows

Shine a flashlight on a wall. Tape a sheet of paper in that spot. Set an object between the wall and the light. Draw its shadow on the paper. Then move the object close to the light and far from the light. Draw and label its shadow each time. How does the shadow change? Why? S1P1b

Vocabulary Review

Use the words to complete the sentences. The page numbers tell you where to look if you need help.

light p. 124 **vibration** p. 137

shadow p. 127 **volume** p. 138

sound p. 136 **pitch** p. 140

1. A ______ is a back and forth motion that can make sound. S1P1c

2. ______ is what you hear. S1P1c

3. The ______ is how high or low a sound is. S1P1d

4. When an object blocks light it makes a ______ . S1P1b

5. ______ is energy that lets us see. S1P1a

6. The ______ is how loud or soft a sound is. S1P1d

Check Understanding

7. Which kind of pitch does a whistle have? S1P1d

A high

B loud

C low

8. Explain how these trees make shadows.

Critical Thinking

9. How do fire truck sirens help keep us safe?

The Big Idea

10. Tell what you know about how sound is made. S1P1c

Chapter 5 Magnets

Georgia Performance Standards in This Chapter

Content

S1P2 Students will demonstrate effects of magnets on other magnets and other objects.

S1P2a S1P2b S1P2c

This chapter also includes these co-requisite standards:

Characteristics of Science

S1CS1 Students will be aware of the importance of curiosity, honesty, openness, and skepticism in science and will exhibit these traits in their own efforts to understand how the world works.

S1CS1a

S1CS2 Students will have the computation and estimation skills necessary for analyzing data following scientific explanations.

S1CS2b S1CS2c S1CS2d

S1CS5 Students will communicate scientific ideas and activities clearly.

S1CS5a S1CS5b S1CS5c

S1CS6 Students will be familiar with the character of scientific knowledge and how it is achieved.

S1CS6b

What's the Big Idea?

Magnets can attract objects made of iron, and can pull through some materials.

Essential Questions

for student eBook www.hspscience.com

Science in Georgia

Athens

Dear Rosa,

Saturday we went to the University of Georgia football game. Mom and Dad let me put a team magnet on the car. The Bulldogs won the game!

Your friend,

Braden

Read Braden's postcard. What did he learn about magnets? How does that help explain the **Big Idea?**

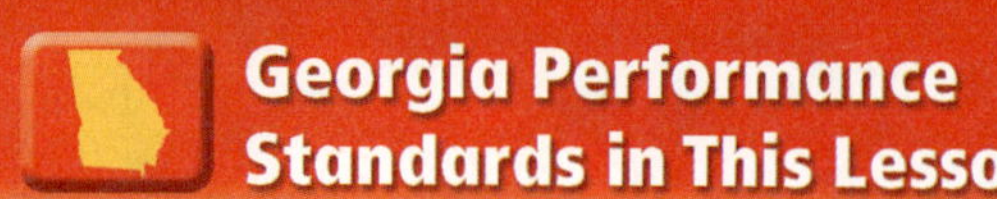

Georgia Performance Standards in This Lesson

Content

S1P2a Demonstrate how magnets attract and repel.

S1P2b Identify common objects that are attracted to a magnet.

Characteristics of Science

S1CS6b

LESSON 1

Essential Question

What Can a Magnet Do?

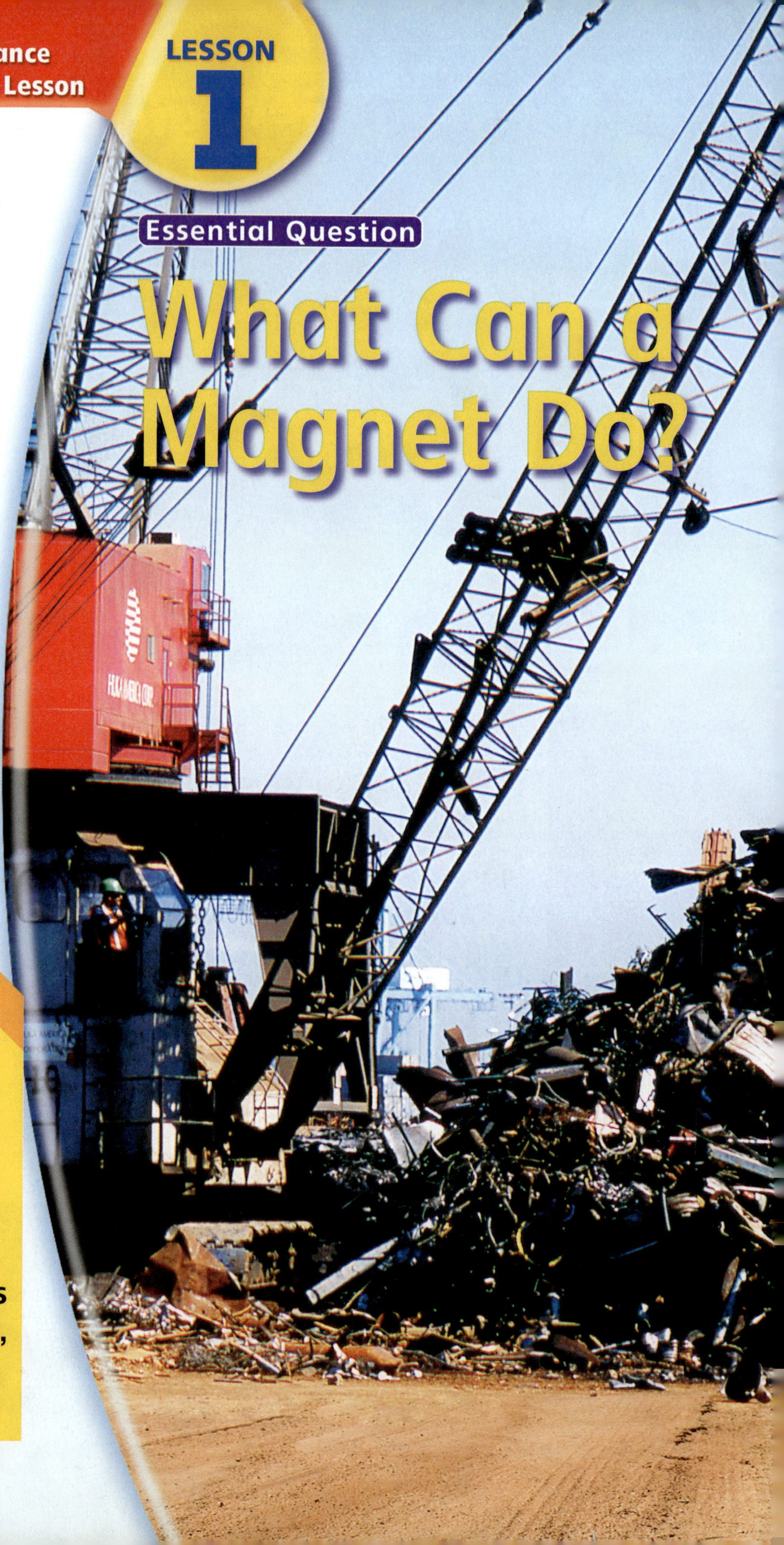

Georgia Fast Fact

Junkyard Magnet

Some magnets are very strong. They can pick up large pieces of metal. This magnet is so strong, it can pick up piles of metal.

magnet moving metal
Vocabulary Preview
magnet p. 160
S
N
S
N
attract p. 160
N
S
pole p. 162
repel p. 163

What Magnets Pull

Guided Inquiry

Ask a Question

What do you think is making things stick to the cabinet below? Investigate to find out. Then read to find out more.

Get Ready

Inquiry Skill Tip

When you hypothesize, you think of an idea.

You need

bar magnet

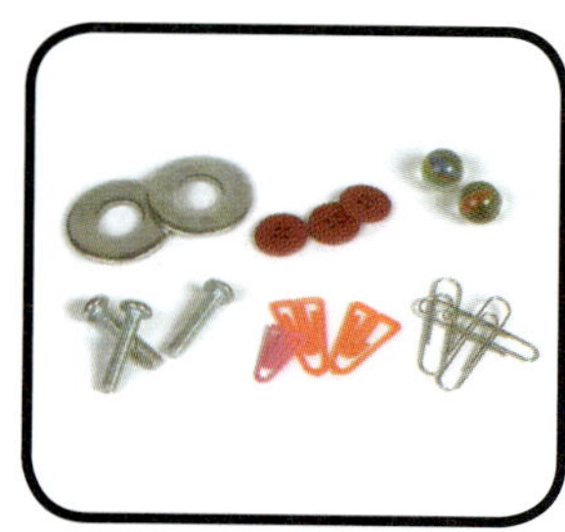

objects

What to Do

Step 1

Look at the objects. Which ones will a magnet pull? **Hypothesize**.

Step 2

Test your hypothesis. Use a magnet. Record your observations.

What a Magnet Can Do

Object	Pulls	Does Not Pull

Step 3

Was your hypothesis correct? How do you know?

Draw Conclusions

What did you find out about magnets? S1P2a

Independent Inquiry

Where are the poles of a magnet? **Hypothesize**. Test your hypothesis. Draw each magnet. Circle the poles. S1CS6b

Understand Science

VOCABULARY
magnet
attract
pole
repel

Focus Skill **MAIN IDEA AND DETAILS**

Find out what magnets are and what they attract.

Magnets

A **magnet** is an object that will **attract**, or pull, things made of iron.

magnets

What does a magnet attract? You can test objects to see. A magnet does not attract all metals. It attracts metals that have iron in them. Steel has iron in it.

What is a magnet?

What Are Magnets Attracted To?

attracted	not attracted
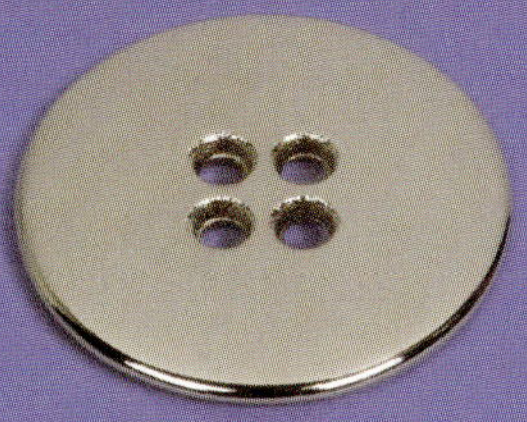 steel button	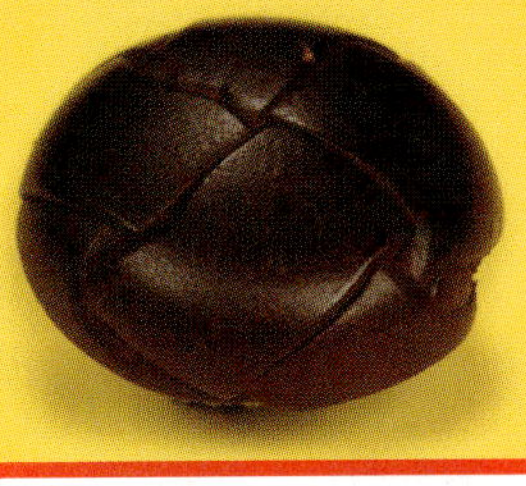 leather button
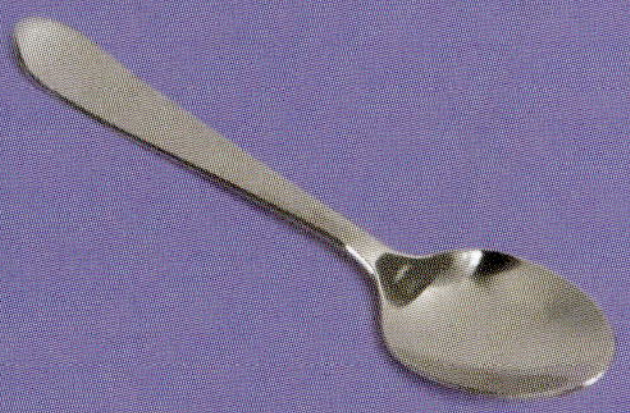 steel spoon	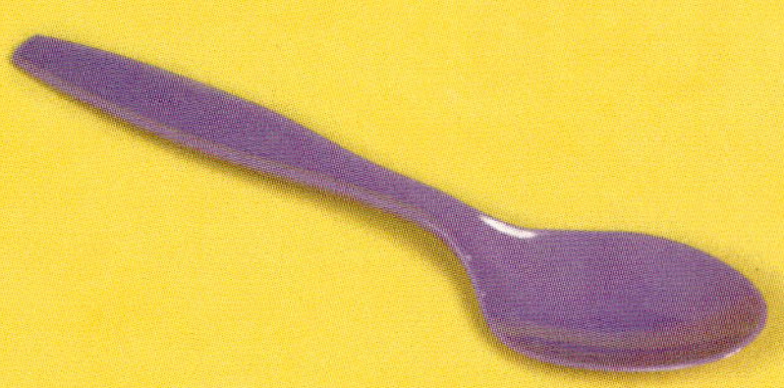 plastic spoon
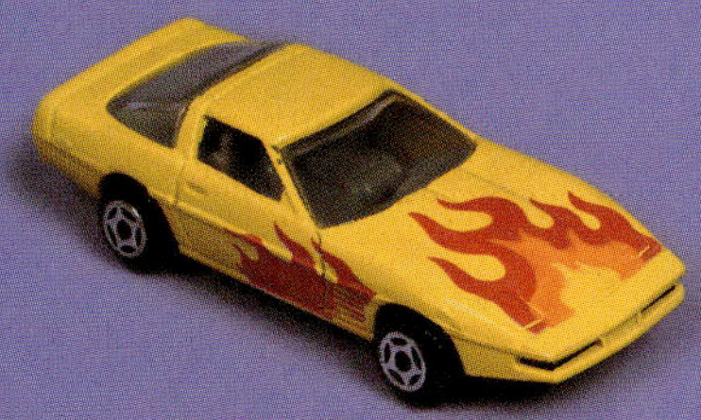 iron car	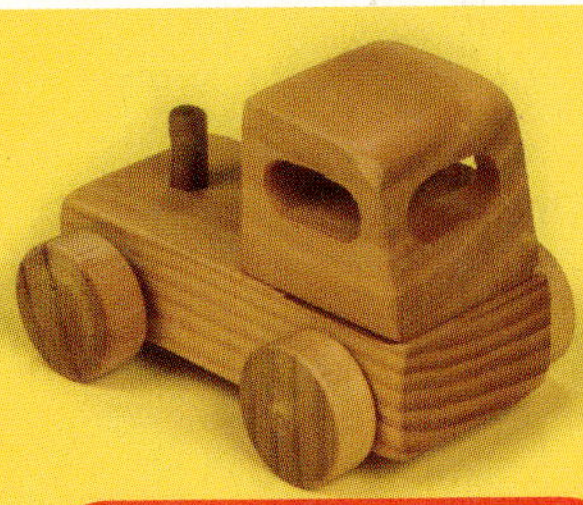 wooden car

Poles of a Magnet

A magnet has an N pole and an S pole. N stands for north. S stands for south. A **pole** is near an end of a bar magnet. The pull is strongest at a magnet's poles.

MAIN IDEA AND DETAILS

What are a magnet's poles?

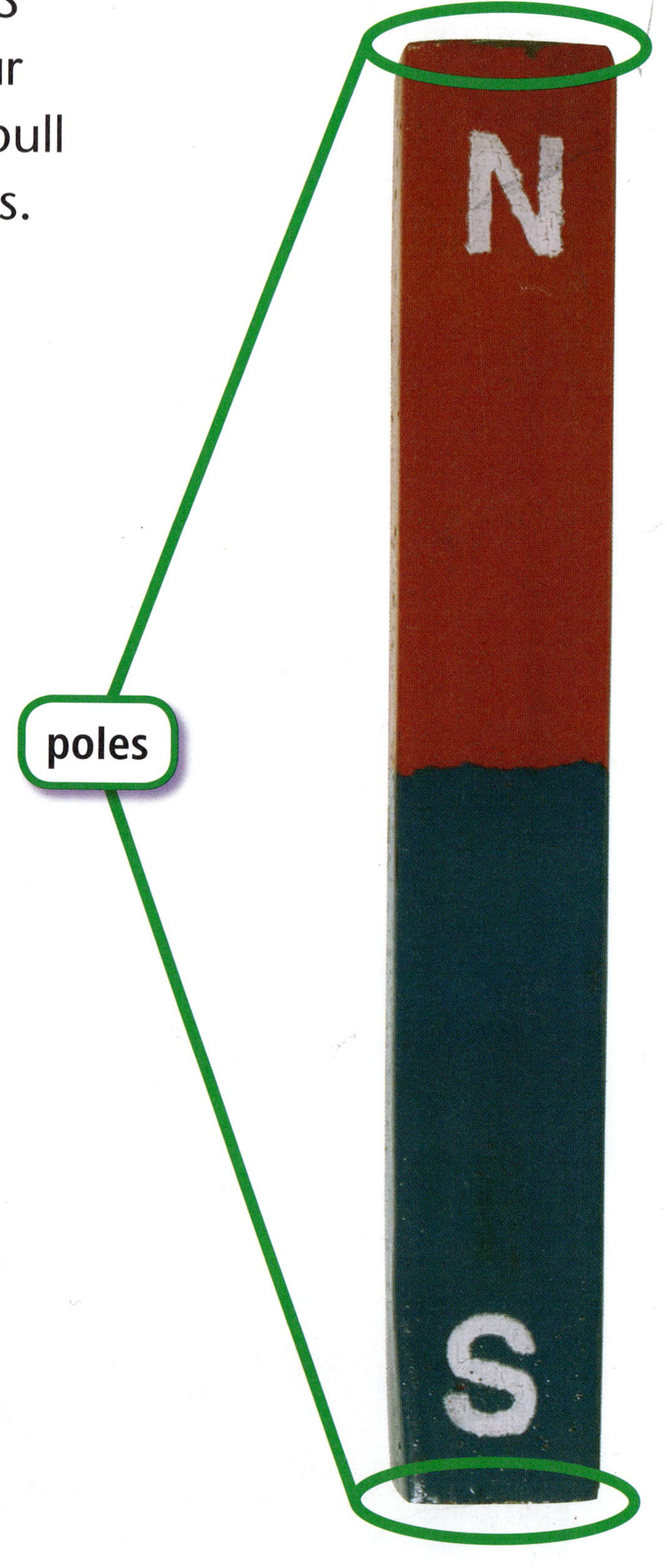

Poles of a Magnet

What will happen when you put together the ends of two magnets? Bring the N end of one magnet toward the S end of the other magnet. Repeat using the two N ends and then the two S ends. What did you find out?

How Magnets Attract and Repel

You can try to put magnets together. If the poles are different, they attract each other. Poles that are the same **repel** each other, or push each other away.

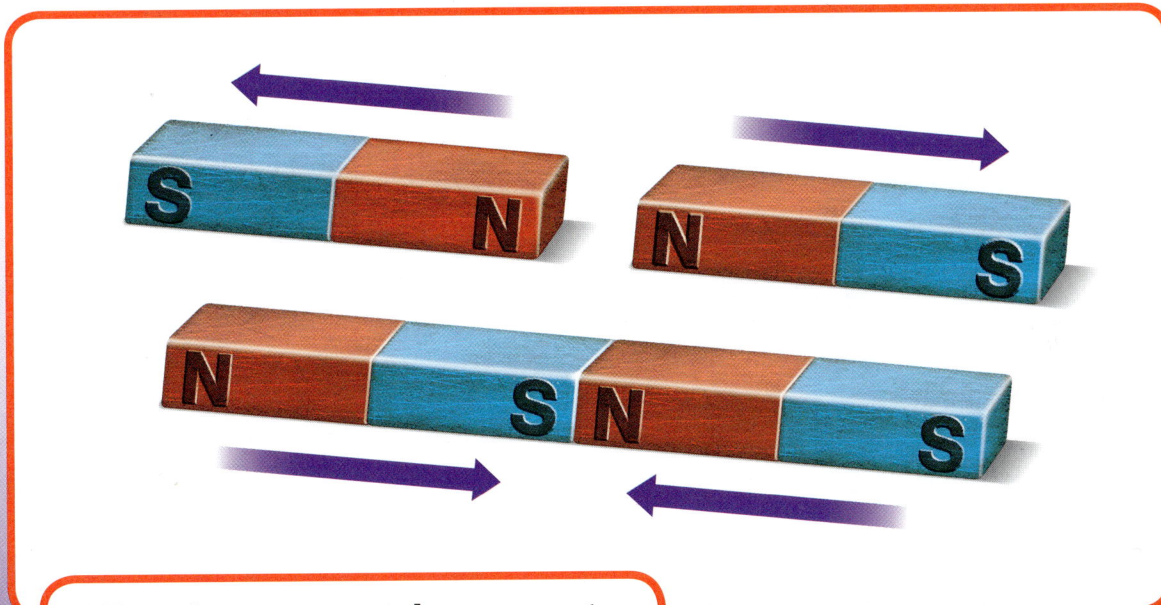

What happens when you try to put magnets together?

GPS Wrap-Up and Lesson Review

Essential Questions

What can a magnet do?

In this lesson, you learned about some things that are attracted to magnets. You also learned how magnets attract and repel.

1. **Focus Skill MAIN IDEA AND DETAILS** Make a chart like this one. Show the details of this main idea. **A magnet will attract things made of iron.** S1P2b

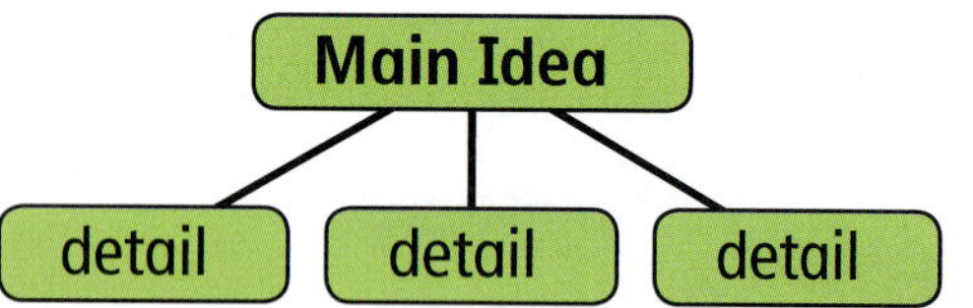

2. **DRAW CONCLUSIONS** Tell what happens when you put the poles of two magnets together. S1P2a

3. **VOCABULARY** Use the word **repel** to tell about this picture. S1P2a

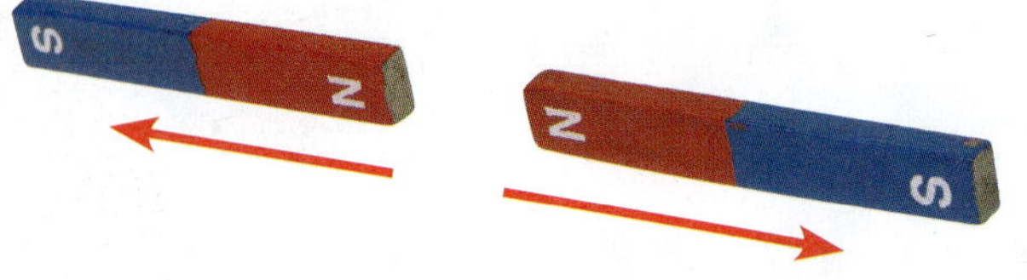

4. A magnet attracts a toy. What do you know about the toy? S1P2b

CRCT Practice

5. Where are the poles of a bar magnet?
   A in the middle
   B near the ends
   C on the back S1P2a

The Big Idea

6. What are some objects that a magnet attracts? S1P2b

Writing ELA1W1k

Write a Report

1. Some objects, such as a compass, use magnets. What other objects use magnets? Research objects that use magnets.
2. Write a report about one object that uses a magnet. How does the magnet help the object work?

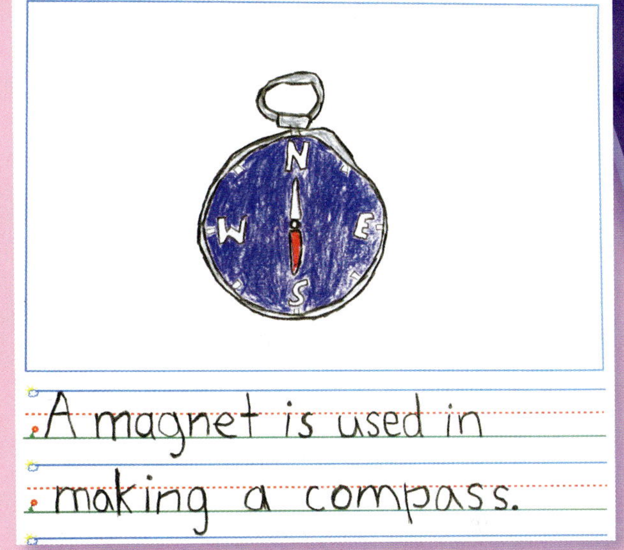

Social Studies  SS1E2

Recycling with Magnets

1. Recycling centers use magnets to sort kinds of metal. See how.
2. Get clean pieces of metal from a recycling bin.
3. Use a magnet to sort them. Make a chart to show your groups.

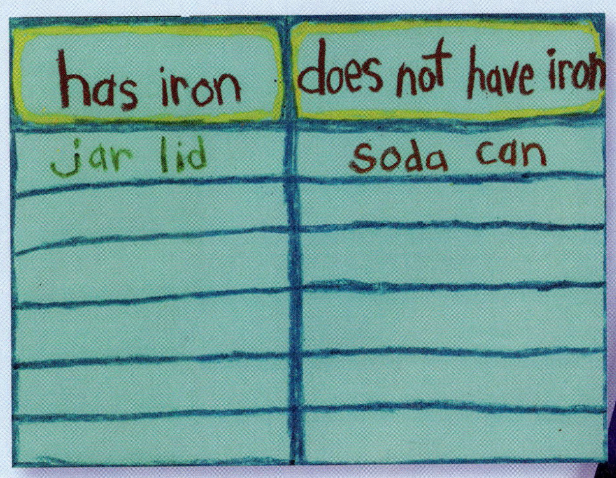

For more links and activities, go to **www.hspscience.com**

Magnetic Toys

This dog was built with magnetic pieces.

Where are the magnets in this toy?

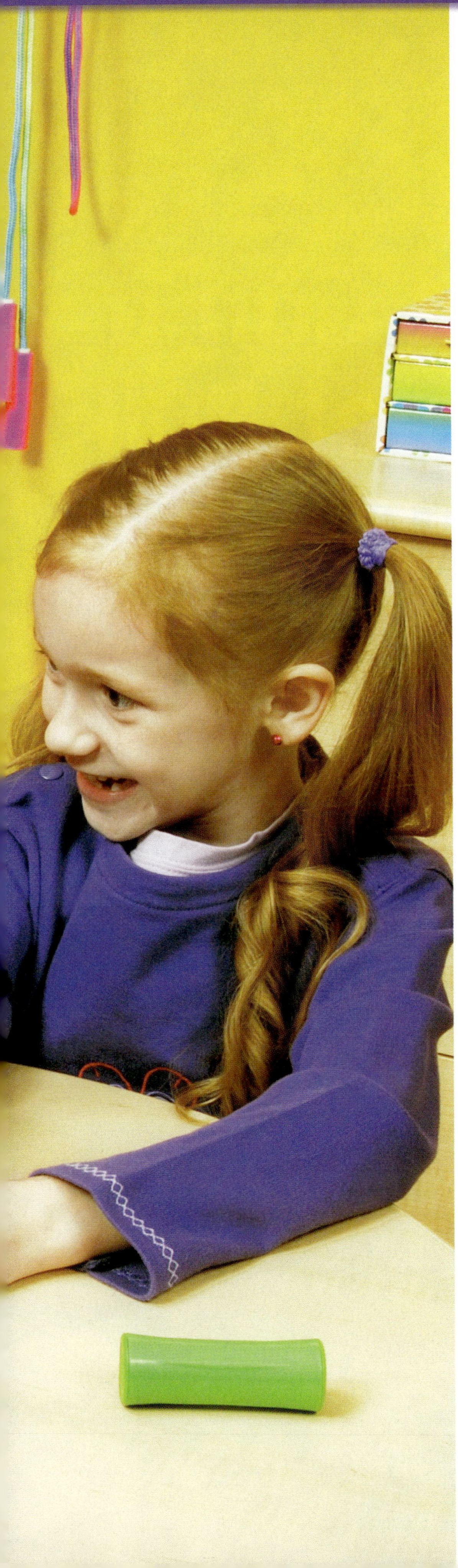

Magnets can make playtime fun. Have you ever built something with magnets? Some building kits use magnets to put the pieces together. The magnets in the pieces attract each other. They stay together until you take them apart. You can make many different shapes.

Magnetic drawing boards are also fun toys. You move iron filings around with a magnet on a stick. The iron is attracted to the magnet. It moves wherever you want it to go!

Think and Write

What does a magnet attract?

S1P2b

Find out more. Log on to **www.hspscience.com**

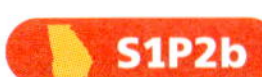

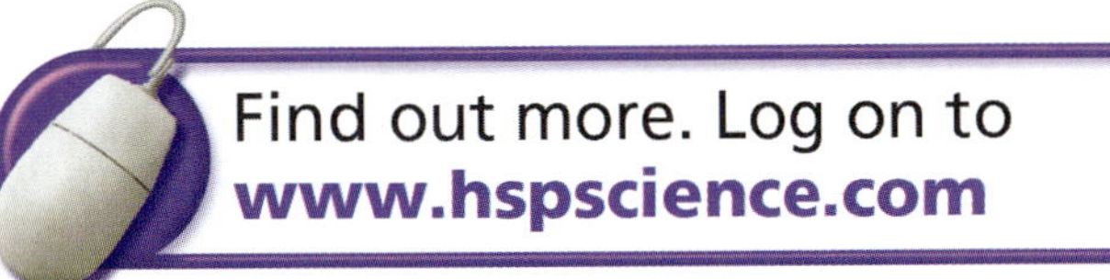

Georgia Performance Standards in This Lesson

Content

S1P2c Identify objects and materials (air, water, wood, paper, your hand, etc.) that do not block magnetic force.

Characteristics of Science

S1CS1a S1CS2a S1CS5a S1CS5b S1CS5c

LESSON 2

Essential Question

What Can a Magnet Pull Through?

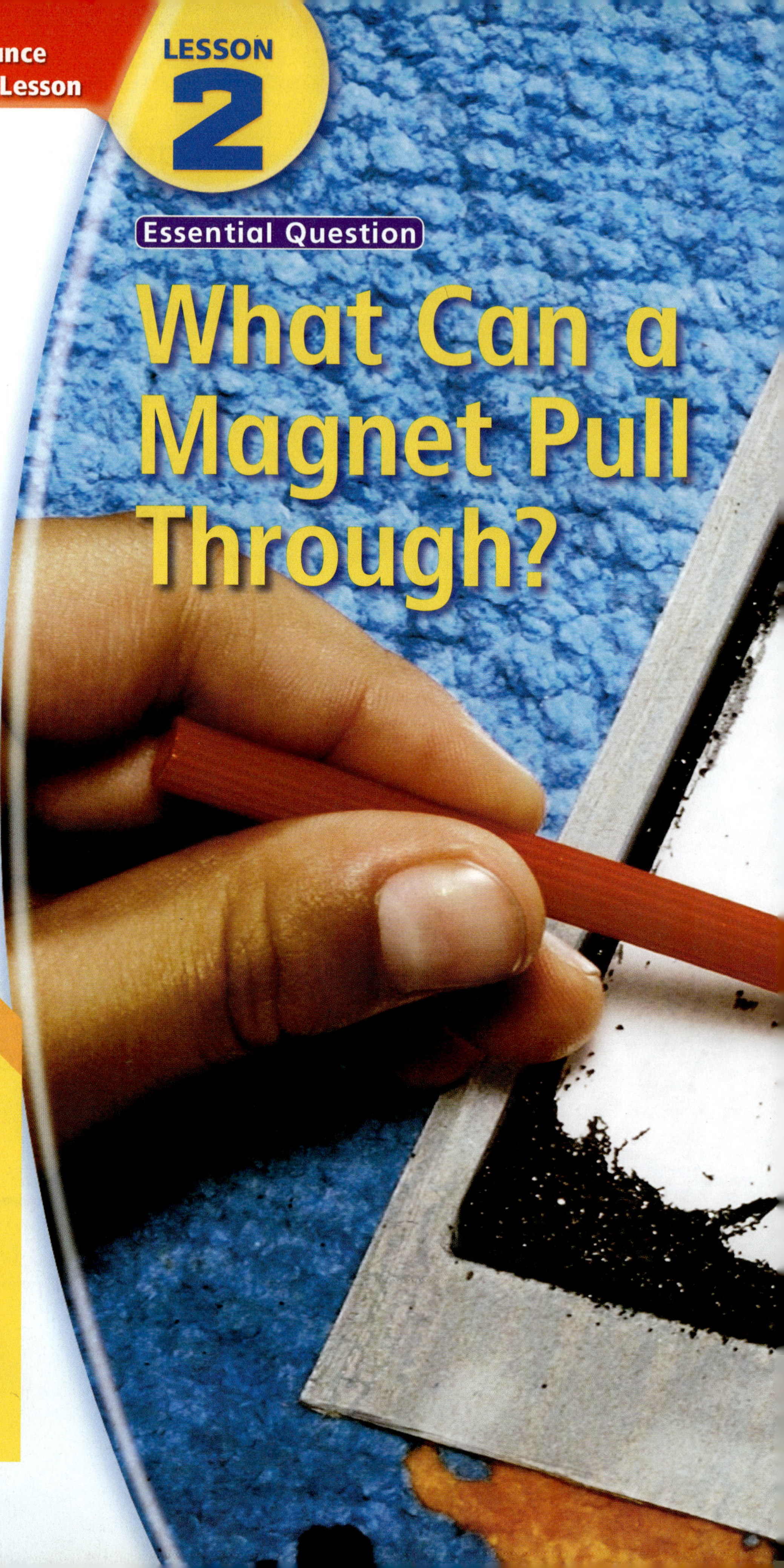

Georgia Fast Fact

Magnetic Force

Magnets can pull through plastic. Iron is under a plastic cover on this toy. You use the magnetic stick to move the iron to change the picture.

Vocabulary Preview
N
S
magnetic force
p. 172
magnetic toy

Investigate

Things Magnets Pull Through

Guided Inquiry

Ask a Question

How do you know that cardboard does not block magnetic force? Investigate to find out. Then read to find out more.

Get Ready

Inquiry Skill Tip

Plan an investigation. Think of ways to answer a question. Find what you need. Try your ideas.

You need

bar magnet

paper clips

different materials

magnet pulling through cardboard

What to Do

Step 1

Can a magnet attract paper clips through things? **Plan an investigation** to find out. Write your plan.

Step 2

Follow your plan to try your ideas. Write about what you see.

Step 3

Use your data to tell what you find out.

Draw Conclusions

What can the force of a magnet pull through?

Independent Inquiry

Plan an investigation. Will a magnet keep attracting a paper clip as you stack more and more cards between them?

S1CS1a

S1P2c

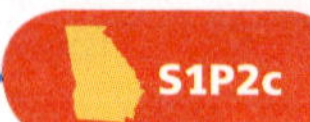

VOCABULARY
magnetic force

Focus Skill **MAIN IDEA AND DETAILS**

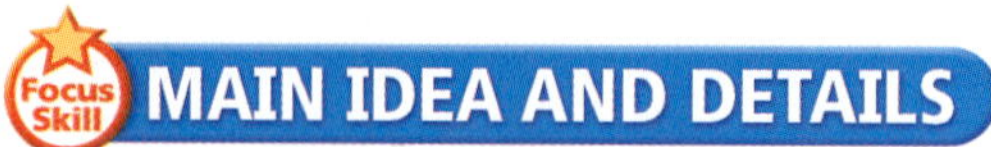

Look for details that tell about magnetic force.

Force of a Magnet

A magnet's pull is called **magnetic force**. Some magnets have a lot of force. They are very strong.

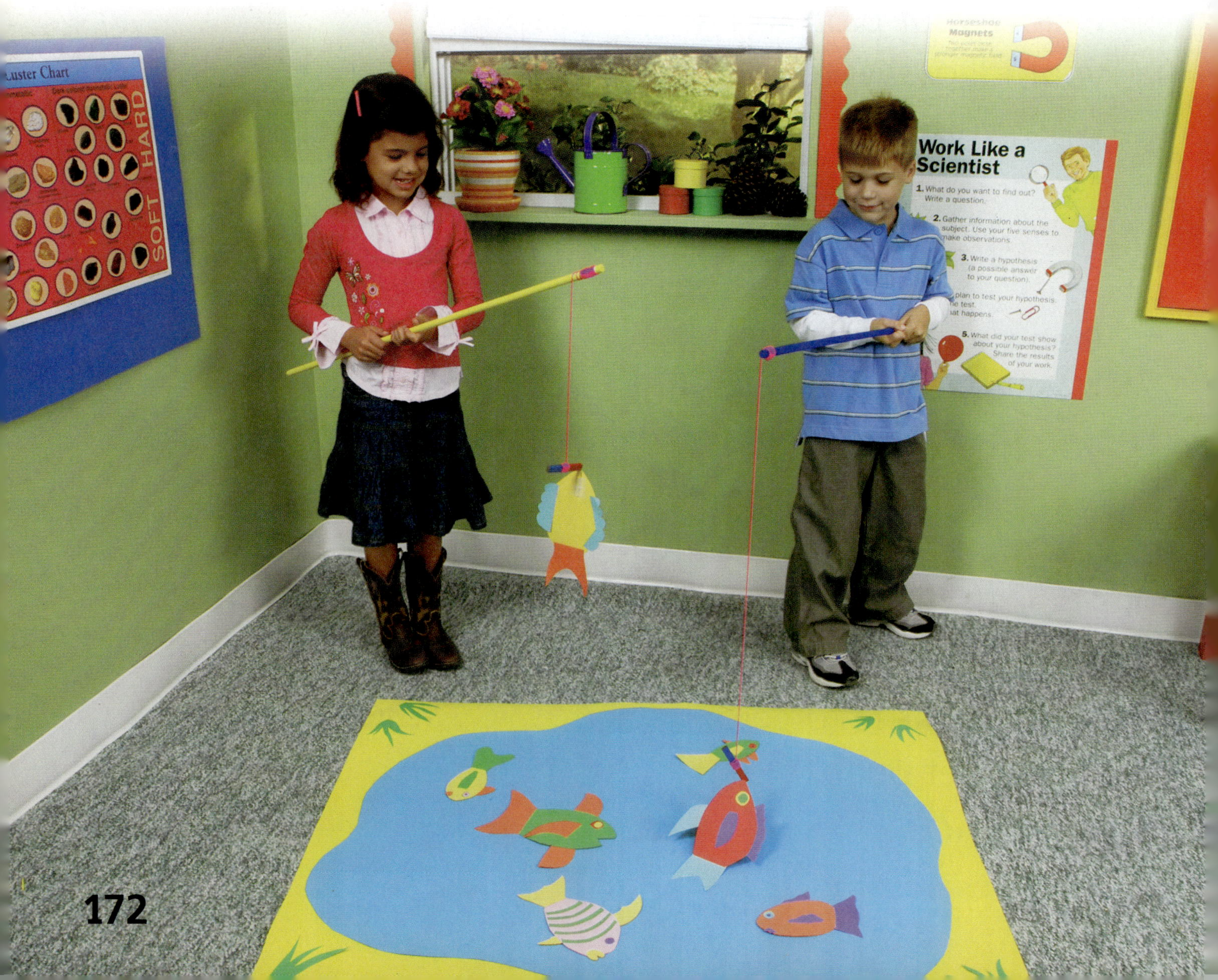

magnet pulling without touching

Magnets can attract objects without touching them. Strong magnets can pull things from far away. This magnet pulls the paper clip on a kite when it is held above it. It can pull through air.

Focus Skill **MAIN IDEA AND DETAILS**

How do you know if a magnet has a strong magnetic force?

What Magnets Pull Through

The magnetic force of some magnets is strong enough to pull through things. This magnet is pulling a toy car through paper. The paper does not block the magnetic force.

magnet pulling through paper

Magnets can pull through other things, too. A magnet can pull a paper clip through water in a plastic cup. A very strong magnet can pull screws through wood. It can even pull paper clips through your hand.

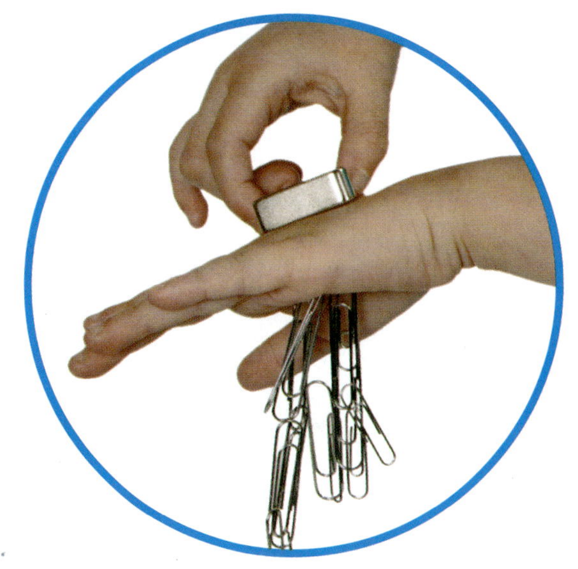

MAIN IDEA AND DETAILS Focus Skill

What are some things that do not block magnetic force?

Insta-Lab

Move It With a Magnet

Find out what a magnet pulls through. Use a strong magnet. Try to attract a metal clip through paper, cloth, and other materials. Tell what you observe.

GPS Wrap-Up and Lesson Review

Essential Question

What can a magnet pull through?

In this lesson, you learned that magnets pull through different things. They can also move objects without touching them.

1. **MAIN IDEA AND DETAILS** Make a chart like this one. Write details of this main idea. **Magnets can pull through different things.** S1P2c

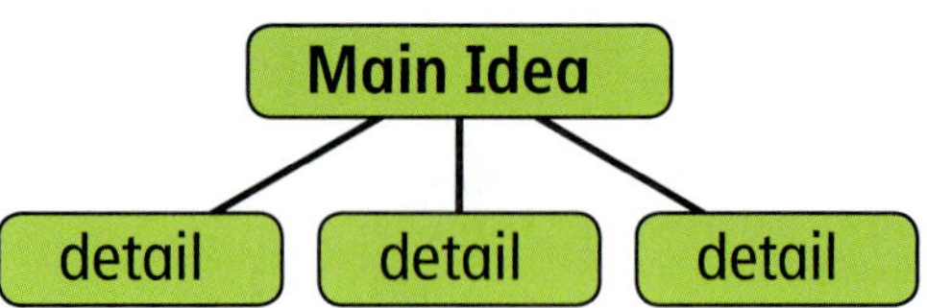

2. **SUMMARIZE** Use the chart to write a summary of the lesson. S1P2c

3. **VOCABULARY** Use the term **magnetic force** to tell about the picture. S1P2c

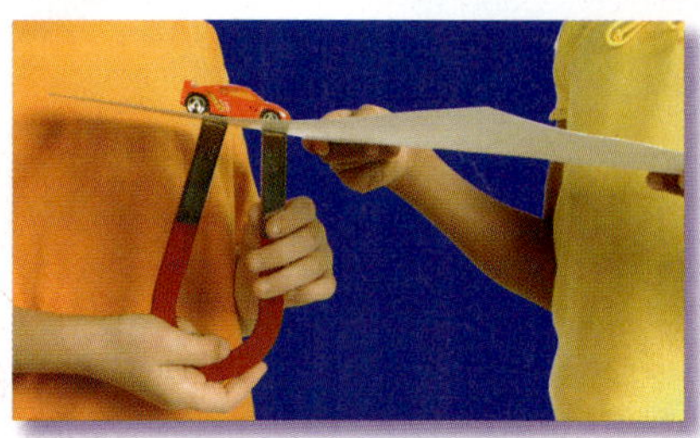

4. What do you know if a magnet can not pull through an object? S1P2c

CRCT Practice

5. What do you know if a magnet pulls a toy through cardboard?
   - **A** The toy is a magnet.
   - **B** The toy does not have iron or steel.
   - **C** The cardboard does not block magnetic force. S1P2c

The Big Idea

6. What things can a magnet pull through? S1P2c

Writing

Write to Describe

1. Think of a toy or tool that uses a magnet.
2. Describe it. Write what it does and how to make it.
3. Draw a picture of it.
4. Share your idea with the class.

Paper Clip Grabber

I made a tool that picks up paper clips that fall on the floor.
I taped a magnet to the end of a ruler.

Math

Magnet Bar Graph

1. Hold a magnet over a pile of paper clips. Count the number of clips the magnet can pick up.
2. Show your findings. Make a tally chart.
3. Repeat with pennies. Then use safety pins.
4. Use the tally chart to make a bar graph.

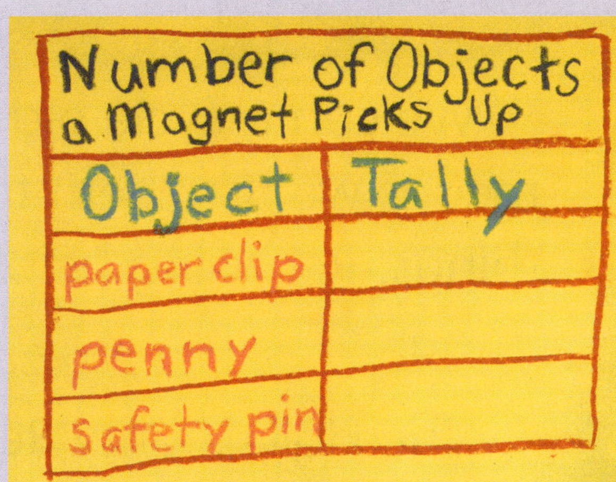

Number of Objects a Magnet Picks Up

Object	Tally
paper clip	
penny	
safety pin	

For more links and activities, go to **www.hspscience.com**

Hall County Recycling Center

We can recycle old things. This means we use them to make new things. Recycling helps us take care of resources.

The Hall County Recycling Center is in Gainesville. It collects paper, glass, and plastic. It also collects different metals. Each kind of material goes through different steps. Then the materials can be recycled.

Steel is the material most often recycled in the United States. Soup cans, pet food cans, and other cans are made of steel.

The Hall County Recycling Center uses magnets to separate steel cans from other materials. The magnets attract steel cans because steel has iron in it. The magnets do not attract other cans or things that do not have iron in them.

Magnets make the job of separating the materials much easier.

Think and Write

How could you use a magnet at home to separate your recycled goods? S1P2b

Wrap-Up

Visual Summary

Tell how each picture helps explain the **Big Idea**.

Magnets can attract objects made of iron, and can pull through some materials.

Lesson 1 S1P2a, b

A magnet will attract things made of iron. Two different poles of a magnet also attract each other. Two poles that are the same repel each other.

Lesson 2 S1P2c

Magnets can pull through some objects. Air, water, wood, paper, and your hand do not block magnetic force.

Show What You Know

Magazine Ads/Write About a Topic

Design a magazine ad for magnets. Form a group of two or three children. Make up a name for a new magnet product. Think of a reason why that product is useful. Then write a slogan for your product. Use the words **attract** and **repel**. Make a colorful poster of the ad.

ELA1W1a

Georgia Performance Task

Make Your Own Compass

Rub a magnet along a straightened paper clip. Rub 50 times in the same direction. Put a piece of plastic foam in a bowl of water. Lay the paper clip on the foam. Observe the direction to which the paper clip points. Turn the bowl. What happens? Write about how a compass works.

S1P2b

Vocabulary Review

Use the words to complete the sentences. The page numbers tell you where to look if you need help.

magnet p. 160 **repel** p. 163

attract p. 160 **magnetic force** p. 172

pole p. 162

1. A _______ is an object that attracts things made of iron. S1P2b

2. For a magnet, to push away is to _______. S1P2a

3. The N pole of a magnet will _______ the S pole of another magnet. S1P2a

4. A magnet's pull is called _______. S1P2c

5. A magnet is strongest at its _______. S1P2a

Check Understanding

6. Which of these objects will a magnet attract? 

A eraser

B paper

C paper clip

7. Look at the picture. What is the magnetic force pulling through? S1P2c

Critical Thinking

8. Why do you think magnets stick to most refrigerators? 

9. Describe how a magnet can move some objects without touching them. S1P2c

The Big Idea

10. Tell how magnets attract and repel. 

CRCT Practice Physical Science

1. Which is a source of light?

A. a toaster

B. a lamp

C. a drum

S1P1a

2. Why is the girl in the picture in a shadow?

A. The sun shines through the windows.

B. The building blocks the sun's light.

C. The paint on the street catches the sun's light.

S1P1b

3. Which sound is soft or quiet?

A. a siren

B. an airplane

C. a whisper

S1P1d

4. **How does a guitar make sounds?**

A. The strings vibrate.

B. The wood vibrates.

C. The wood does not vibrate.

S1P1c

5. **Look at these two magnets. What will happen if you try to put them together?**

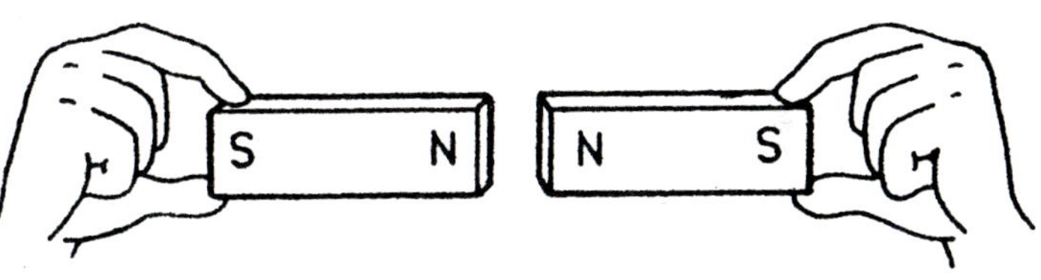

A. They will attract.

B. They will move fast.

C. They will repel.

S1P2a S1P2b

6. **A magnet can not pull a toy through cardboard. What do you know?**

A. The toy is a magnet.

B. The magnet is very strong.

C. The toy is not made of iron or steel.

UNIT
C
LIFE SCIENCE
dolphins
Chapter 6 All About Plants
Chapter 7 All About Animals
GO online
for student eBook
www.hspscience.com

What do you wonder?
These dolphins are swimming underwater. How do they get air?
Unit Inquiry
Plants and Light How does light change the way plants grow? Plan and do a test to find out.

CHAPTER 6
All About Plants

Georgia Performance Standards in This Chapter

Content

S1L1 Students will investigate the characteristics and basic needs of plants and animals.

S1L1a S1L1c

This chapter also addresses these co-requiste standards:

Characteristics of Science

S1CS2 Students will have the computation and estimation skills necessary for analyzing data and following scientific explanations.

S1CS2a

S1CS3 Students will use tools and instruments for observing, measuring, and manipulating objects in scientific activities.

S1CS3a

S1CS5 Students will communicate scientific ideas and activities clearly.

S1CS5b

S1CS7 Students will understand important features of the process of scientific inquiry.

S1CS7d

What's the Big Idea?

Plants need air, water, light, and nutrients to live and grow. Different parts of plants help plants get what they need.

Essential Questions

for student eBook www.hspscience.com

Science in Georgia

Dear Emily,

It is fall here. All of the leaves are changing color. You should see the Chattahoochee National Forest. I hope you can visit soon.

Your friend,

Martin

Read Martin's postcard. What did Martin learn about plants? How do you think that helps explain the **Big Idea?**

Georgia Performance Standards in This Lesson

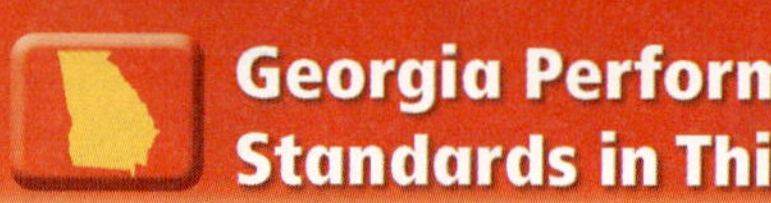

LESSON 1

Essential Question

What Do Plants Need?

Content

S1L1a Identify the basic needs of a plant.

1. Air
2. Water
3. Light
4. Nutrients

Characteristics of Science

S1CS5b S1CS7d

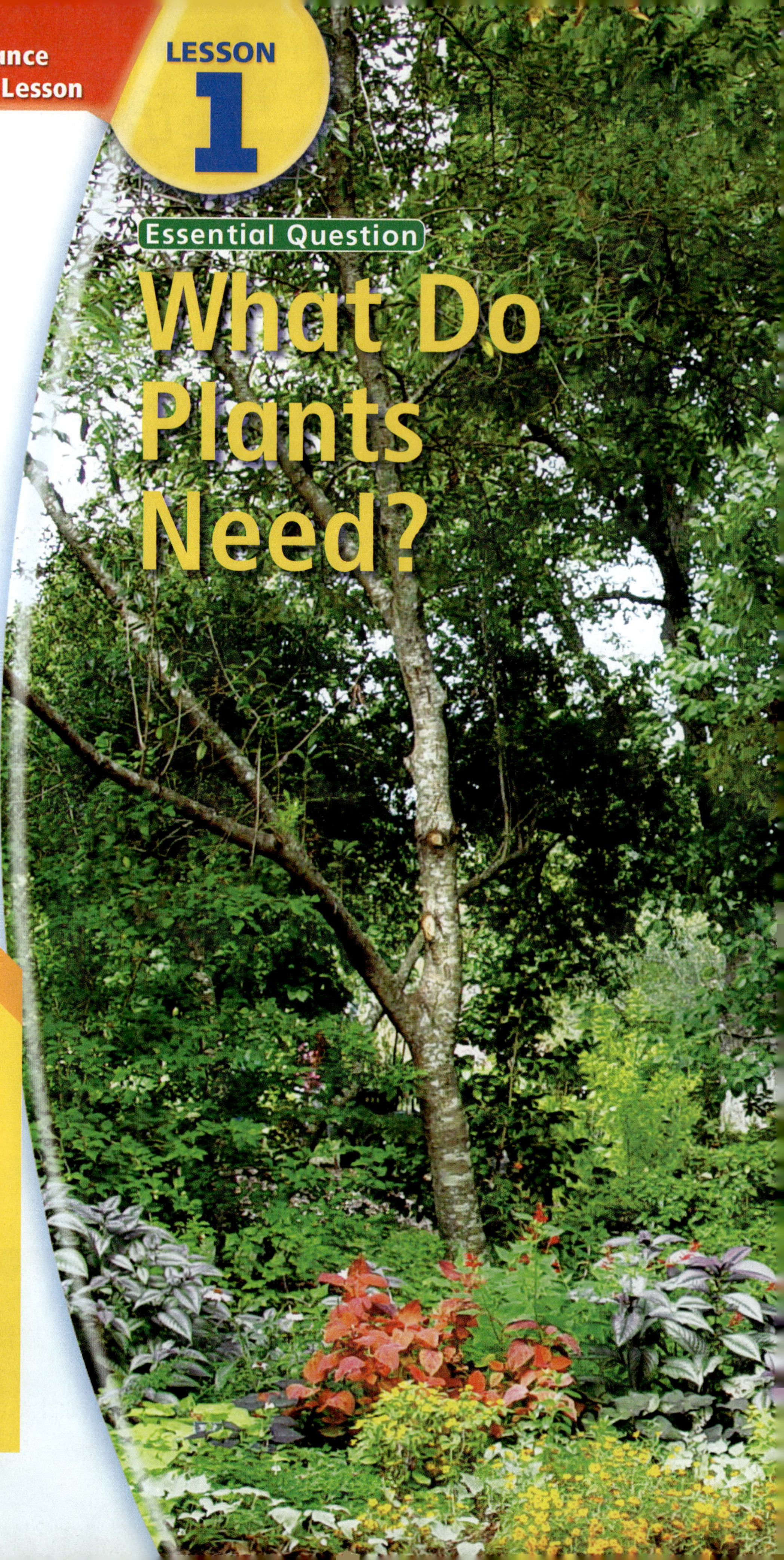

Georgia Fast Fact

Botanical Garden

At this botanical garden, you can plant seeds. You can give them what they need to grow. Then you can harvest the vegetables.

What to Do

Step 1

Label the plants. Put both plants in a sunny place.

Step 2

Water only one of the plants. **Predict** what will happen to each plant.

Step 3

After four days, check the plants. Did you predict correctly?

Draw Conclusions

What did you find out about the needs of plants?

Independent Inquiry

Measure the height of a plant. **Predict** how tall the plant will be in two weeks. After two weeks, check your prediction. S1CS7d

VOCABULARY
sunlight
nutrients

Look for all the things that cause plants to grow.

Light

Plants take in **sunlight**, or light from the sun. A plant needs light, air, and water to make its own food. The food helps the plant grow and stay healthy.

What would happen to a plant that did not have light, air, or water?

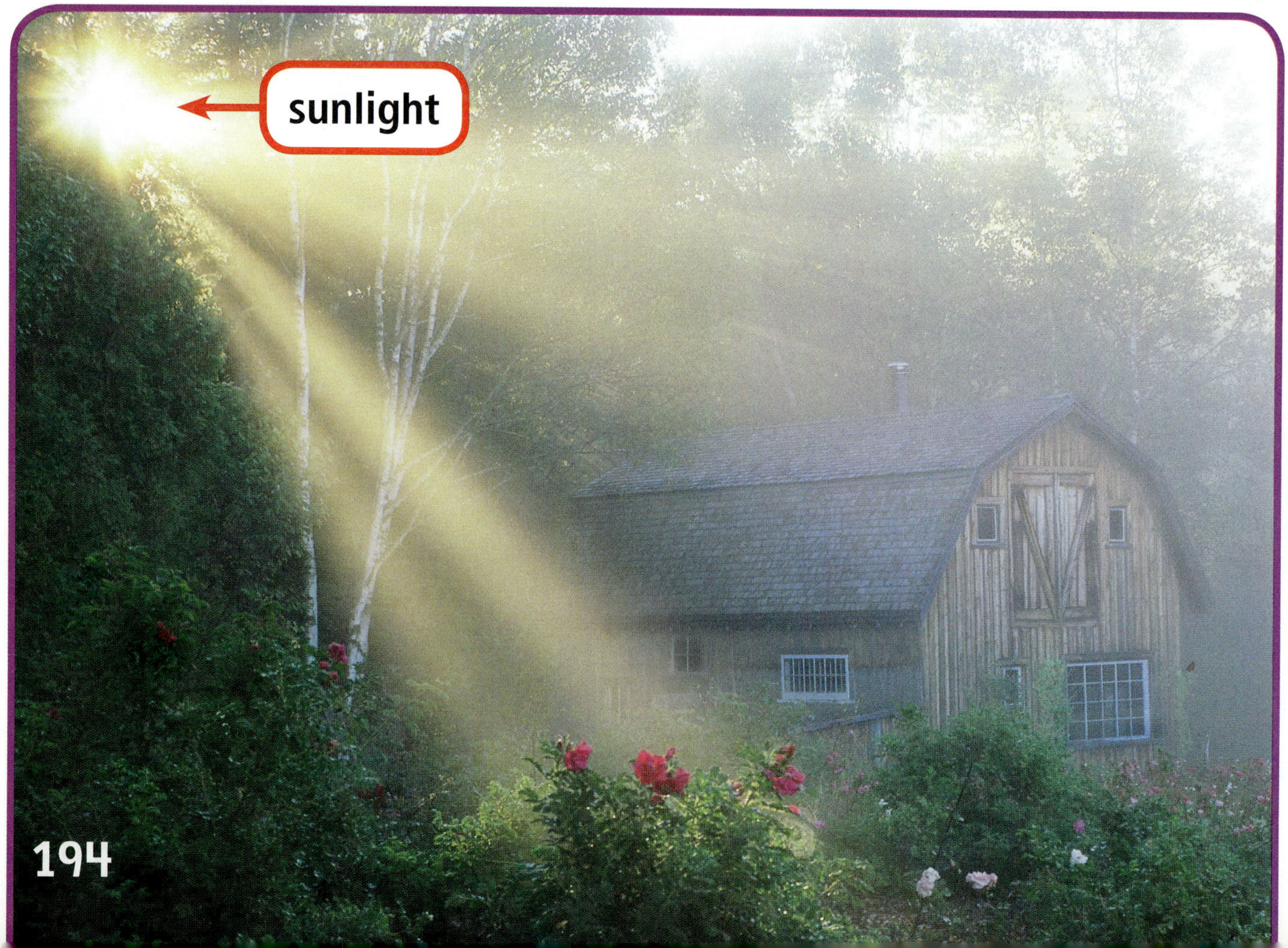

sunlight

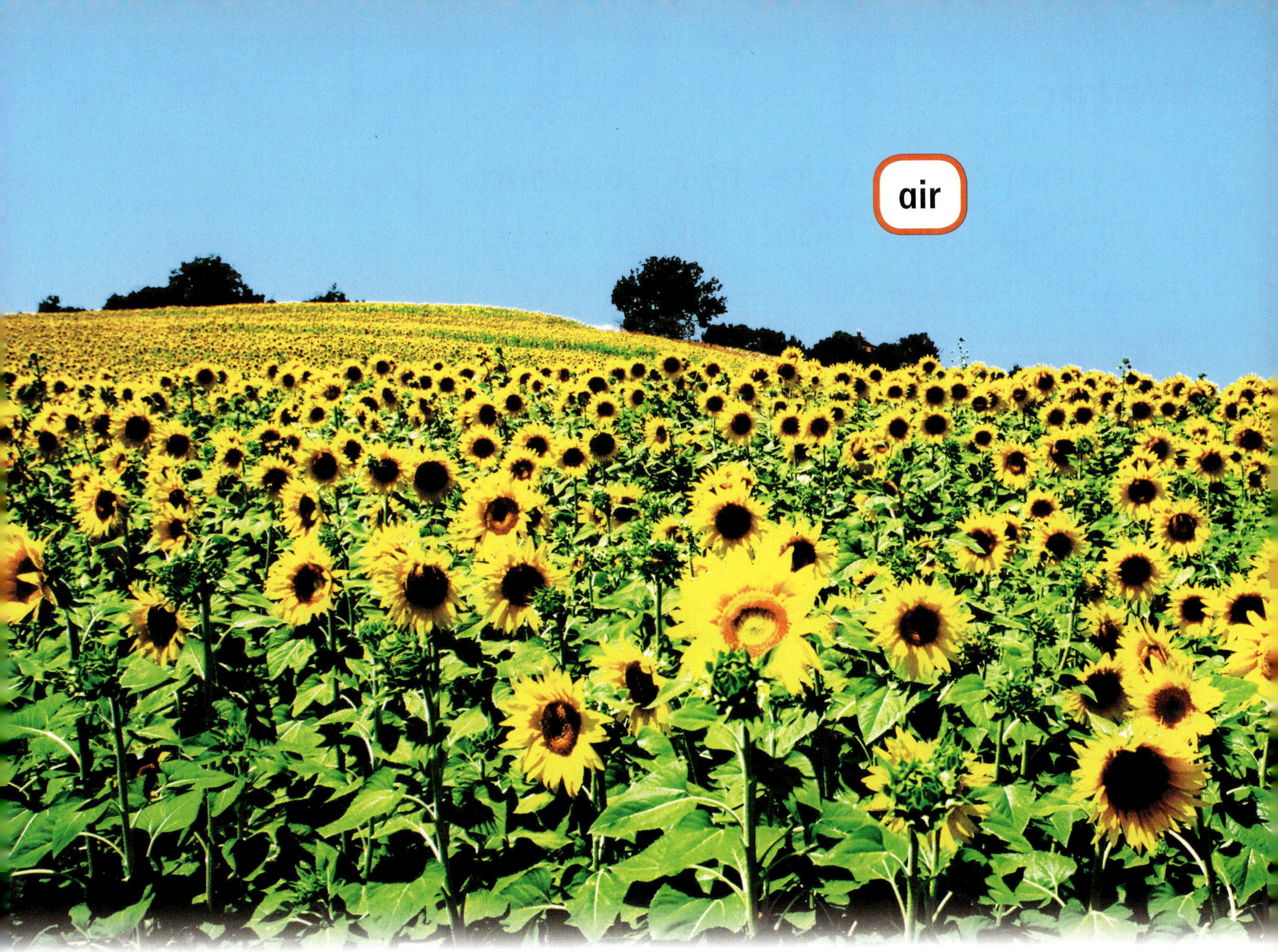

air

Air

Plants need air to live and grow. Plants use gases from the air to make food. They also use gases from the air to give off oxygen.

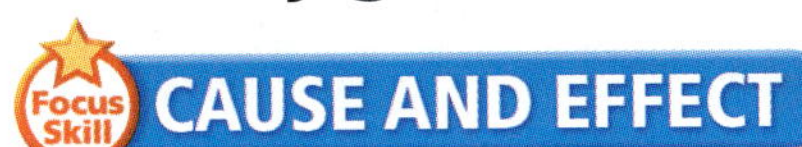

Why do plants need air?

Make a Model Plant

Use paper, clay, craft sticks, and other art materials to make a model plant. Then tell about what a real plant needs to live.

Water

A plant needs water to move food to all of its parts. Plants take in water mostly from the soil.

Why does a plant need water?

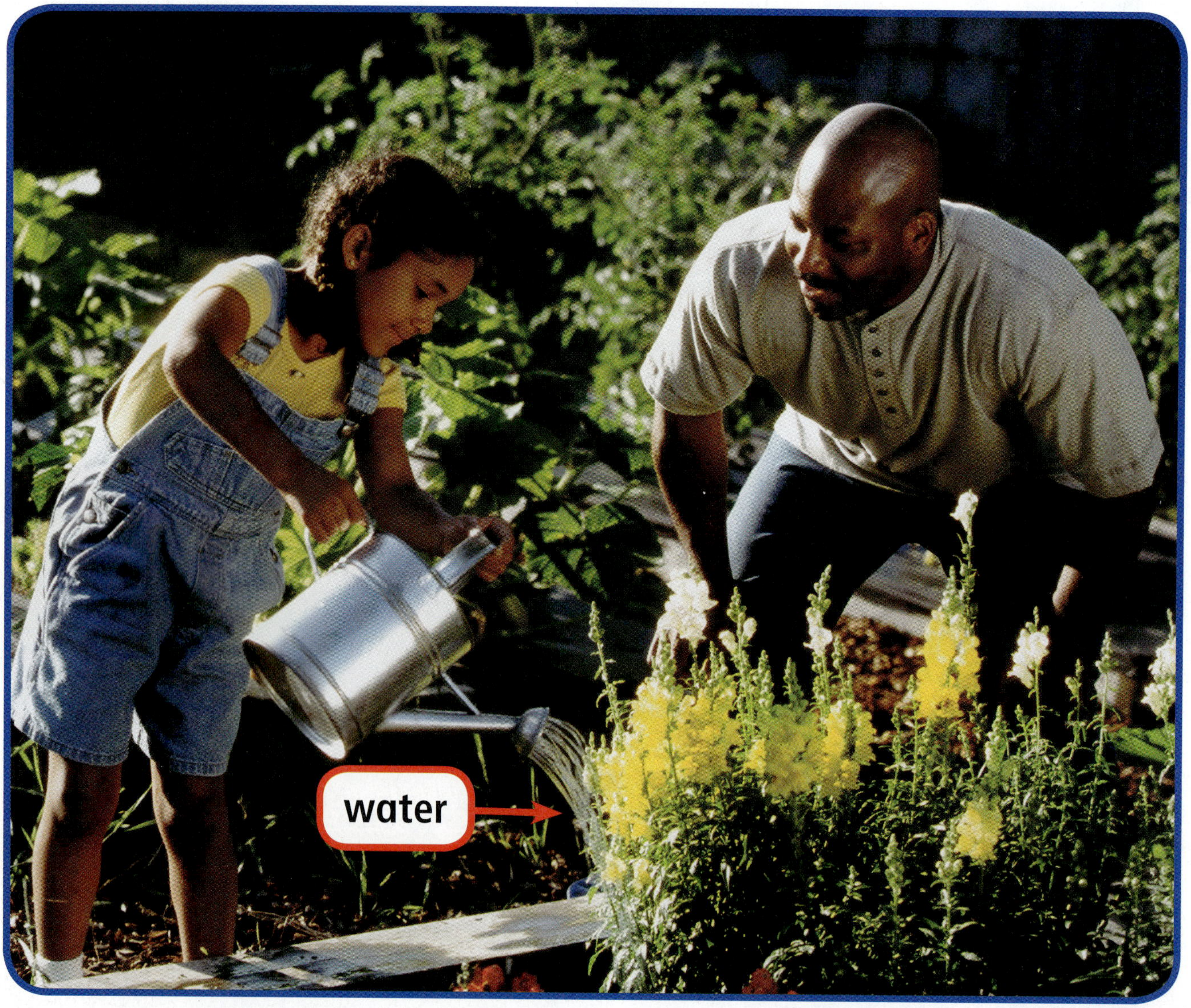

water

Nutrients

Plants take in nutrients from the soil. **Nutrients** are minerals that plants use to grow.

Why does a plant need nutrients?

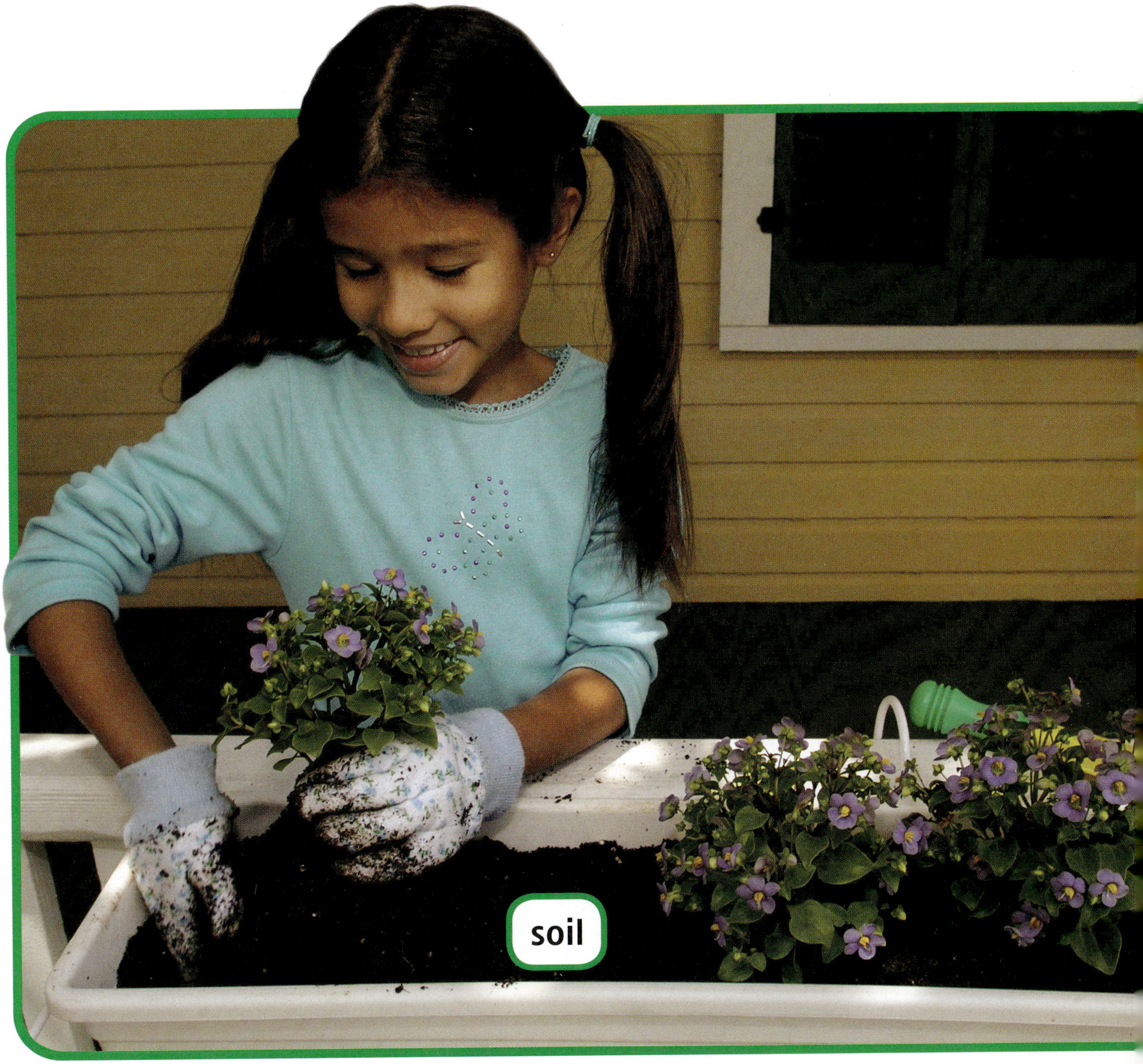

soil

GPS Wrap-Up and Lesson Review

Essential Question

What do plants need?

In this lesson, you learned that plants need light, air, water, and nutrients to live and grow.

1. **CAUSE AND EFFECT** Make a chart like this one. When a plant gets all the things it needs, what is the effect? S1L1a

cause → effect

2. **SUMMARIZE** Use the vocabulary words to write a lesson summary.

3. **VOCABULARY** Use the word **nutrients** to tell about this picture. S1L1a

4. Why is soil important to plants? S1L1a

CRCT Practice

5. What would happen if a plant did not get all the things it needs?
   A It would die.
   B It would grow.
   C It would live. S1L1a

The Big Idea

6. What things does a plant need to grow and stay healthy? S1L1a

Writing

ELA1W1a

Write How To Take Care of Plants

1. What could you do for a plant that does not look healthy? Write a plan.
2. Draw a picture to show your plan.
3. Share your plan and your drawing with the rest of the class.

Social Studies

SS1E1

Plant Product Collage

1. Cut out pictures of things people get from plants.
2. Make groups of food, clothing, and things from a home.
3. Glue the pictures on poster board to make a collage.

For more links and activities, go to **www.hspscience.com**

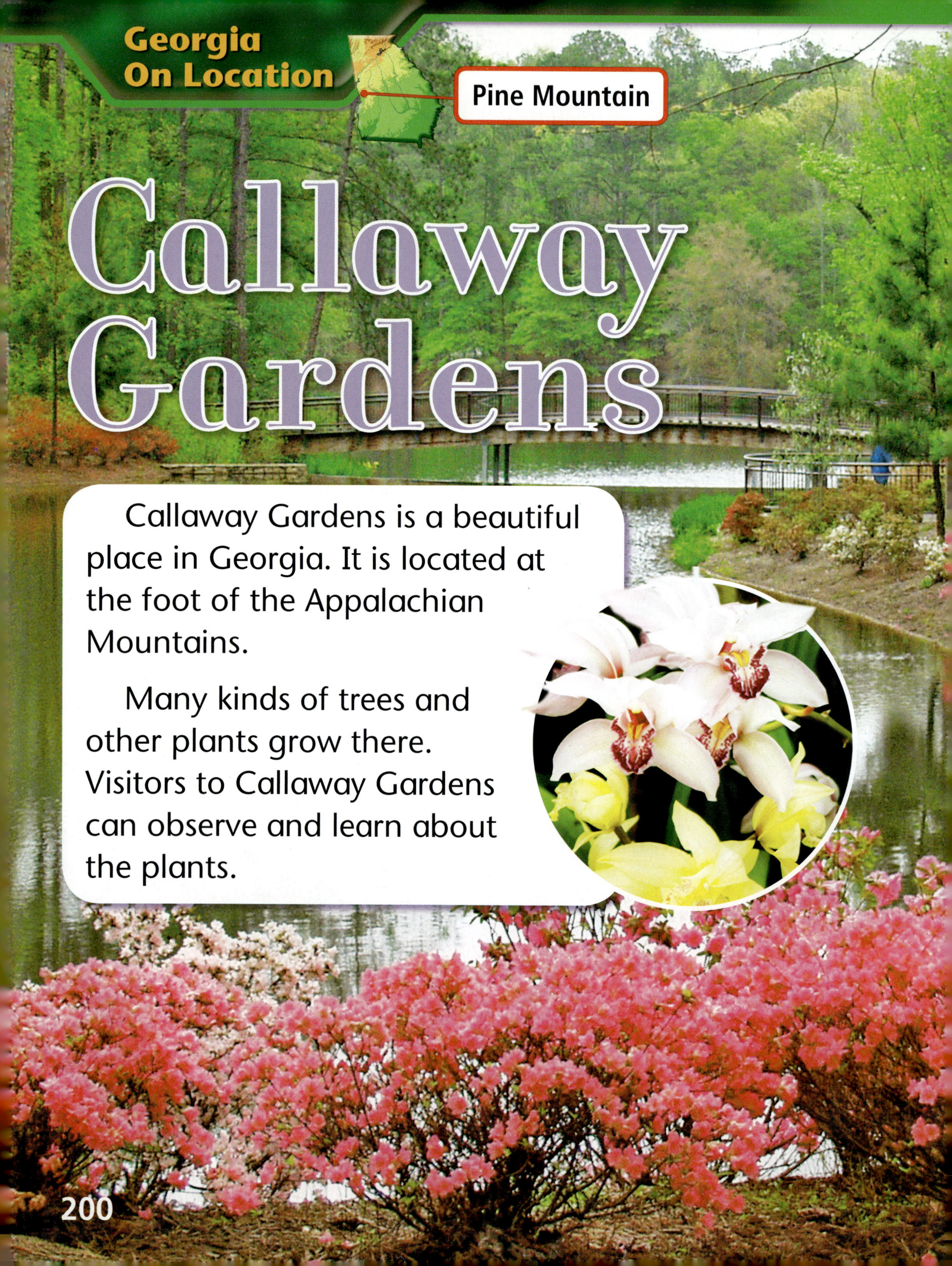

Callaway Gardens

Callaway Gardens is a beautiful place in Georgia. It is located at the foot of the Appalachian Mountains.

Many kinds of trees and other plants grow there. Visitors to Callaway Gardens can observe and learn about the plants.

All Kinds of Plants

The Sibley Horticulture Center is a garden and greenhouse. There you can see plants that grow in Georgia. You can also see plants that come from far-away places.

Mr. Cason's Vegetable Garden grows more than vegetables. There are also fruits, herbs, and flowers. The gardeners at Callaway Gardens make sure that their plants get what they need to live and grow.

Think and Write

How are the needs of the plants grown at Callaway Gardens the same as the needs of the plants that grow where you live? S1L1a

Georgia Performance Standards in This Lesson

Content

S1L1c Identify the parts of a plant—root, stem, leaf, and flower.

Characteristics of Science

S1CS2a S1CS3a S1CS5b

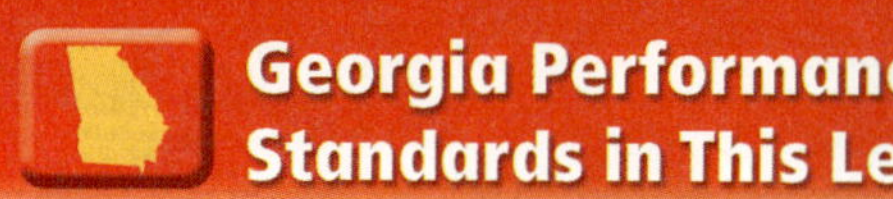

LESSON 2

Essential Question

What Are the Parts of Plants?

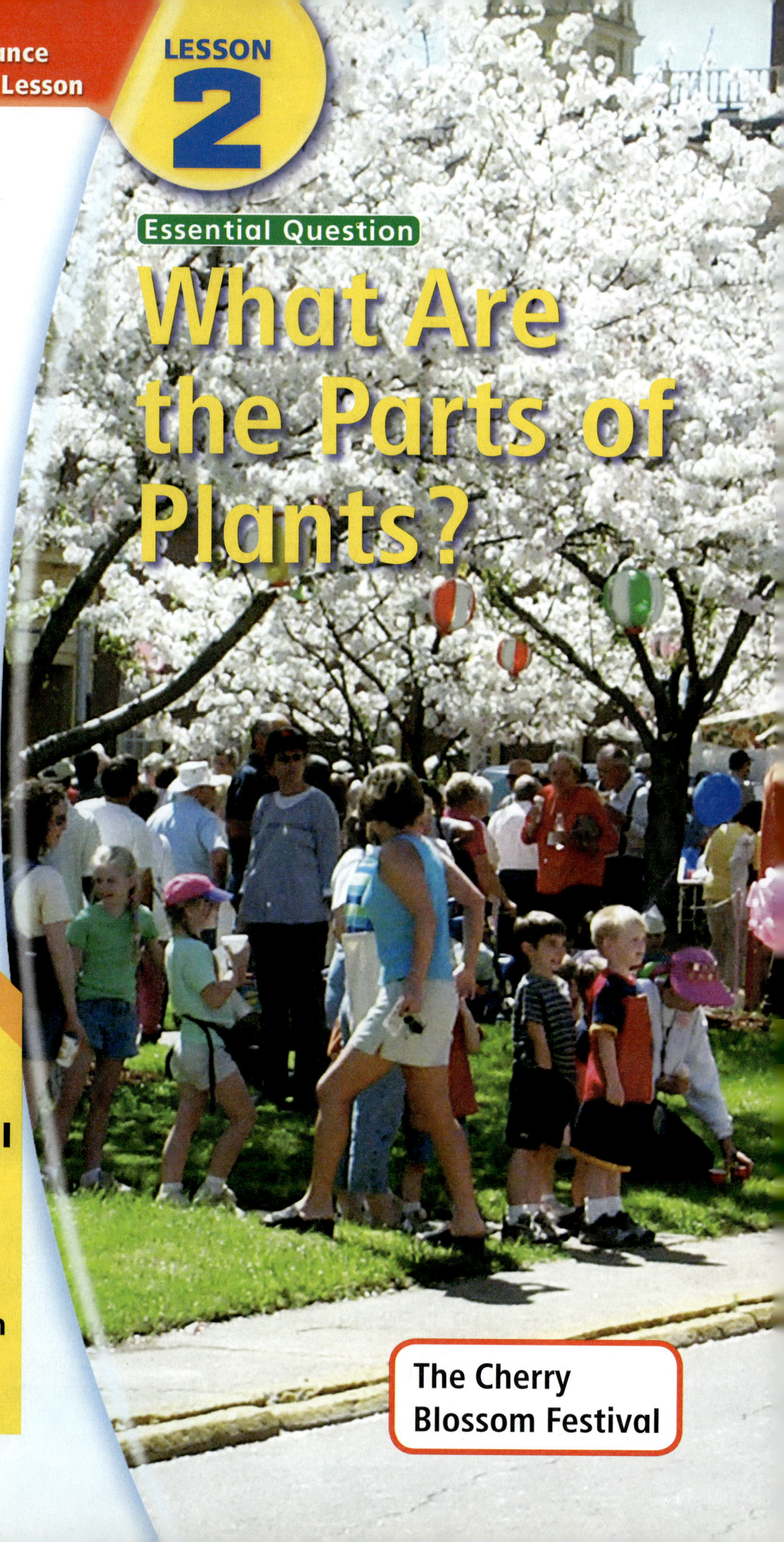

The Cherry Blossom Festival

Georgia Fast Fact

The Cherry Blossom Festival
Each spring, this festival is held in Macon. People can go to see the beautiful flowers on the cherry blossom trees.

Vocabulary Preview

roots p. 208

stem p. 209

leaves p. 210

flowers p. 211

fruits p. 211

seeds p. 211

Investigate

Parts of a Plant

Guided Inquiry

Ask a Question

What part of this plant do we eat? Investigate to find out. Then read to find out more.

Get Ready

Inquiry Skill Tip

You can use drawing, writing, and talking to communicate what you observe.

You need

hand lens

plant

What to Do

Step 1

Observe the parts of the plant. Use a hand lens.

Step 2

Draw what you see. Write about your picture.

Step 3

Share your work with a partner. **Communicate** what you observed.

Draw Conclusions

What did you find out about the parts of plants? S1L1c

Independent Inquiry

Put a flower in colored water. **Communicate** what happens to the flower. S1CS3c S1CS5b

Understand Science

VOCABULARY
roots
stem
leaves
flowers
fruits
seeds

MAIN IDEA AND DETAILS

Look for the parts of a plant and details about what the parts do.

Parts of a Plant

Plants have different parts. The parts help the plant live and grow.

How do the parts of a plant help it?

dogwood tree

Science Up Close

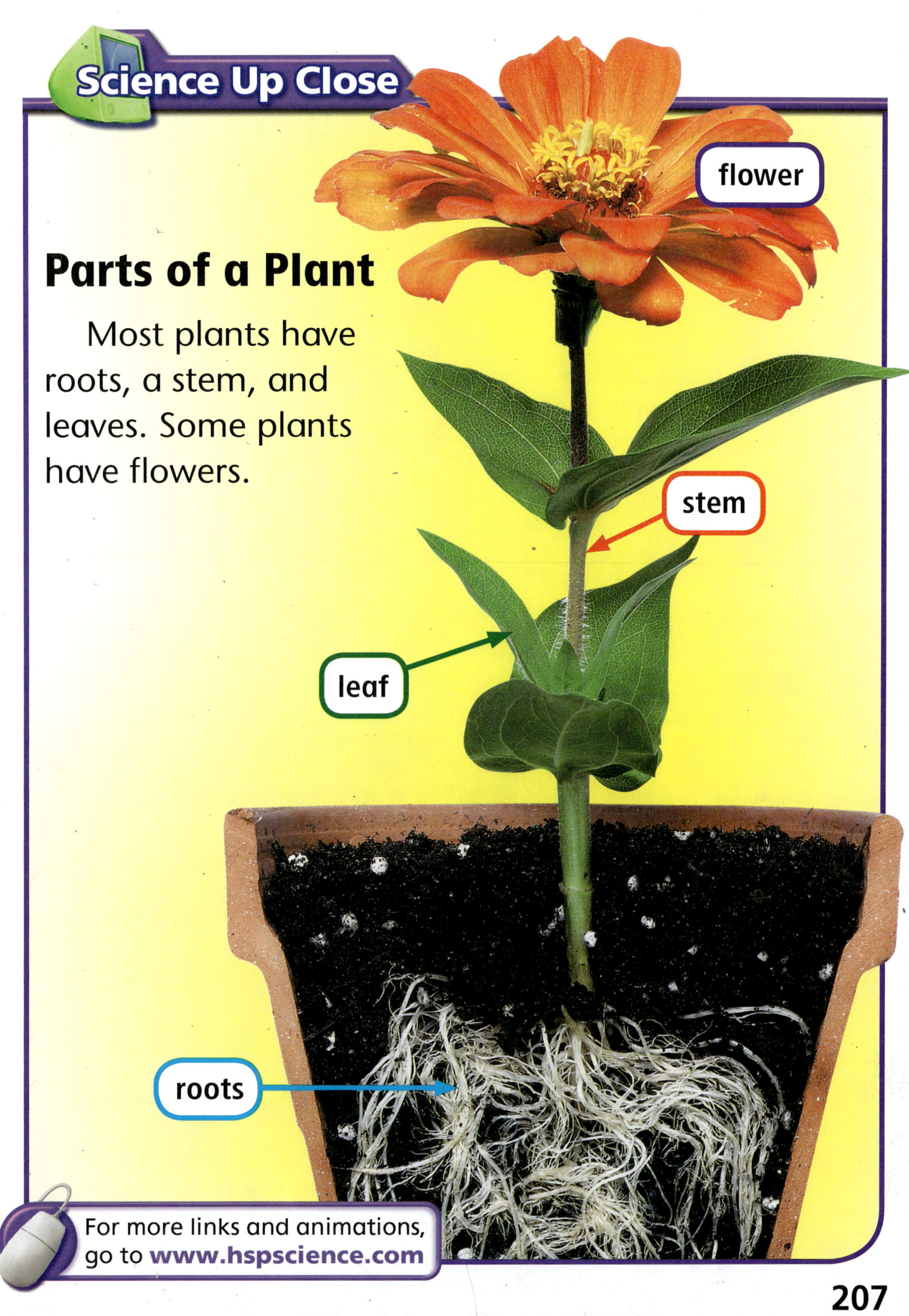

Parts of a Plant

Most plants have roots, a stem, and leaves. Some plants have flowers.

For more links and animations, go to **www.hspscience.com**

Roots

The **roots** hold the plant in the soil. They also take in the water and nutrients the plant needs.

MAIN IDEA AND DETAILS

What are two ways roots help a plant?

How Roots Help

Push a craft stick deep into clay. Push another craft stick into clay just a little. Tap the side of each stick. What happens? How is the first stick like a plant with roots? How do roots hold a plant in place?

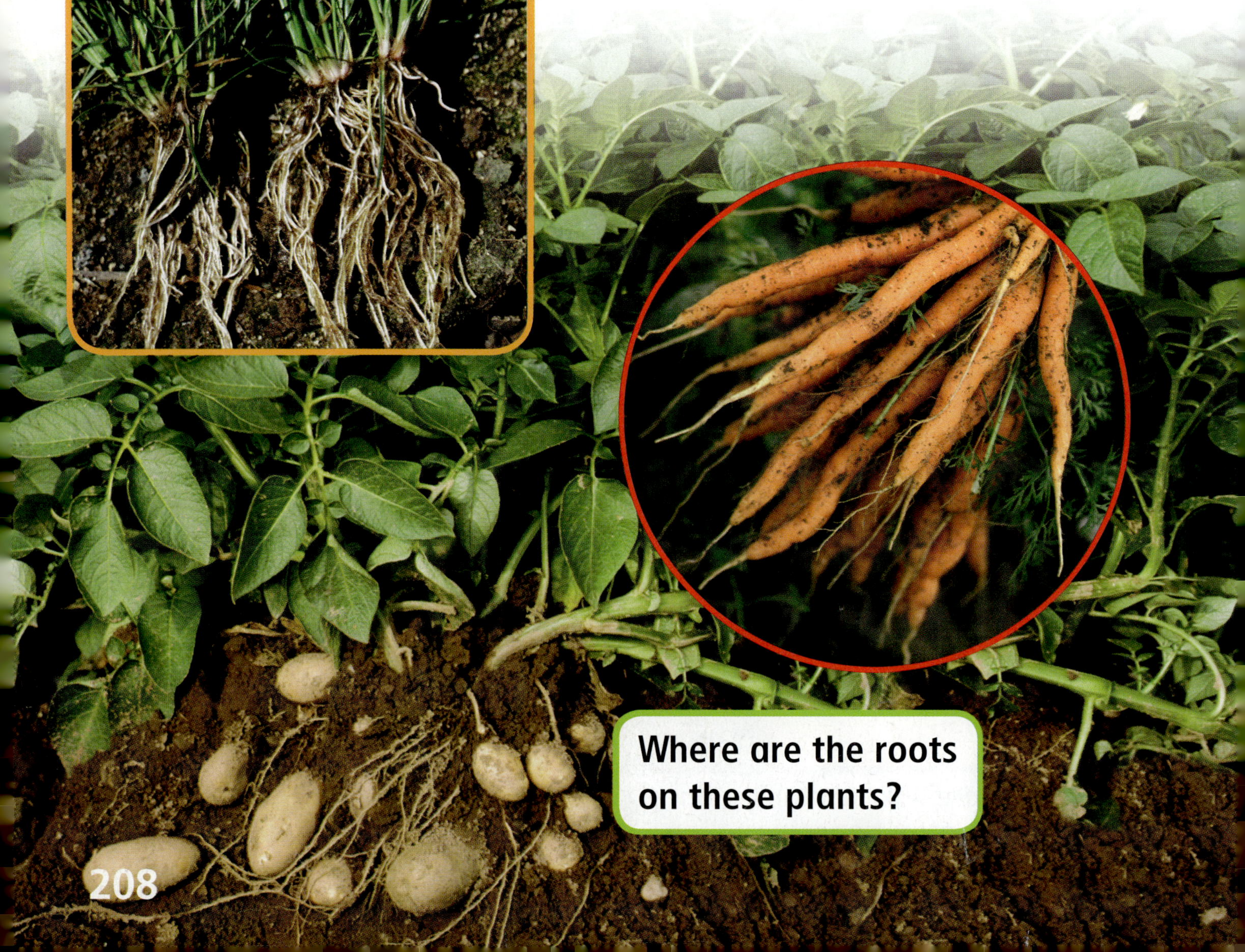

Where are the roots on these plants?

Stems

The **stem** holds up the plant. It carries food and water through the plant.

Stems may be green or woody. The trunks of trees are woody stems.

MAIN IDEA AND DETAILS

What are two ways the stem helps a plant?

Where are the stems on these plants?

Leaves

Leaves take in light and air. They need these things to make food for the plant. Different kinds of plants have leaves that look different. Leaves have different patterns.

What do leaves do?

What shapes and patterns do these leaves have?

Flowers, Fruits, and Seeds

Many plants have flowers. The **flowers** make fruits. The **fruits** hold seeds.

New plants may grow from the **seeds**. The new plants look like the plants that made the seeds.

Focus Skill **MAIN IDEA AND DETAILS**

What do flowers do?

GPS Wrap-Up and Lesson Review

Essential Question

What are the parts of plants?

In this lesson, you learned that plants have different parts that help them live and grow.

1. **MAIN IDEA AND DETAILS** Make a chart like this one. Show details of this main idea. **Plants have different parts**. S1L1c

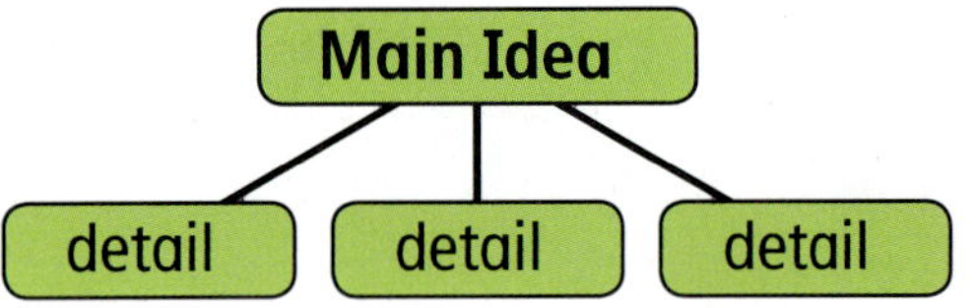

2. **SUMMARIZE** Use the vocabulary words to write a lesson summary. S1L1c

3. **VOCABULARY** Use the words **roots** and **leaves** to tell about this picture. S1L1c

4. What would happen to a plant if an animal ate all of its leaves? S1L1c

CRCT Practice

5. What part of a plant carries food and water through the plant?
   A flower
   B stem
   C roots S1L1c

The Big Idea

6. How do the different parts of a plant help it meet its needs? S1L1c

Writing ELA1W1k

Make a Plant Guide

1. Research plants that live in Georgia.
2. Make a guide. Write about and draw pictures of plants that live near you.
3. Share your guide with others.

Math  M1M1b

Measuring Leaves

1. Put some leaves under a sheet of paper.
2. Rub the paper over the leaves with the sides of crayons.
3. Use small blocks to measure the rubbings. Record how long each leaf is.

For more links and activities, go to **www.hspscience.com**

George Washington Carver

- Plant Scientist
- Invented many things using peanuts

George Washington Carver

Dr. George Washington Carver was a plant scientist. He worked with farmers who grew crops. He showed them a way to plant that would keep their soil healthy. When they did this, they had bigger and better crops.

Dr. Carver did experiments with plants such as sweet potatoes, cotton, soybeans, and peanuts. He thought of more than 300 things to make with peanut plants!

Think and Write

Why is it important for farmers to keep their soil healthy? S1L1a

peanuts

Ynes Enriquetta Julietta Mexia

Ynes Enriquetta Julietta Mexia was a scientist. She collected plants from around the world. She studied where they lived and what they needed to grow. Many of these plants had never been collected before.

Ynes Enriquetta Julietta Mexia

- Botanist
- Collected plants

Ynes Enriquetta Julietta Mexia brought thousands of plants to a college. The plants are in the herbarium there. A herbarium is a place where dried plants are kept. Now other scientists can study the plants.

Think and Write

How did Ynes Enriquetta Julietta Mexia help other scientists learn about the world's plants? S1L1a

Chapter 6 Wrap-Up

Visual Summary

Tell how each picture helps explain the **Big Idea**.

Plants need air, water, light, and nutrients to live and grow. Different parts of plants help plants get what they need.

Lesson 1 S1L1a

Plants have four needs. They need air, water, light, and nutrients from the soil to live and grow.

Lesson 2 S1L1c

Plants have different parts. Plants have roots, a stem, and leaves. Many plants have flowers, fruits, and seeds.

Show What You Know

Chapter Writing Activity

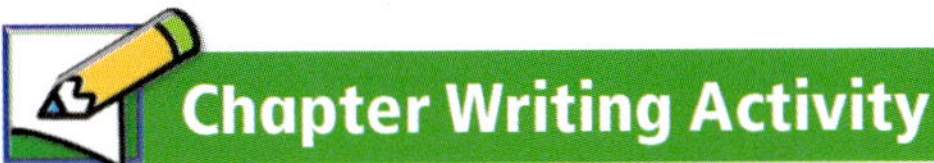

Plant a Seed/Write a Letter

Plant a seed. See if you can meet its needs to keep it alive. Write a letter to a friend telling what you needed to do to meet the needs of your plant.

ELA1W1b

Georgia Performance Task

Show Plant Parts

We eat some parts of plants. Cut pictures out of old magazines of plant parts we eat. Compare your pictures with the pictures your classmates cut out. Work together to make a class bulletin board. Show what parts of plants we eat.

S1L1c

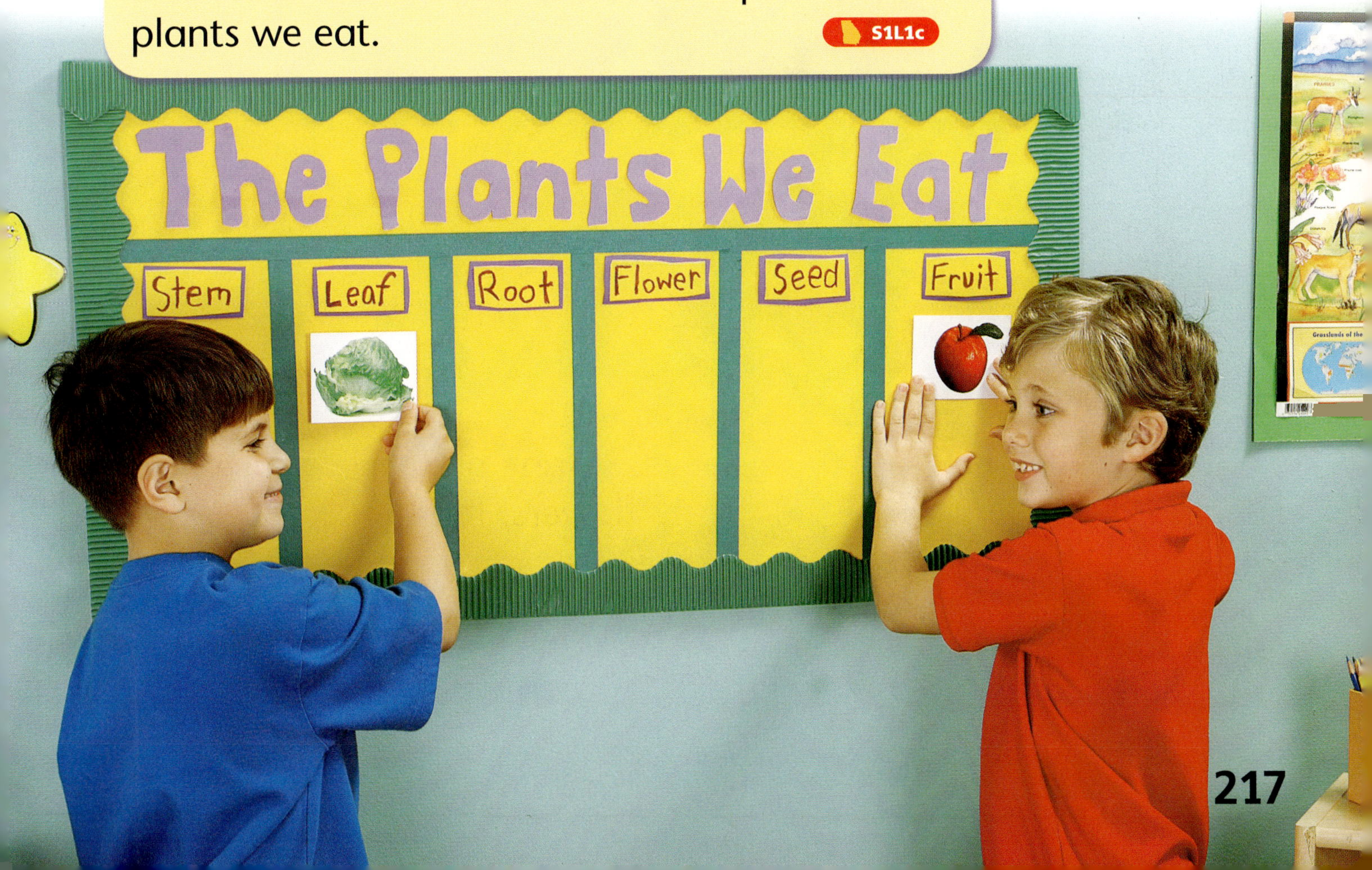

Vocabulary Review

Look at the numbers next to the plant parts. Tell the number and the name of each part. S1L1c

roots p. 208
stem p. 209
leaves p. 210
flowers p. 211
fruit p. 211
seeds p. 211

1.
2.
3.
4.
5.
6.

Check Understanding

7. What happens to a plant that gets air, light, water, and nutrients? Tell how you know. S1L1a

8. Which plant part makes food? S1L1c

A flower

B leaves

C roots

Critical Thinking

9. What is happening in each picture. 

The Big Idea

10. What things does a plant need? How do the different parts of a plant help it meet its needs? S1L1a

CHAPTER 7

All About Animals

Georgia Performance Standards in This Chapter

Content

S1L1 Students will investigate the characteristics and basic needs of plants and animals.

S1L1b S1L1d

This chapter also addresses these co-requisite standards:

Characteristics of Science

S1CS2 Students will have the computation and estimation skills necessary for analyzing data and following scientific explanations.

S1CS2a S1CS2b

S1CS3 Students will use tools and instruments for observing, measuring, and manipulating objects in scientific activities.

S1CS3a

S1CS4 Students will use the ideas of system, model, change, and scale in exploring scientific and technological matters.

S1CS4a S1CS4c

S1CS5 Students will communicate scientific ideas and activities clearly.

S1CS5a S1CS5b

S1CS7 Students will understand important features of the process of scientific inquiry.

S1CS7d

What's the Big Idea?

Animals need air, water, food, and shelter to live and grow. You can compare animals.

Essential Questions

for student eBook
www.hspscience.com

Science in Georgia

Dear Ben,

Our class went to the Chehaw Wild Animal Park. We saw many kinds of animals. None of them looked the same. Some were running. Some were climbing trees.

Your friend,

Amy

Read Amy's postcard. What did Amy learn about animals? How do you think that helps explain the **Big Idea?**

Georgia Performance Standards in This Lesson

LESSON 1

Essential Question

What Do Animals Need?

Content

S1L1b Identify the basic needs of an animal.

1. Oxygen
2. Water
3. Food
4. Shelter

S1L1d Compare and describe various animals—appearance, motion, growth, basic needs.

Characteristics of Science

S1CS2a  S1CS2b

 S1CS5a  S1CS5b

S1CS7d

Georgia Fast Fact

White-tailed Deer

A male deer is a buck. Bucks grow antlers. A female deer is a doe. A young deer is a fawn. Most does and fawns do not have antlers.

Vocabulary Preview
shelter p. 229
white-tailed deer

Investigate

Observe an Animal Home

Guided Inquiry

Ask a Question

What do these animals need to live and grow? Investigate to find out. Then read to find out more.

Get Ready

Inquiry Skill Tip

When you observe, you use your senses to find out about things. You can draw pictures to record what you see.

You need

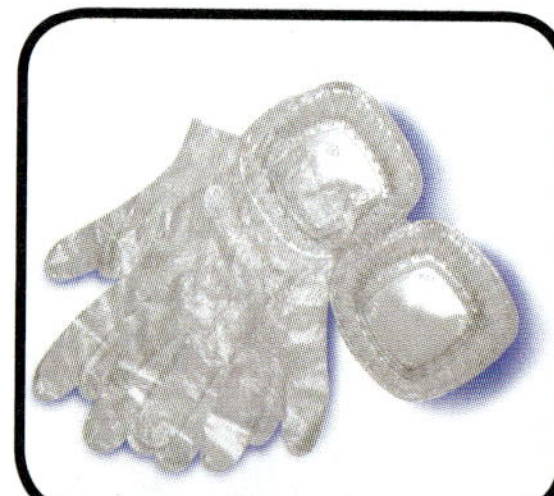

plastic box and gloves

soil, twig, leaf, rocks

water in a bottle cap

small animals

What to Do

Step 1

Put the soil, twig, leaf, rocks, and water in the box. Add the animals.

Step 2

Observe. Draw pictures to record what you see.

Step 3

Tell how the home that you made gives the animals food, water, and a place to live.

Draw Conclusions

What did you find out about the needs of animals?

Independent Inquiry

Go for a nature walk. **Observe** how animals meet their needs. Record what you observe. S1CS7d

VOCABULARY
shelter

Look for all the things that animals need to live.

Animals Need Food and Water

Animals need food to live and to grow. Animals can not make their own food. They have to find it. An elephant eats grasses, branches, and fruits.

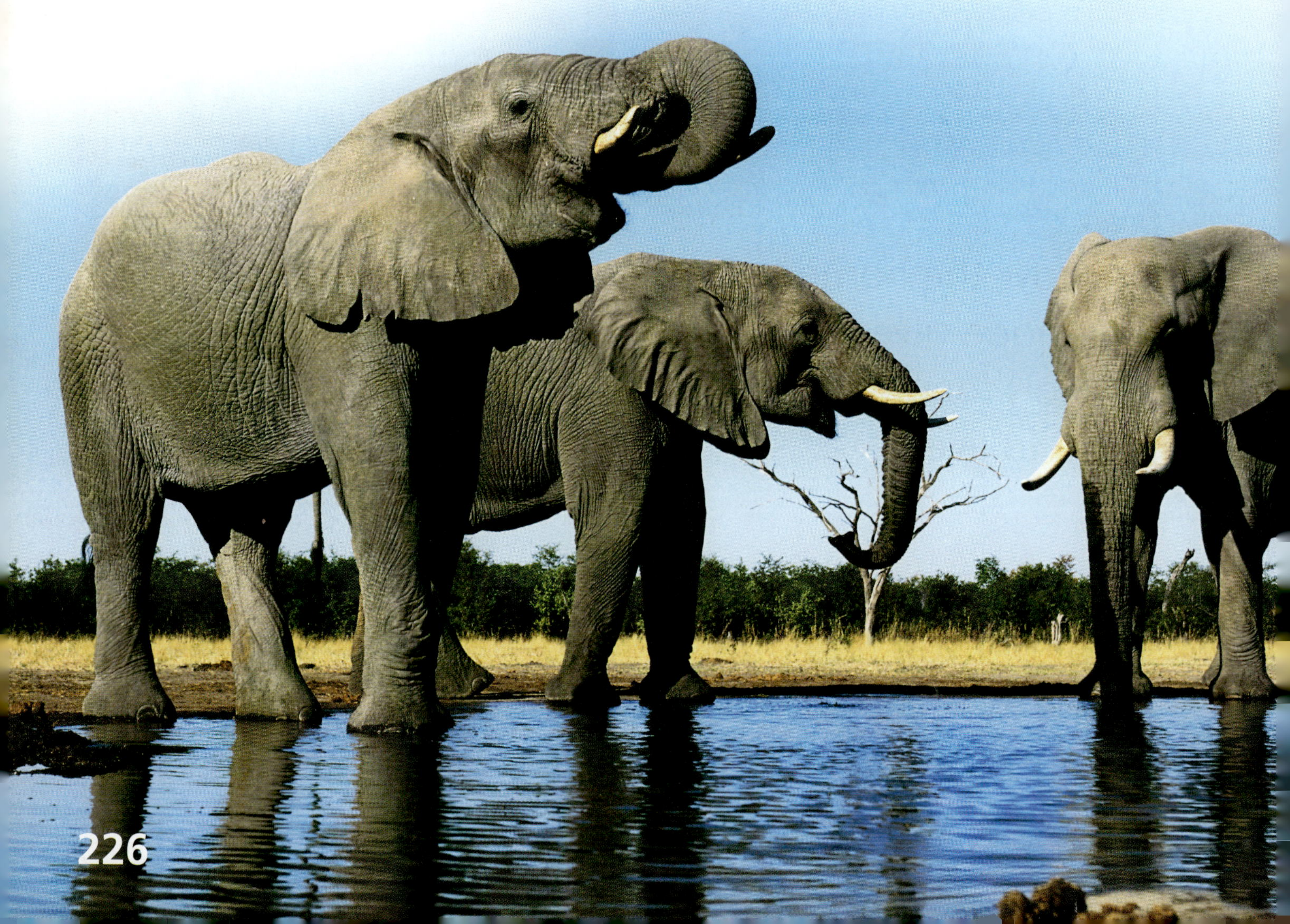

Animals need water, too. Elephants drink from ponds. They also get water from the foods that they eat.

Focus Skill **MAIN IDEA AND DETAILS**

What are two things that animals need to live?

Insta-Lab

Pet Food Survey

Take a survey. List some pet foods. Then ask your classmates what their pets eat. Make a tally mark next to each food. Which food do the most pets eat?

A panda eats bamboo.

A horse drinks water from a pond.

Animals Need Oxygen

All animals need oxygen. They have body parts that help them get oxygen. Lungs help some animals take in air. A porcupine has lungs. Some animals, such as fish, have gills. Gills take in oxygen from water.

fish

MAIN IDEA AND DETAILS **What are two body parts animals use to take in oxygen?**

porcupine

Animals Need Shelter

Most animals need shelter. A **shelter** is a place where an animal can be safe. Some birds use trees as shelters. Foxes dig holes in the ground for shelter.

MAIN IDEA AND DETAILS

What is a shelter?

GPS Wrap-Up and Lesson Review

Essential Question

What do animals need?

In this lesson, you learned that animals need food, water, air, and shelter.

1. **MAIN IDEA AND DETAILS** Make a chart like the one below. Tell the things animals need to live and grow. S1L1b

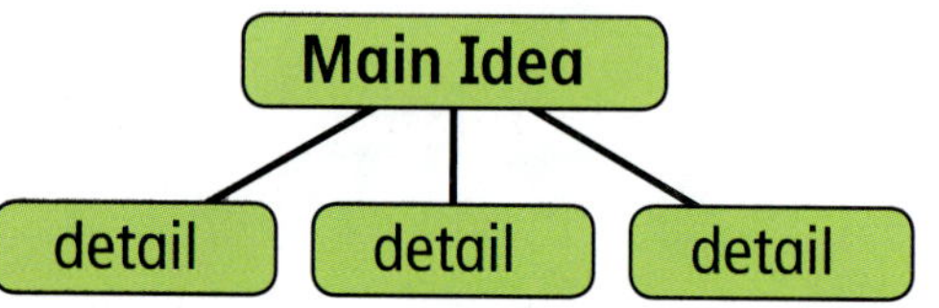

2. **DRAW CONCLUSIONS** Why do different kinds of animals need different kinds of shelter? S1L1b

3. **VOCABULARY** Use the word **shelter** to tell about this picture. S1L1b

4. Draw a picture of a pet you would like to have. List the things it would need. Tell how you would help it meet its needs. S1L1b

CRCT Practice

5. What do lungs and gills help animals get?
   A oxygen
   B food
   C shelter
   S1L1b

The Big Idea

6. List four things animals need. S1L1b

Writing

ELA1W1c

Write to Inform

1. Use a mirror to look at your teeth.
2. Write about which teeth you use to eat different foods.
3. Share your writing with the rest of the class.

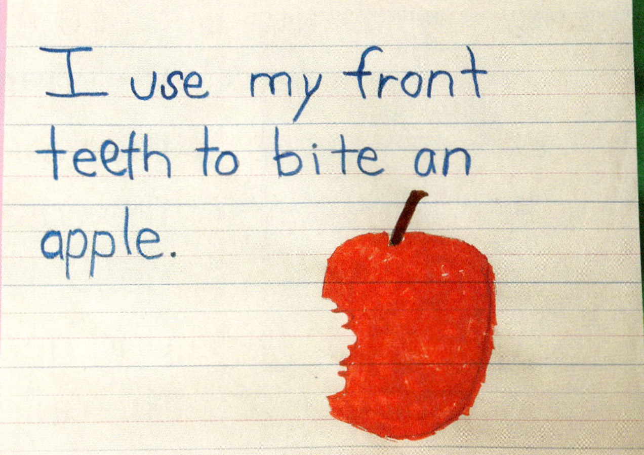

Math

M1N1c,3f

Compare Amounts

1. Different animals need different amounts of food. Use the chart to compare how much food three dogs eat each day.
2. Which eats the most? The least? How much would each dog eat in 3 days?

Dog	Amount of Food
Sandy	1 cup
Rosey	2 cups
Bo	3 cups

For more links and activities, go to **www.hspscience.com**

Dr. Maria Crane

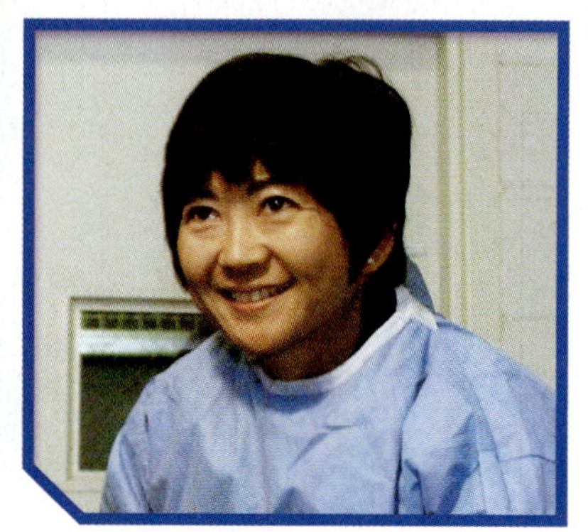

Dr. Maria Crane
- **Georgia Veterinarian**
- **Works to keep animals healthy**

Zoo Atlanta has about 900 animals from around the world. Think about the care all those animals need! Dr. Maria Crane and her team help keep the animals healthy.

Dr. Crane gives the animals check-ups. She gives animals that seem sick or hurt tests to help find out what is wrong. Dr. Crane helps with big events. She helps when a new panda is born. She also teaches people about the importance of animals in the wild.

Think and Write

How would Dr. Crane's job be different from a veterinarian who treats pets? S1L1b

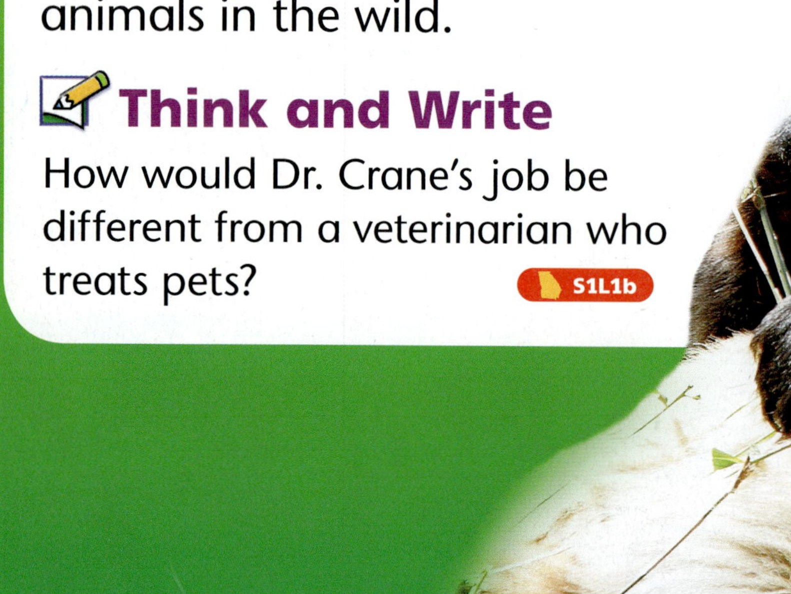

Ray Davis

The Georgia Aquarium is one of the world's largest aquariums. It is home to over 100,000 animals.

Ray Davis

- Georgia Marine Biologist
- Works with marine animals

Ray Davis helps plan and design the exhibits in the aquarium. This includes making sure that the animals have everything they need to stay healthy.

Ray Davis helps oversee special projects at the aquarium. He hopes the work at the Georgia Aquarium can help scientists learn more about animals from the ocean.

Think and Write

Ray Davis has traveled to oceans around the world to study animals. How would that experience help in planning an aquarium? S1L1b

LESSON 2

Essential Question

How Can We Compare Animals?

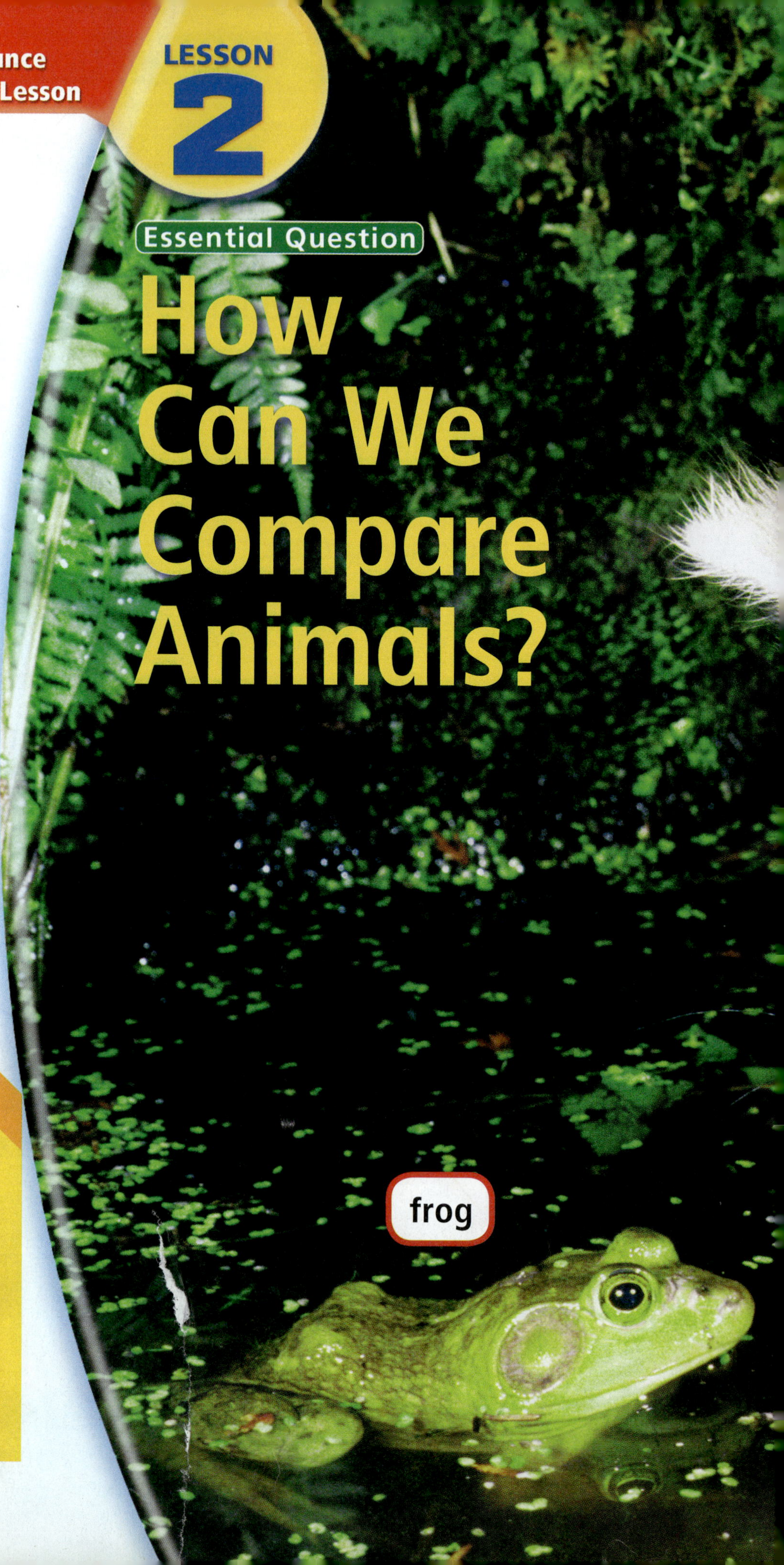

Content

S1L1d Compare and describe various animals—appearance, motion, growth, basic needs.

Characteristics of Science

S1CS3a S1CS4a S1CS4c S1CS5a S1CS5b

frog

Georgia Fast Fact

Animal Coverings

A raccoon is a mammal. It has fur. A frog is an amphibian. It has wet, smooth skin.

Vocabulary Preview
appearance p. 238
growth p. 240
raccoon

Investigate

Compare Hair and Feathers

Guided Inquiry

Ask a Question

Look at the animals. How do they look alike? How do they look different? Investigate to find out. Then read to find out more.

Get Ready

Inquiry Skill Tip

To compare hair and a feather helps you understand how animals are different.

You need

feather

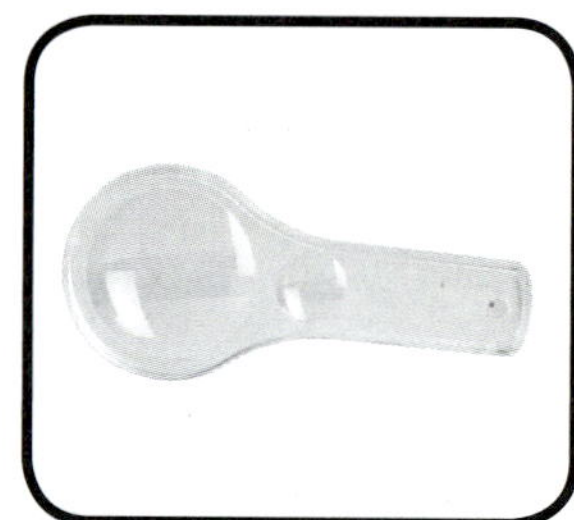

hand lens

What to Do

Step 1

Observe the feather with the hand lens. What does it look like and feel like?

Step 2

Observe the hair on your arm. **Compare** the hair with the feather.

Step 3

Draw pictures of what you observed. Write about how the feather and hair are alike and different.

Draw Conclusions

What did you find out about feathers and hair?

Independent Inquiry

Compare several birds. Tell two or three ways they are alike. Then tell two or three ways they are different. S1CS4c S1CS5a

S1L1d

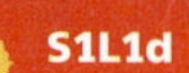

VOCABULARY
appearance
growth

COMPARE AND CONTRAST

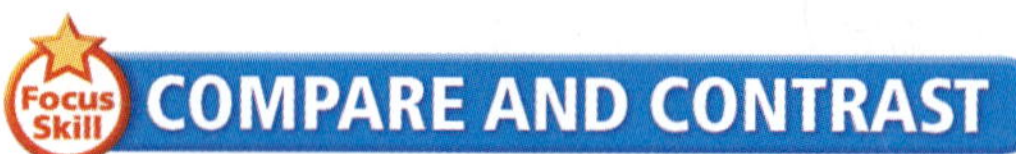

Look for ways animals are alike and different.

Compare How Animals Look

Every kind of animal has a certain **appearance**, or way it looks. Some animals have fur. Some have feathers. Some animals have scaly, dry skin. Some have smooth, wet skin. Some have scales.

COMPARE AND CONTRAST

How do these animals look alike? How do they look different?

fish

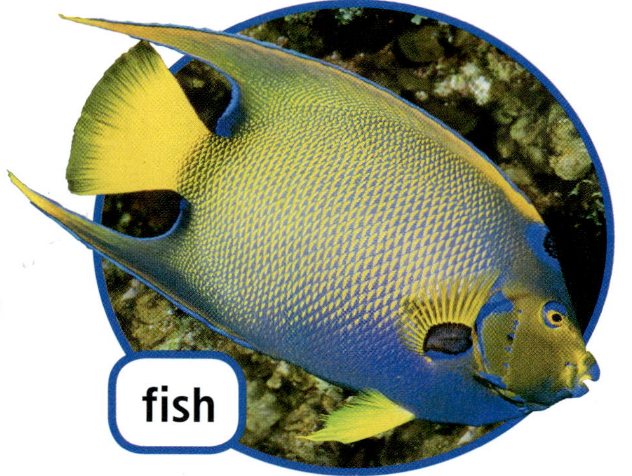

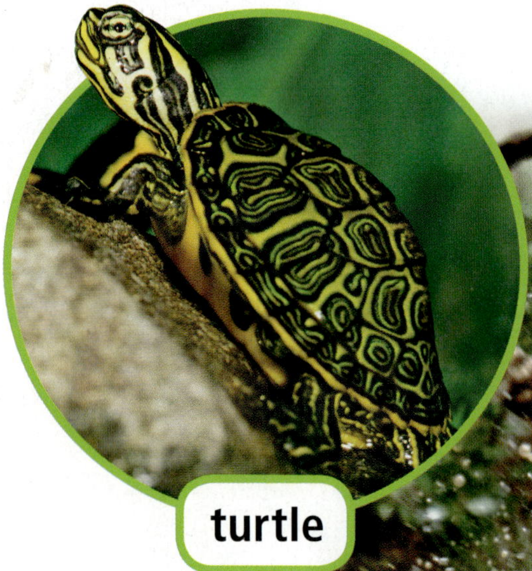

turtle

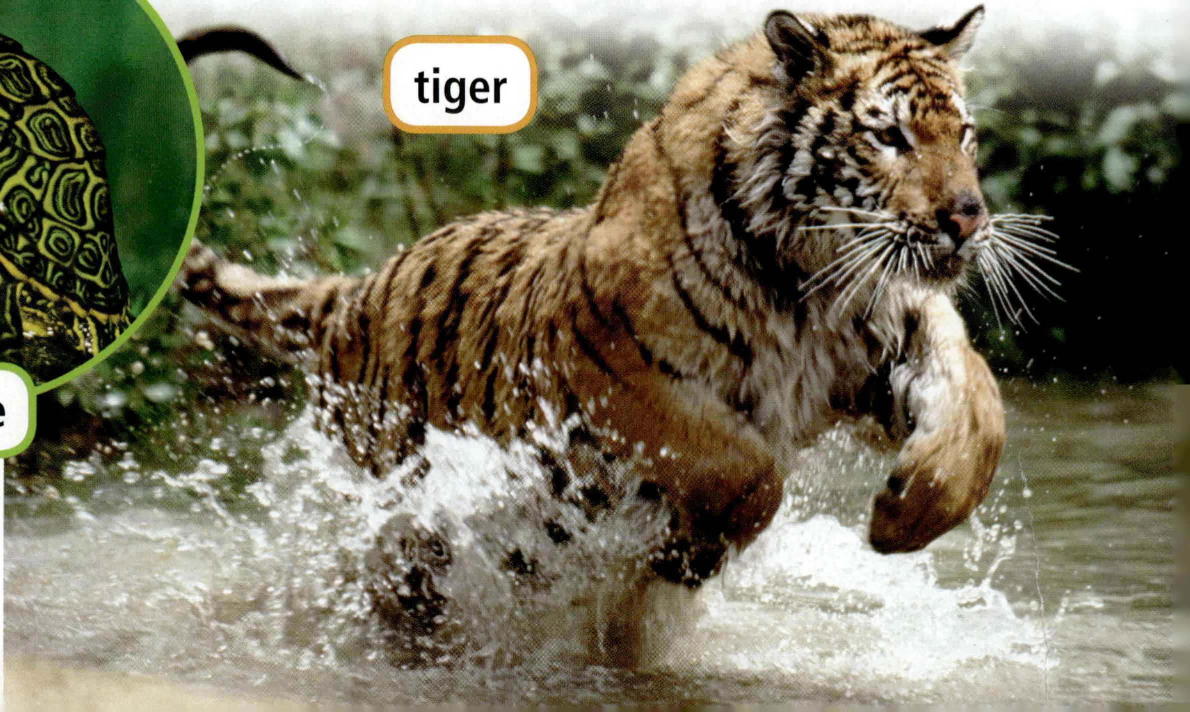

tiger

Compare How Animals Move

Animals move in different ways. Some have wings to fly. Some have flippers or fins to swim. Some animals have legs to walk, hop, or leap. Some crawl or slither.

COMPARE AND CONTRAST

How are a frog and an eagle alike? How are they different?

Make a Model

Make a model of an animal. Use chenille sticks. Ask a classmate to guess the animal you made. Tell why you made the model as you did.

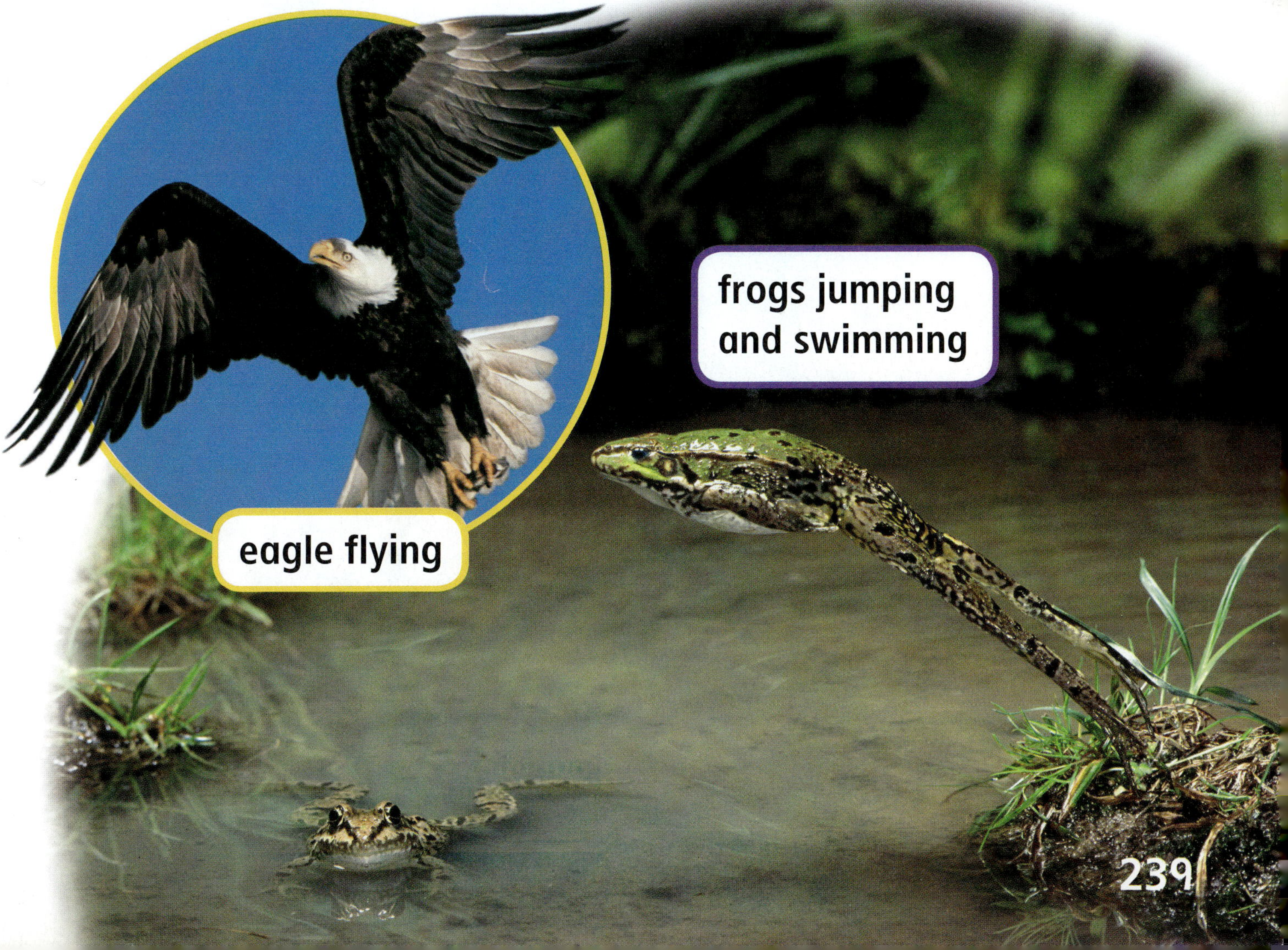

eagle flying

frogs jumping and swimming

Compare How Animals Grow

Most living things change as they get older. This change is called **growth**. Some young animals look like their parents. They grow and change in size. Some young animals do not look like their parents. They change in shape and size as they grow.

COMPARE AND CONTRAST

Compare the growth of these animals.

Compare the Needs of Animals

All animals need food, water, and air to live and grow. The amount an animal needs is different. Some animals need a lot of food and water. Some can live on only a little. Most animals need a safe place to live.

What do all animals need?

Science Up Close

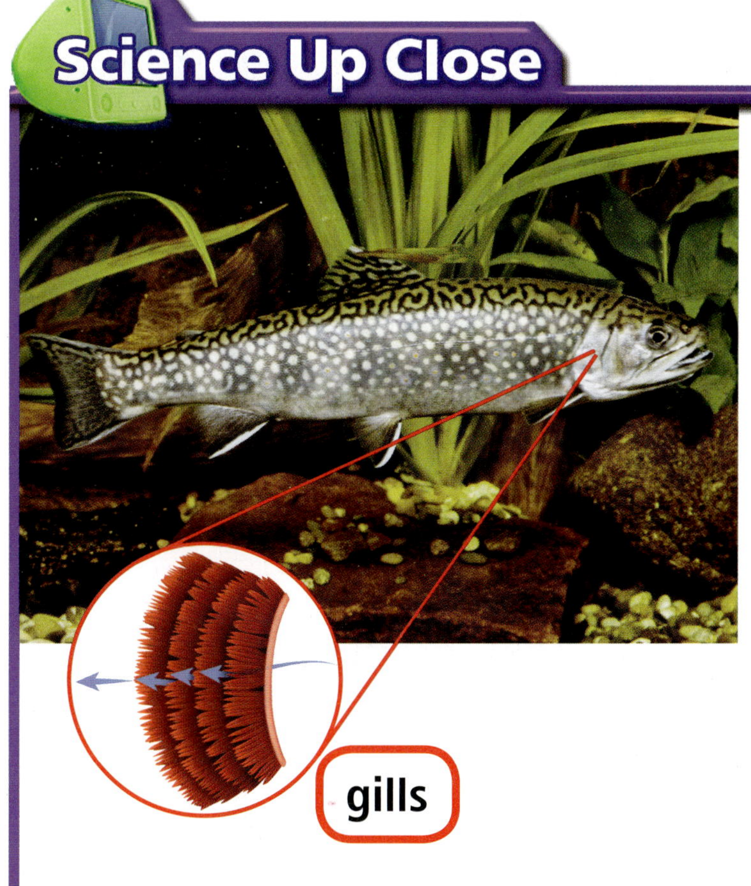

How Fish Get Oxygen

All animals need oxygen, but they get it in different ways. People and many animals use lungs to get oxygen from the air. Fish use gills to take in oxygen from water.

For more links and animations, go to **www.hspscience.com**

GPS Wrap-Up and Lesson Review

Essential Question

How can we compare animals?

In this lesson, you learned that you can compare different animals. Observe how they look, move, grow, and meet their needs.

1. Focus Skill **COMPARE AND CONTRAST** Make a chart like the one below. Use the chart to tell how a polar bear cub and its mother are alike and different. S1L1d

alike — different

2. **DRAW CONCLUSIONS** Can a fish live out of water? Tell why or why not. S1L1d

3. **VOCABULARY** Use the word **growth** or **appearance** to tell about the cub and its mother. S1L1d

4. Why do most small animals need less food and water than larger animals? S1L1d

CRCT Practice

5. You see an animal with flippers and an animal with fins. What do you know about both animals?

A They swim.
B They fly.
C They hop. S1L1d

The Big Idea

6. List four ways you can compare a rabbit and a butterfly. S1L1d

Writing

Animal Information

1. Draw a picture of an animal.
2. Write its name, what kind of animal it is, what its body covering is, and where it lives.
3. Share your work with a friend.

animal	robin
kind of animal	bird
body covering	feathers
where it lives	park

Art

Patterned Wrapping Paper

1. Make wrapping paper. Use patterns found on animals.
2. Look at butterfly wings or an animal's skin. Choose a pattern you like.
3. Draw it on a large sheet of paper. Then color it.

For more links and activities, go to **www.hspscience.com**

Science Spin™ From Weekly Reader TECHNOLOGY

Traveling Turtles

A Trip Across the Atlantic

In late spring, huge sea turtles crawl onto a beach in Florida. Each turtle digs a nest in the sand. The mother turtle then lays about 100 eggs. Two months later, tiny turtles hatch.

The young turtles crawl out of their holes and into the ocean.

A Long Trip

The tiny turtles set out on a long trip. They swim across the Atlantic Ocean and back again. The trip takes between five and ten years. The trip is thousands of miles long.

Scientists wanted to know how turtles made their way across the ocean. To find out, scientists put "bathing suits" on some young sea turtles. The suits were tied to special machines. The special machines can follow how the turtles swim.

Think and Write

How long will it take for a young turtle to swim across the Atlantic Ocean? S1L1d

Find out more. Log on to **www.hspscience.com**

Wrap-Up

Visual Summary

Tell how each picture helps explain the **Big Idea**.

Animals need oxygen, water, food, and shelter to live and grow. You can compare animals.

Lesson 1 S1L1b; S1L1d

Animals have four needs. They need oxygen, water, food, and shelter to live and grow.

Lesson 2 S1L1d

You can compare and describe animals in different ways. You can compare animals by how they look and how they move. You can compare animals by what they need to live. You can also compare animals by how they grow.

Show What You Know

Chapter Writing Activity

Taking Care of Pets/Write a Story

Write a story about how to take care of a pet. Make sure you tell about how the needs of the pet are met. Draw pictures to go with your story. Share your story with classmates. ELA1W1a

Georgia Performance Task

Make a Terrarium

A terrarium is a closed container in which small plants and animals can meet their needs. You can make one with a plastic bottle or a tank. Put in some soil and some plants that grow where you live. Add insects or other animals. Put a lid on the terrarium. Observe it each week. Write about ways the plants help the animals. S1L1b

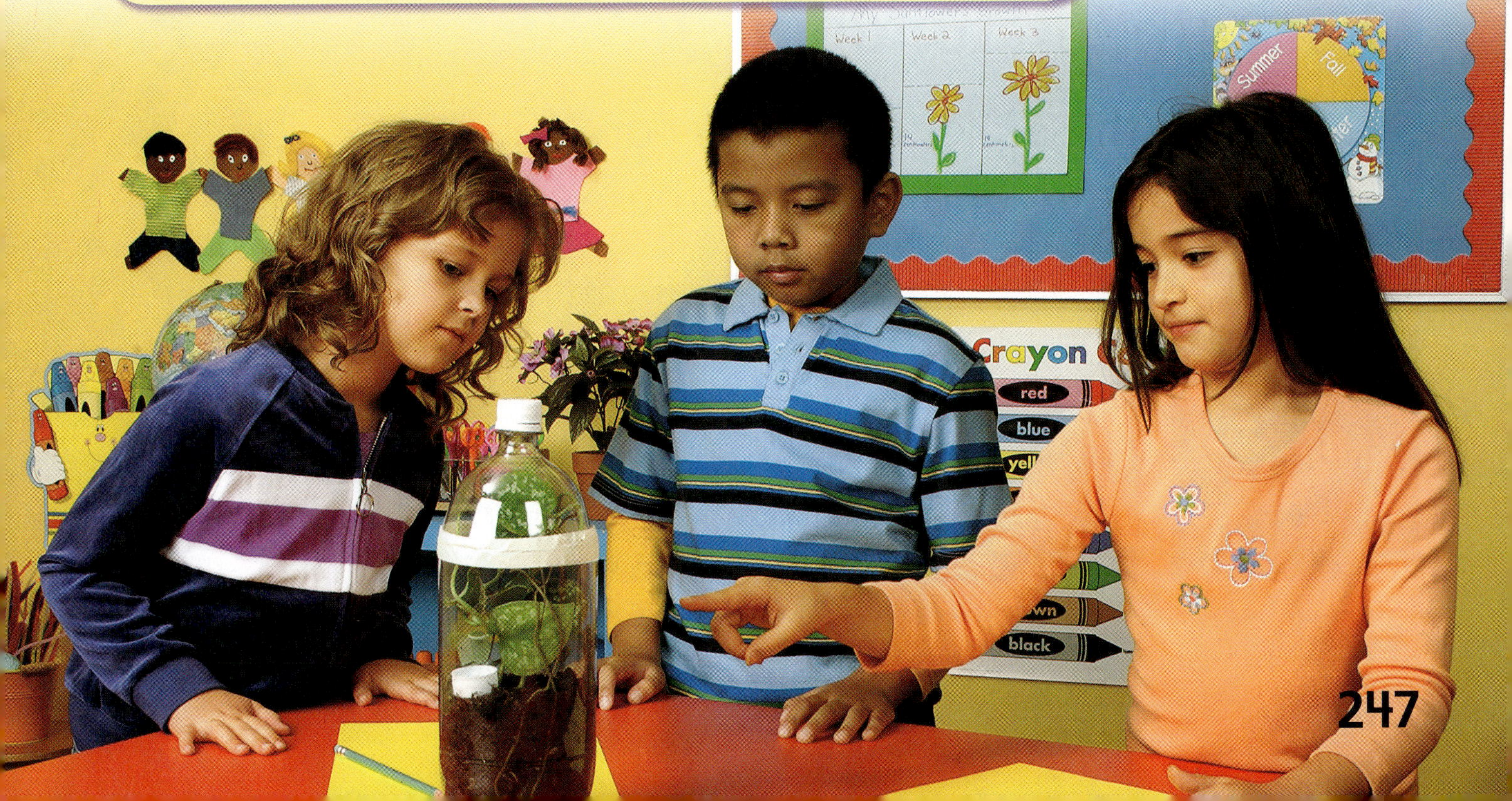

Vocabulary Review

Use the words to complete the sentences. The page numbers tell you where to look if you need help.

shelter p. 229 **growth** p. 240

appearance p. 238

1. ______ is what something looks like. S1L1d
2. ______ is an increase in size. S1L1d
3. A ______ is a place where an animal can be safe. S1L1b

Check Understanding

4. Look at these pictures. How can you compare and describe these animals? S1L1d

5. Some animals have lungs. Other animals have gills. What does this tell you? S1L1b
   - **A** They can swim.
   - **B** They can move on land.
   - **C** They can get the oxygen they need.

Critical Thinking

6. How are animals like plants? S1L1b

7. Describe how a fox and a fish are alike and different. S1L1d

The Big Idea

8. What four things do animals need to live and grow? How can you compare and describe animals by their needs and growth? S1L1b S1L1d

CRCT Practice Life Science

1. Look at the picture. Which letter shows an adult frog?
   A. A
   B. B
   C. C

S1L1d

2. You are growing a plant. Which does your plant need to make its food?
   A. flowers
   B. seeds
   C. sunlight

3. Where do plants get nutrients?
   A. from the air
   B. from the soil
   C. from sunlight

S1L1a

4. Look at the picture of a plant. Which letter shows the stem?

A. A

B. B

C. C

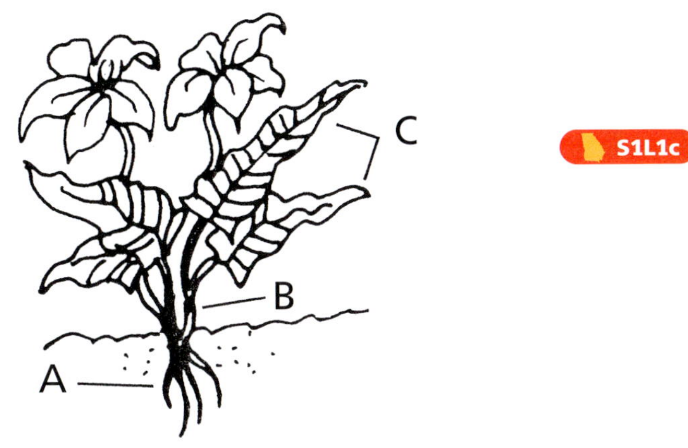

S1L1c

5. What do animals need to grow?

A. food

B. love

C. shelter

6. How would you describe the body covering of a peacock?

A. It has fur.

B. It has scaly skin.

C. It has feathers.

CRCT Practice Cumulative

1. **It is cold. It might snow. What season is it?**

A. fall

B. winter

C. summer

2. **The pictures show the weather. Which day would be best to go to the beach?**

A. Monday

B. Tuesday

C. Wednesday S1E1a

3. **Which tool can you use to measure how much rain falls?**

A. wind vane

B. weather gauge

C. rain gauge

4. **Which is liquid precipitation?**

A. rain

B. sleet

C. hail S1E2b

5. **What happens when water changes from a solid to a liquid?**

A. It freezes.

B. It melts.

C. It evaporates S1E2a

6. **What will happen to the puddle?**

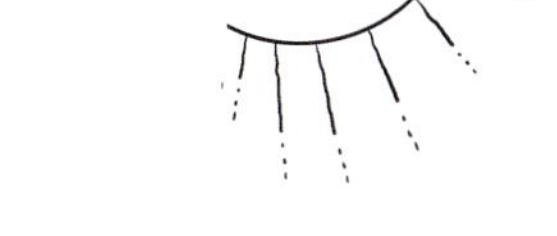

A. It will freeze.

B. It will evaporate.

C. It will melt. S1E2d

7. **Which is a source of light?**

A. a thermometer

B. a vibration

C. the sun S1P1a

8. **How is sound made?**

A. when something vibrates

B. when something stops vibrating

C. when something does not move

9. **What is a dark place made when an object blocks light?**

A. space

B. light

C. shadow

10. **What is a sound that can help you stay safe?**

A. a whisper

B. an airplane landing

C. a siren

11. **One sound is high. One sound is low. What do you know?**

A. They have a different pitch.

B. They have the same volume.

C. They have the same pitch. 

12. **Which object will a magnet attract?**

SIP2b

A. 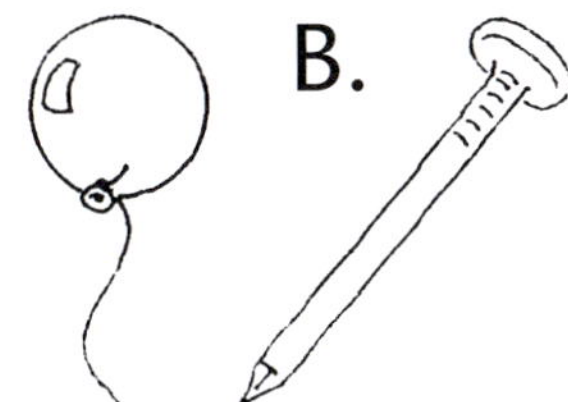

B. 

C.

13. **What will happen if you put together two S poles?**

A. They will repel.

B. They will vibrate.

C. They will make sound. 

14. **A magnet will pull a paper clip through water. What do you know?**

A. A paper clip is not made of steel.

B. Water blocks magnetic force.

C. Water does not black magnetic force.

S1P2a–c

15. **What part of a plant makes fruits?**

A. the seeds

B. the flowers

C. the roots

S1L1c

16. **What are minerals that plants need to make their food?**

A. nutrients

B. sunlight

C. water

S1L1a

17. **Look at the arrow. What does this part help the plant do?**

A. collect light

B. hold the plant in the soil

C. make food

S1L2c

18. What do animals need to live and grow?

A. food, water, sunlight, and oxygen

B. food, water, oxygen, and shelter

C. food, water, nutrients, and sunlight

19. How would you compare a turtle and a dog by appearance?

A. A dog moves faster than a turtle.

B. A turtle has a hard shell and a dog has fur.

C. A turtle has different needs than a dog.

S1L1d

20. Look at the picture. What will this animal look like when it is an adult?

A. a butterfly

B. a fly

C. a fish

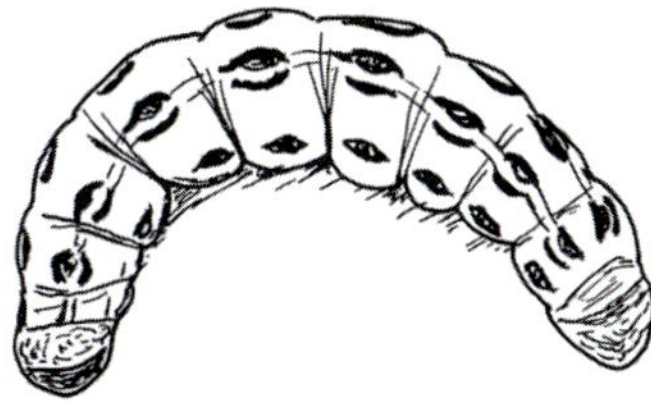

References

Contents

Your Senses

You have five senses that tell you about the world. Your five senses are sight, hearing, smell, taste, and touch.

Your Eyes

If you look at your eyes in a mirror, you will see an outer white part, a colored part called the iris, and a dark hole in the middle. This hole is called the pupil.

Inside of Eye

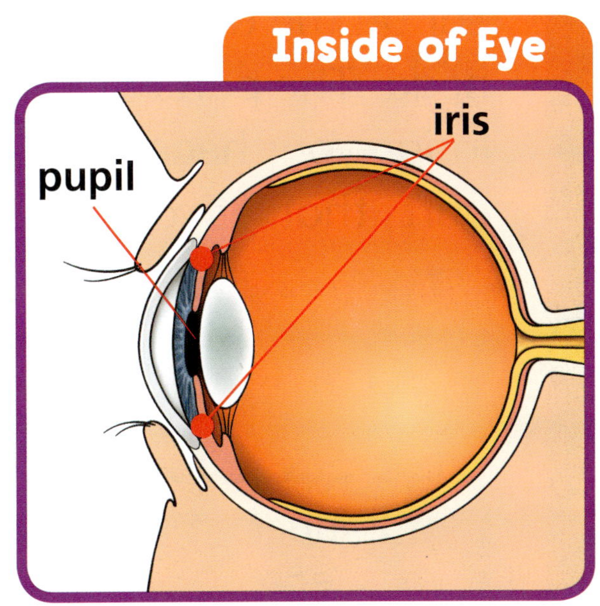

Caring for Your Eyes

- Have a doctor check your eyes to find out if they are healthy.
- Never look directly at the sun or at very bright lights.
- Wear sunglasses outdoors in bright sunlight and on snow and water.
- Don't touch or rub your eyes.
- Protect your eyes when you play sports.

Outside of Eye

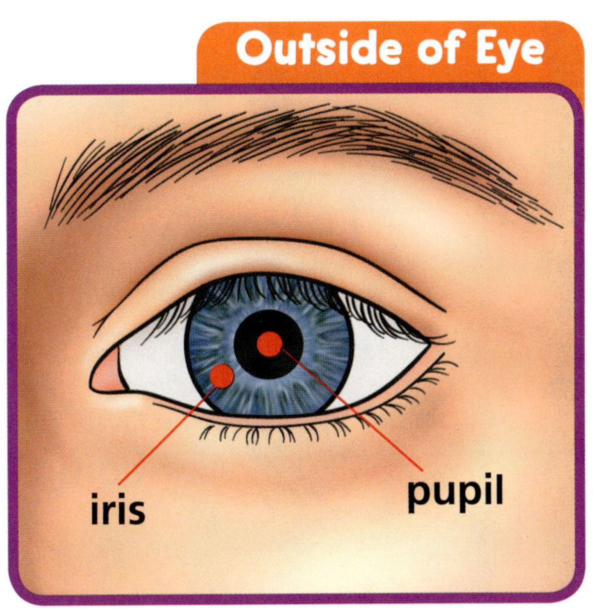

Your Senses

Your Ears

Your ears let you hear the things around you. You can see only a small part of the ear on the outside of your head. The parts of your ear inside your head are the parts that let you hear.

Caring for Your Ears

- Have a doctor check your ears.
- Avoid very loud noises.
- Never put anything in your ears.
- Protect your ears when you play sports.

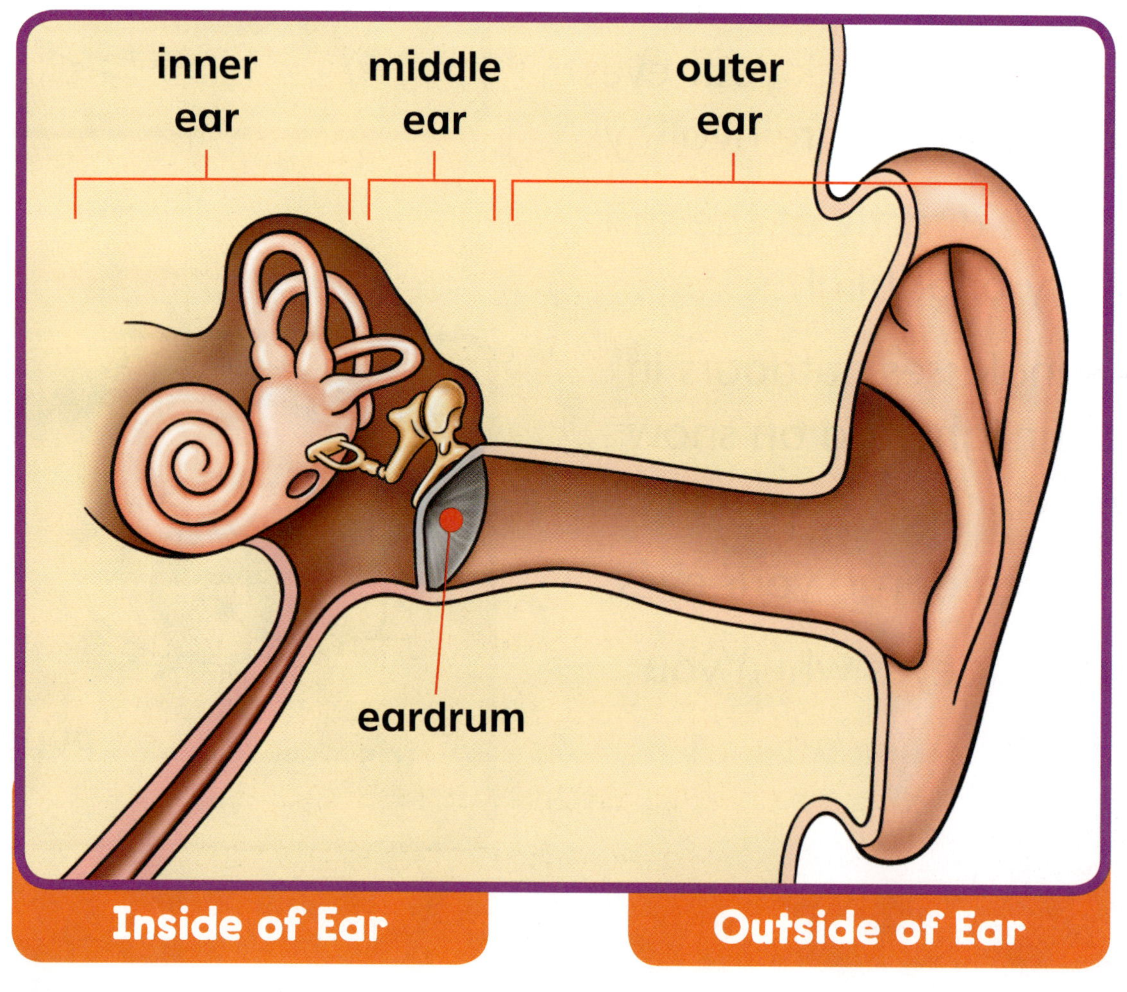

Your Senses of Smell and Taste

Your nose cleans the air you breathe and lets you smell things. Your nose and tongue help you taste things you eat and drink.

Your Skin

Your skin protects your body from germs. Your skin also gives you your sense of touch.

Caring for Your Skin

- Always wash your hands after coughing or blowing your nose, touching an animal, playing outside, or using the restroom.
- Protect your skin from sunburn. Wear a hat and clothes to cover your skin outdoors.
- Use sunscreen to protect your skin from the sun.
- Wear proper safety pads and a helmet when you play sports, ride a bike, or skate.

Your Skeletal System

Inside your body are many hard, strong bones. They form your skeletal system. The bones in your body protect parts inside your body.

Your skeletal system works with your muscular system to hold your body up and to give it shape.

Caring for Your Skeletal System

- Always wear a helmet and other safety gear when you skate, ride a bike or a scooter, or play sports.
- Eat foods that help keep your bones strong and hard.
- Exercise to help your bones stay strong and healthy.
- Get plenty of rest to help your bones grow.

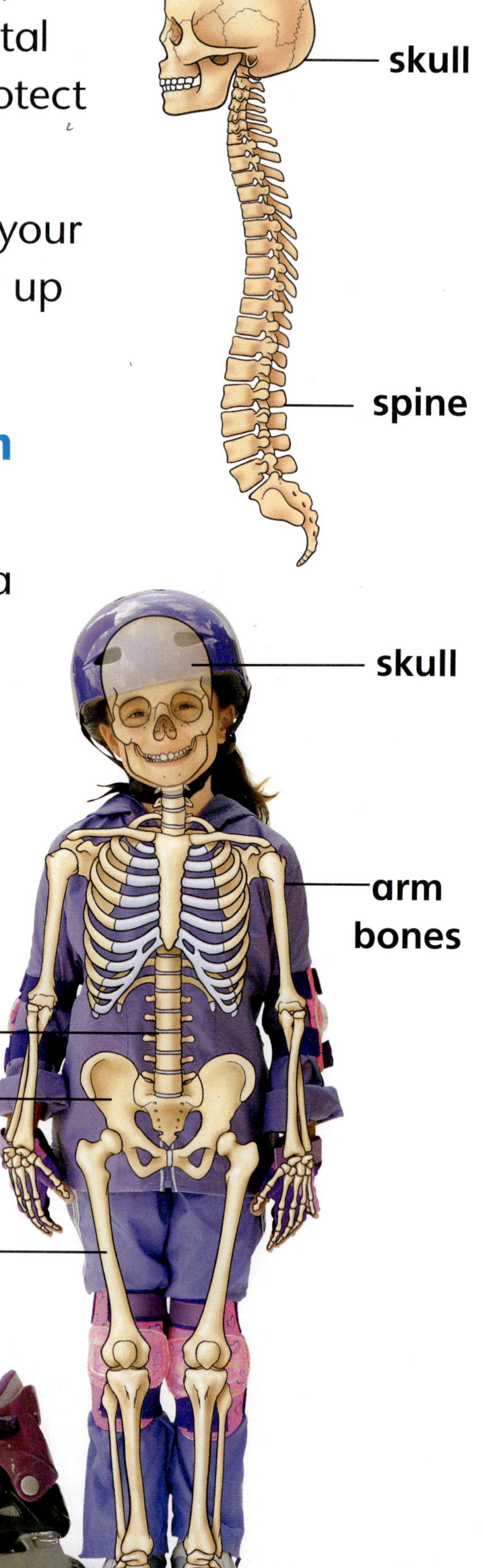

Your Muscular System

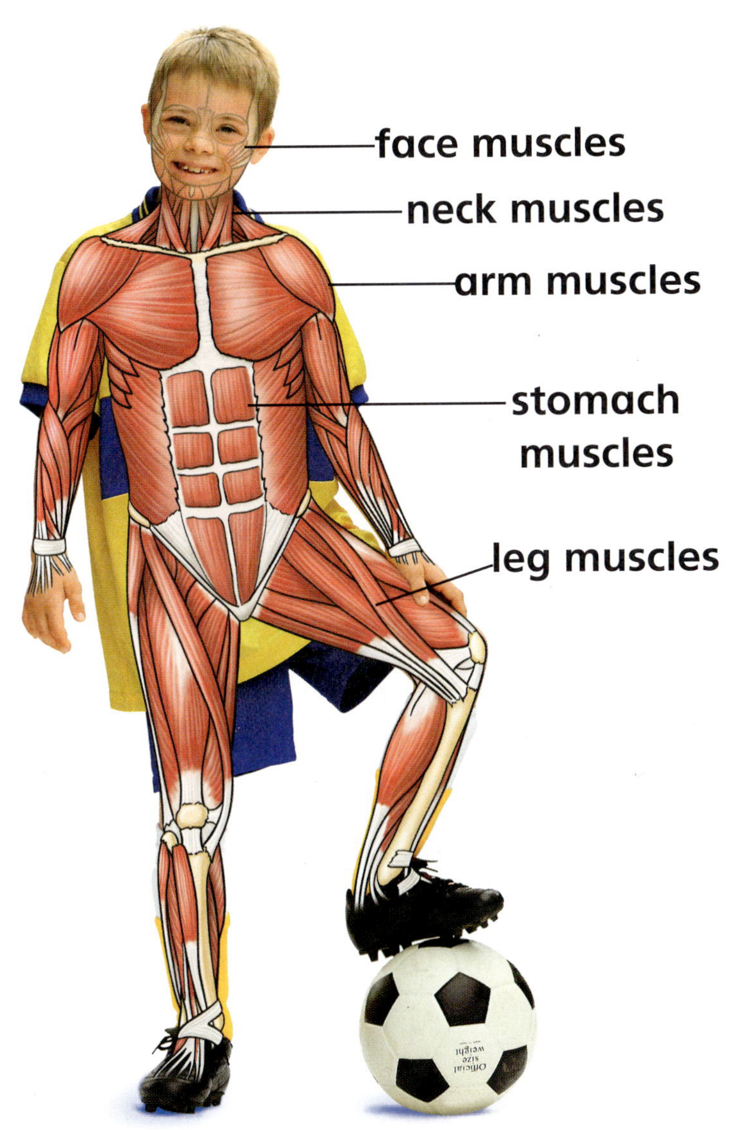

Your muscular system is made up of the muscles in your body. Muscles are body parts that help you move.

Caring for Your Muscular System

- Exercise to keep your muscles strong.
- Eat foods that will help your muscles grow.
- Drink plenty of water when you play sports or exercise.
- Rest your muscles after you exercise or play sports.

Your Nervous System

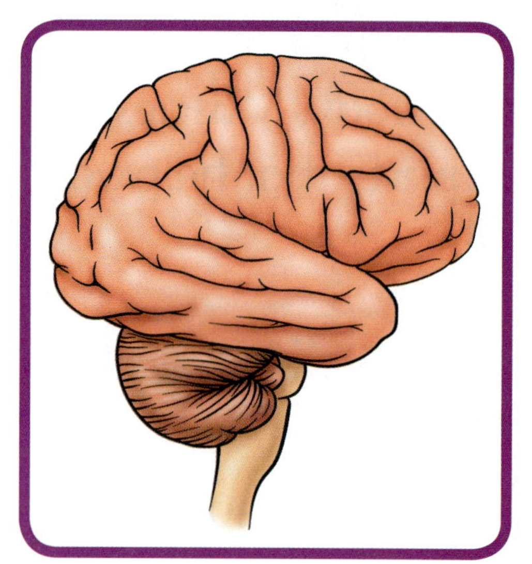

Your brain and your nerves are parts of your nervous system. Your brain keeps your body working. It tells you about the world around you. Your brain also lets you think, remember, and have feelings.

Caring for Your Nervous System

- Get plenty of sleep. Sleeping lets your brain rest.
- Always wear a helmet to protect your head and your brain when you ride a bike or play sports.

Your Digestive System

Your digestive system helps your body get energy from the foods you eat. Your body needs energy to do things.

When your body digests food, it breaks the food down. Your digestive system keeps the things your body needs. It also gets rid of the things your body does not need to keep.

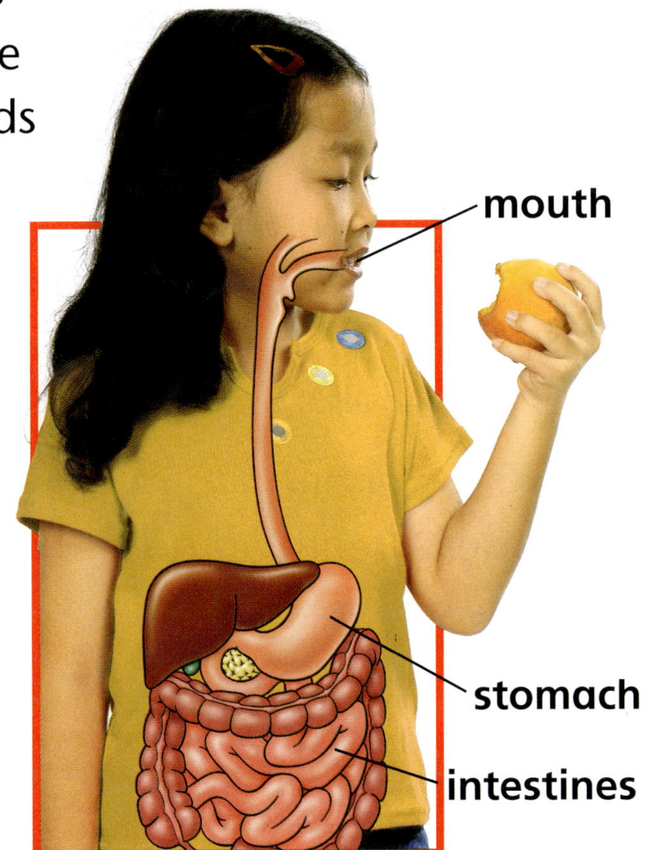

Caring for Your Digestive System

- Brush and floss your teeth every day.
- Wash your hands before you eat.
- Eat slowly and chew your food well before you swallow.
- Eat vegetables and fruits. They help move foods through your digestive system.

Your Respiratory System

You breathe using your respiratory system. Your mouth, nose, and lungs are all parts of your respiratory system.

Caring for Your Respiratory System

- Never put anything in your nose.
- Never smoke.
- Exercise enough to make you breathe harder. Breathing harder makes your lungs stronger.

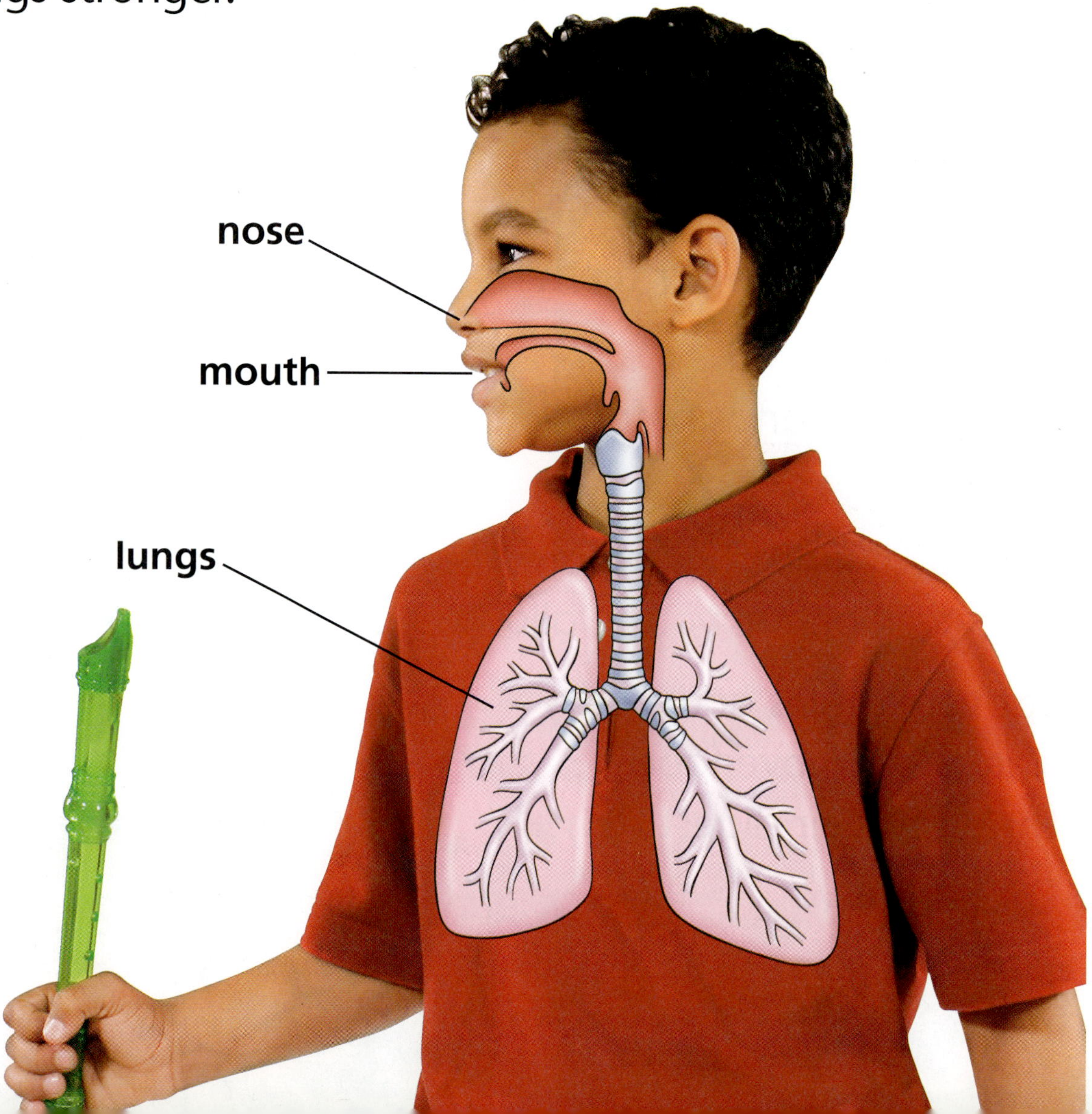

nose
mouth
lungs

Your Circulatory System

Your circulatory system is made up of your heart and your blood vessels. Your blood carries food energy and oxygen to help your body work. Blood vessels are small tubes. They carry blood from your heart to every part of your body.

Your heart is a muscle. It is beating all the time. As your heart beats, it pumps blood through your blood vessels.

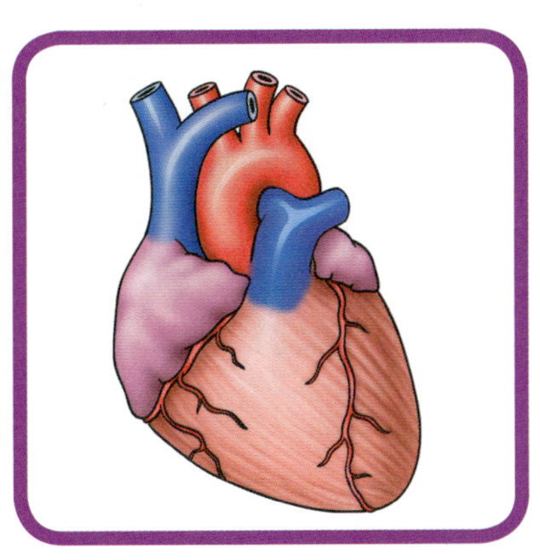

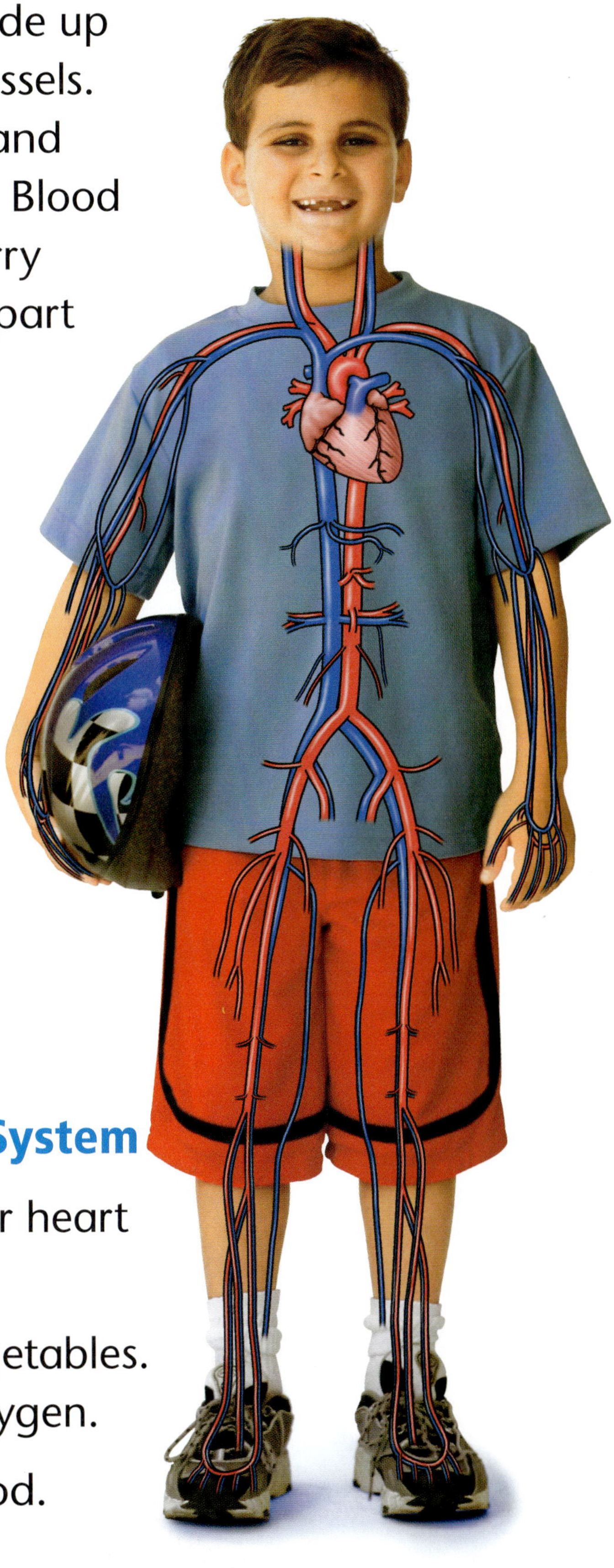

Caring for Your Circulatory System

- Exercise every day to keep your heart strong.
- Eat meats and green leafy vegetables. They help your blood carry oxygen.
- Never touch anyone else's blood.

Staying Healthy

You can do many things to help yourself stay fit and healthy.

You can also avoid doing things that can harm you.

If you know ways to stay safe and healthy and you do these things, you can help yourself have good health.

Getting enough rest

Staying away from alcohol, tobacco, and other drugs

Eating right

Keeping Clean

Keeping clean helps you stay healthy. You can pick up germs from the things you touch. Washing with soap and water helps remove germs from your skin.

Wash your hands for as long as it takes to say your ABCs. Always wash your hands at these times.

- Before and after you eat
- After coughing or blowing your nose
- After using the restroom
- After touching an animal
- After playing outside

Caring for Your Teeth

Brushing your teeth and gums keeps them clean and healthy. You should brush your teeth at least twice a day. Brush in the morning. Brush before you go to bed at night. It is also good to brush your teeth after you eat if you can.

Brushing Your Teeth

Use a soft toothbrush that is the right size for you. Always use your own toothbrush. Use only a small amount of toothpaste. It should be about the size of a pea. Be sure to rinse your mouth with water after you brush your teeth.

❶ Brush the outsides of all of your teeth.

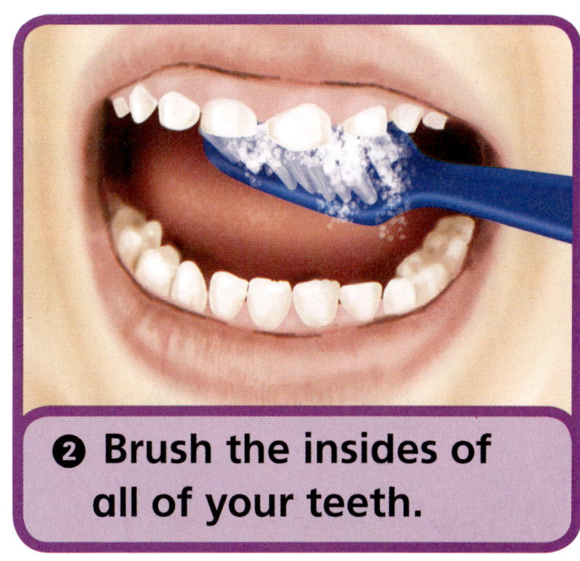

❷ Brush the insides of all of your teeth.

❸ Brush the flat parts of your back teeth.

❹ Brush your tongue.

Identify the Main Idea and Details

Some lessons in this science book are written to help you find the main idea. Learning how to find the main idea can help you understand what you read. The main idea of a paragraph is what it is mostly about. The details tell you more about it.

Read this paragraph.

Lions are hunters. They hunt for meat to eat. Lions can run very fast. They see and hear very well. They need sharp teeth to catch animals. They have sharp teeth to eat the meat they catch.

This chart shows the main idea and details.

Detail:
Lions can run very fast.

Detail:
Lions see and hear very well.

Main Idea: Lions are hunters.

Detail:
Lions hunt for meat to eat.

Detail:
Lions have sharp teeth.

Focus Skill

Compare and Contrast

Some science lessons are written to help you see how things are alike and different. Learning how to compare and contrast can help you understand what you read.

Read this paragraph.

Birds and mammals are kinds of animals. Birds have a body covering of feathers. Mammals have a body covering of fur. Both birds and mammals need food, air, and water to live. Most birds can fly. Most mammals walk or run.

Here is how you can compare and contrast birds and mammals.

Ways They Are Alike	Ways They Are Different
Compare	**Contrast**
Both are kinds of animals. Both need food, air, and water to live.	Birds have feathers. Mammals have fur. Most birds fly. Most mammals walk or run.

Cause and Effect

Focus Skill

Some science lessons are written to help you understand why things happen. You can use a chart like this to help you find cause and effect.

Cause	→	Effect
A cause is why something happens.	→	An effect is what happens.

Some paragraphs have more than one cause or effect. Read this paragraph.

Water can be a solid, a liquid, or a gas. When water is very cold, it turns into solid ice. When water is heated, it turns into water vapor, a gas.

This chart shows two causes and their effects in the paragraph.

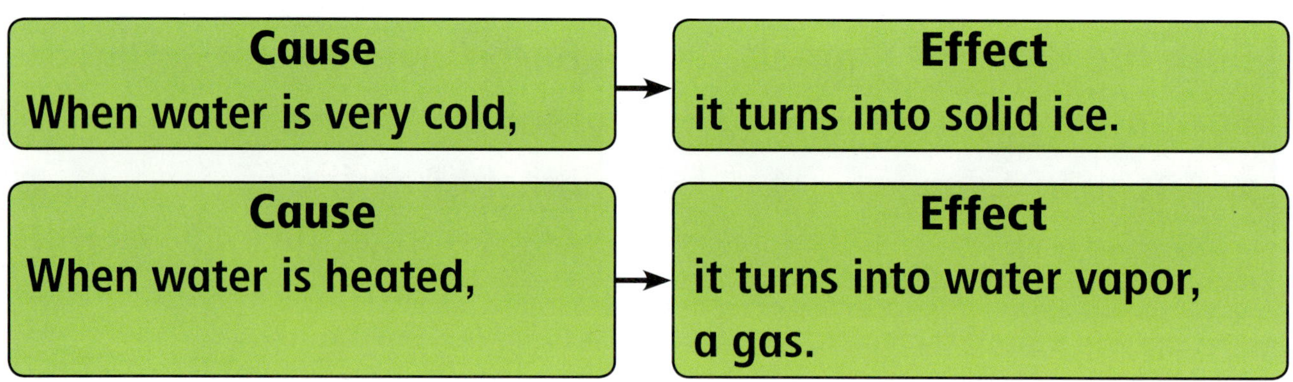

Sequence

Learning how to find sequence can help you understand what you read. You can use a chart like this to help you find sequence.

1. The first step → **2. The next step** → **3. The last step**

Some paragraphs use words that help you understand order. Read this paragraph. Look at the underlined words.

Each day begins when the sun appears. Then the sun slowly climbs into the sky. At midday, the sun is straight overhead. Then the sun slowly falls back to the horizon. At last, the sun is gone. It is nighttime.

This chart shows the sequence of the paragraph.

1. Day begins when the sun appears. → **2. The sun climbs until midday.** → **3. The sun falls back again. It is night.**

Draw Conclusions

Focus Skill

At the end of some lessons, you will be asked to draw conclusions. When you draw conclusions, you figure something out. To do this, you use what you have learned and your own ideas.

Read this paragraph.

Birds use their bills to help them get food. Each kind of bird has its own kind of bill. Birds that eat seeds have strong, short bills. Birds that eat bugs have long, sharp bills. Birds that eat water plants have wide, flat bills.

This chart shows how you can draw conclusions.

What I Read		What I Know		Conclusion:
Birds use their bills to get food. The bills have different shapes.	+	I have seen ducks up close. They have wide, flat bills.	=	Ducks are birds that eat water plants.

Focus Skill

Summarize

At the end of some lessons, you will be asked to summarize what you read. In a summary, some sentences tell the main idea. Some sentences tell details.

Read this paragraph.

Honey is made by bees. They gather nectar from flowers. Then they fly home to their beehive with the nectar inside special honey stomachs. The bees put the nectar into special honeycomb holes. Then the bees wait. Soon the nectar will change into sweet, sticky honey. The bees cover the holes with wax that they make. They eat some of the honey during the cold winter.

This chart shows how to summarize what the paragraph is about.

Recall Detail	Recall Detail	Recall Detail
Honey is made by bees.	Bees gather nectar from flowers.	The nectar turns into honey in the beehive.

Summary

Bees make honey. They collect nectar from flowers. They bring the nectar to their beehive. The nectar turns to honey in the beehive.

Using Tables, Charts, and Graphs

Gather Data

When you investigate in science, you need to collect data.

Suppose you want to find out what kinds of things are in soil. You can sort the things you find into groups.

Things I Found in One Cup of Soil

Parts of Plants

Small Rocks

Parts of Animals

By studying the circles, you can see the different items found in soil. However, you might display the data in a different way. For example, you could use a tally table.

Reading a Tally Table

You can show your data in a tally table.

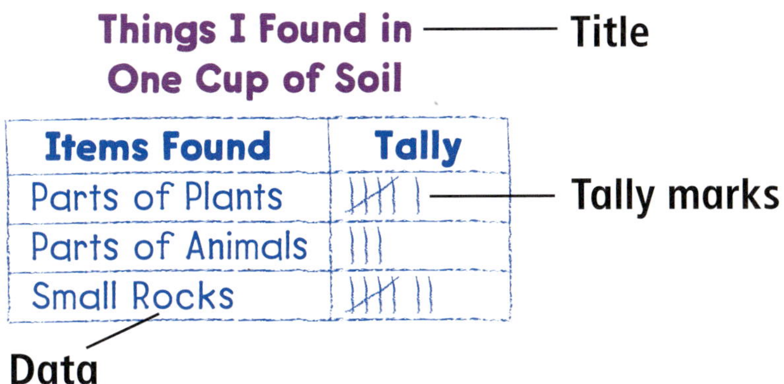

How to Read a Tally Table

1. **Read** the tally table. Use the labels.
2. **Study** the data.
3. **Count** the tally marks.
4. **Draw conclusions**. Ask yourself questions like the ones on this page.

Skills Practice

1. How many parts of plants were found in the soil?
2. How many more small rocks were found in the soil than parts of animals?
3. How many parts of plants and parts of animals were found?

Using Tables, Charts, and Graphs

Reading a Bar Graph

People keep many kinds of animals as pets. This bar graph shows the animal groups pets belong to. A bar graph can be used to compare data.

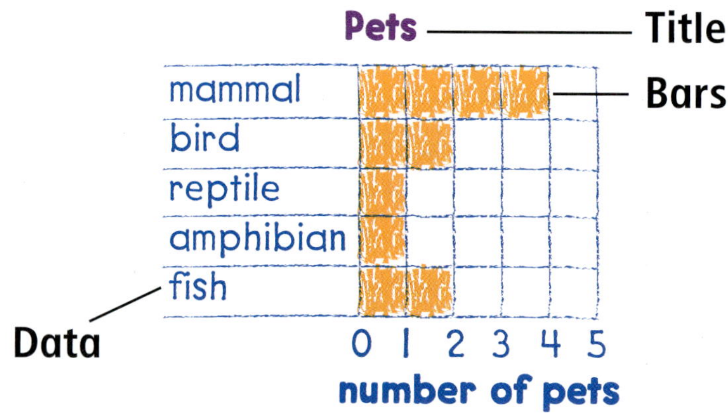

How to Read a Bar Graph

1. **Look** at the title to learn what kind of information is shown.
2. **Read** the graph. Use the labels.
3. **Study** the data. Compare the bars.
4. **Draw conclusions**. Ask yourself questions like the ones on this page.

Skills Practice

1. How many pets are mammals?
2. How many pets are birds?
3. How many more pets are mammals than fish?

Reading a Pictograph

A second-grade class was asked to choose their favorite season. A pictograph was made to show the results. A pictograph uses pictures to show information.

How to Read a Pictograph

1. **Look** at the title to learn what kind of information is shown.
2. **Read** the graph. Use the labels.
3. **Study** the data. Compare the number of pictures in each row.
4. **Draw conclusions**. Ask yourself questions like the ones on this page.

Skills Practice

1. Which season did the most classmates choose?
2. Which season did the fewest classmates choose?
3. How many classmates in all chose summer or winter?

Measurements

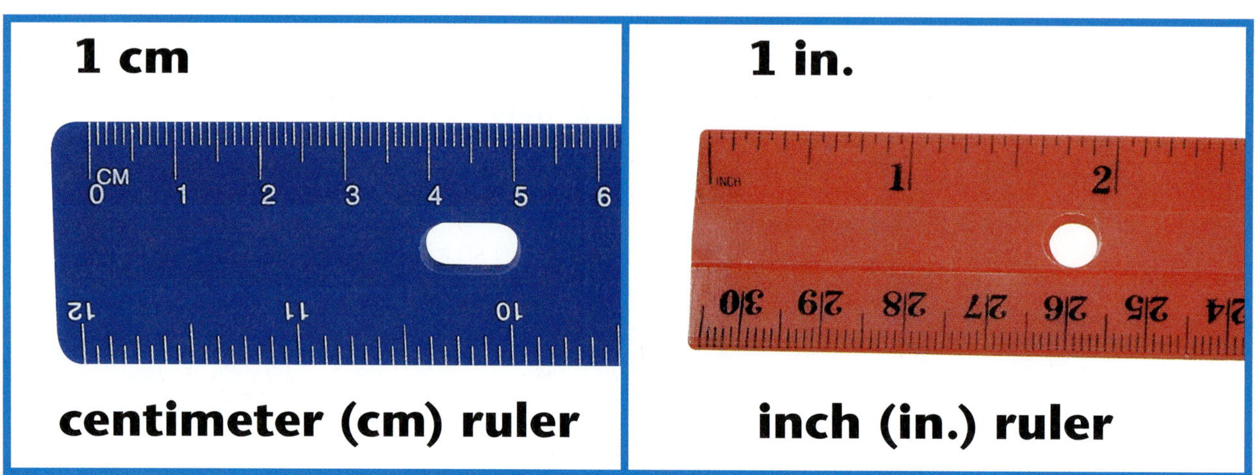

centimeter (cm) ruler

inch (in.) ruler

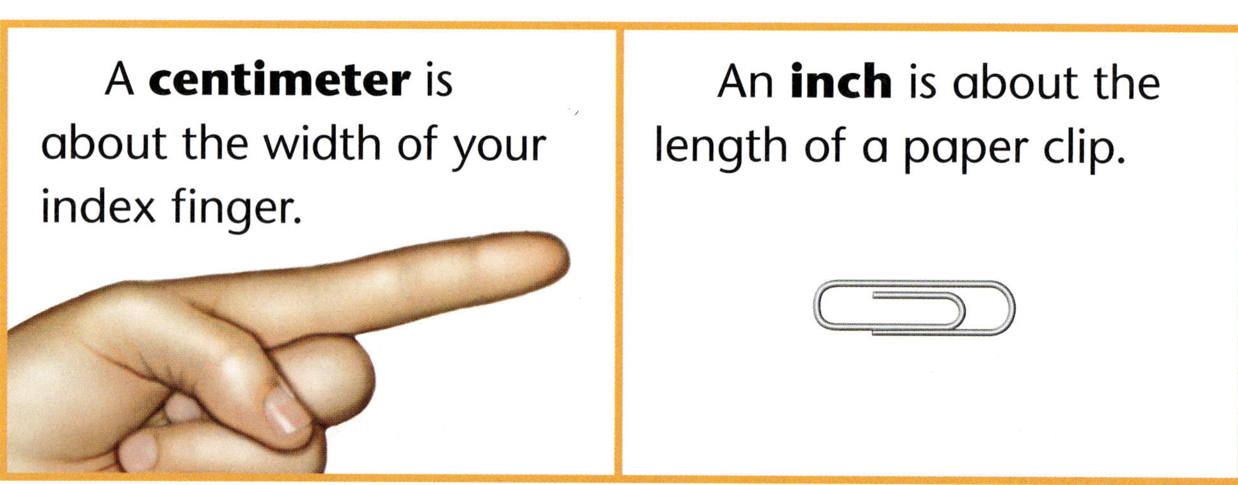
A **centimeter** is about the width of your index finger.

An **inch** is about the length of a paper clip.

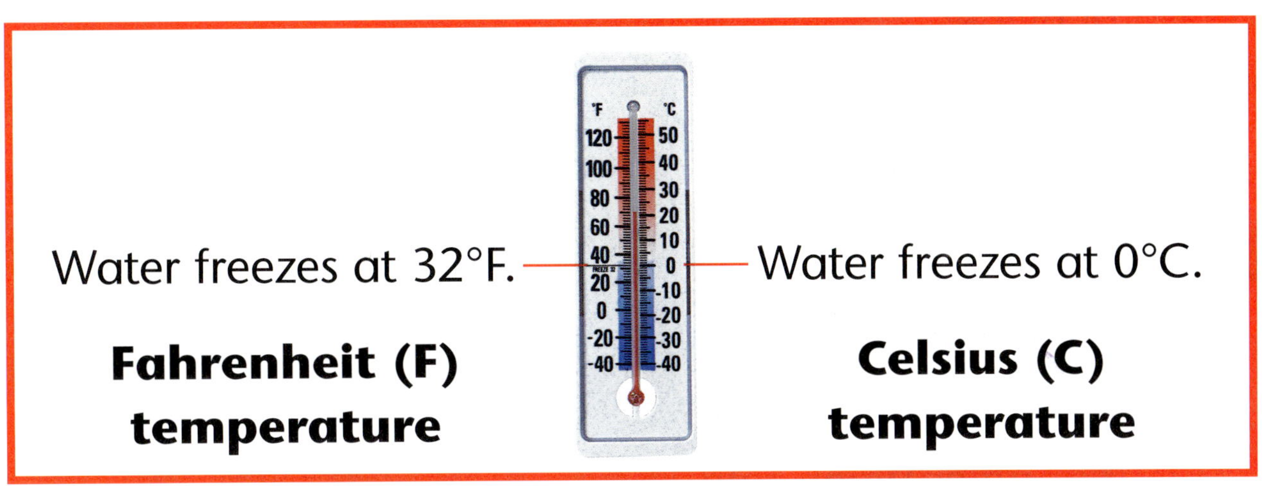

Water freezes at 32°F.

Water freezes at 0°C.

Fahrenheit (F) temperature

Celsius (C) temperature

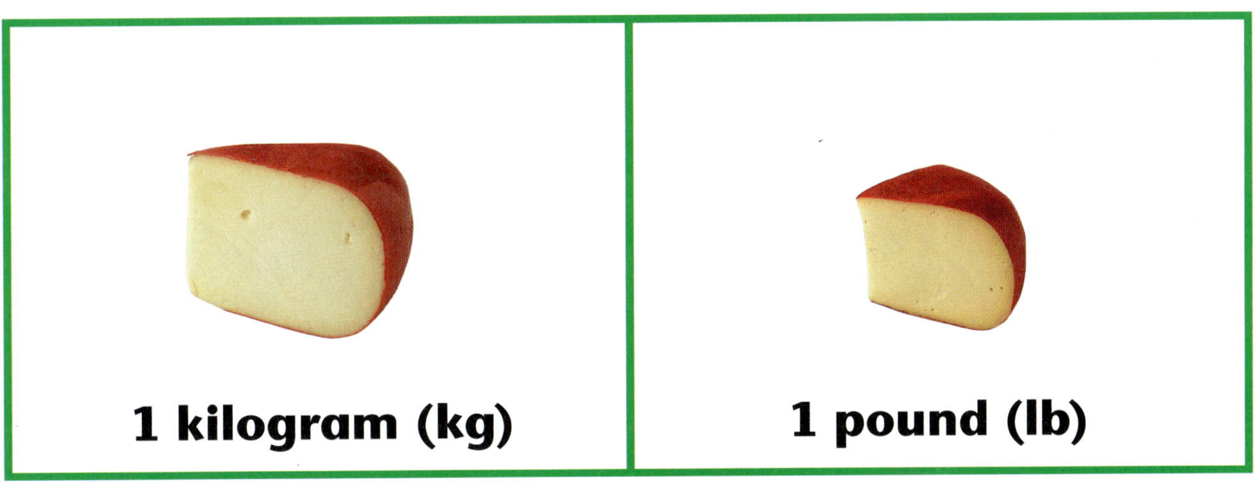
1 kilogram (kg)

1 pound (lb)

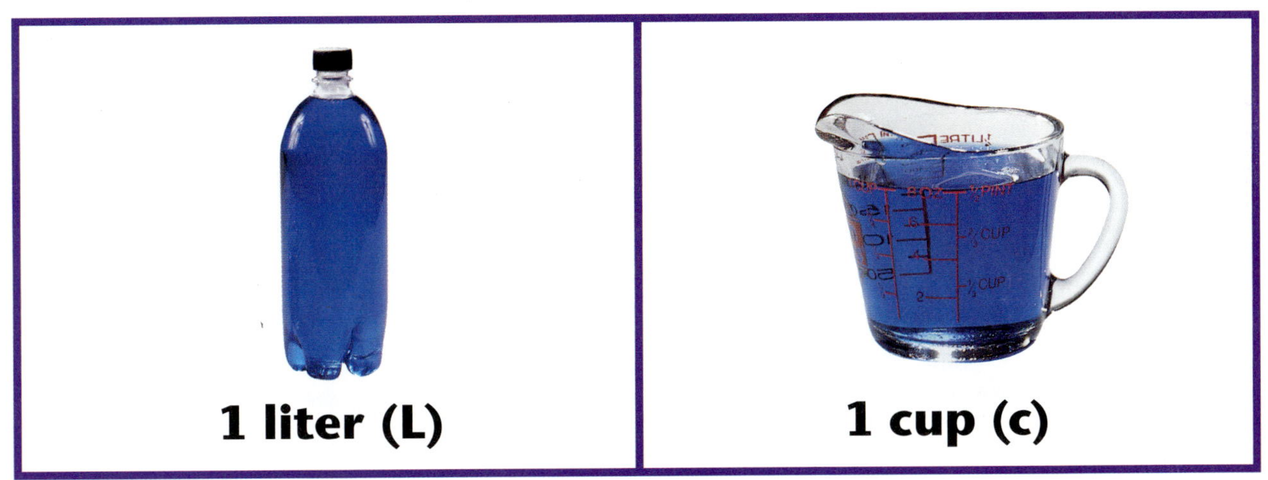
1 liter (L)

1 cup (c)

Safety in Science

Here are some safety rules to follow when you do activities.

1. **Think ahead.** Study the steps and follow them.
2. **Be neat and clean.** Wipe up spills right away.
3. **Watch your eyes.** Wear safety goggles when told to do so.
4. **Be careful with sharp things.**
5. **Do not eat or drink things.**

A glossary lists words in alphabetical order. To find a word, look it up by its first letter or letters.

A

appearance
What something looks like. A porcupine has quills. (238)

attract
To pull something. A magnet attracts things made of iron. (160)

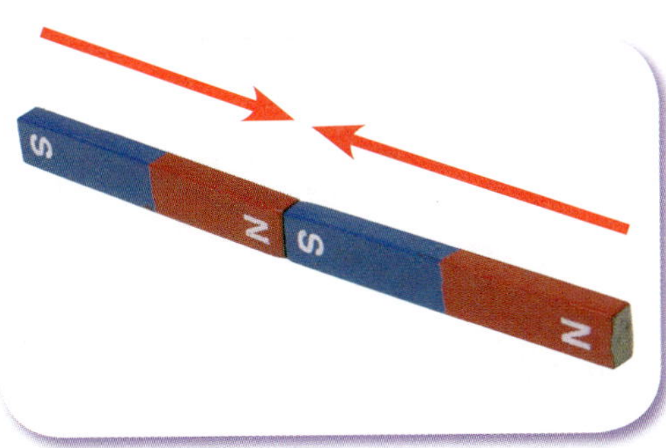

B

bar graph
A graph that uses bars to help you compare numbers of things (33)

C

condense
To change from a gas to a liquid (103)

E

evaporate

To change from a liquid to a gas (103)

F

flowers

The parts of a plant that make fruits (211)

freeze

To change from a liquid to a solid (102)

fruits

The parts of a plant that hold the seeds (211)

G

growth

An increase in size (240)

H

hail

Balls of ice that fall from the sky (91)

inquiry skills
The skills people use to find out things (6)

leaves
The parts of a plant that take in light and air and make food (210)

light
A kind of energy that lets us see (124)

magnet
An object that will attract things made of iron (160)

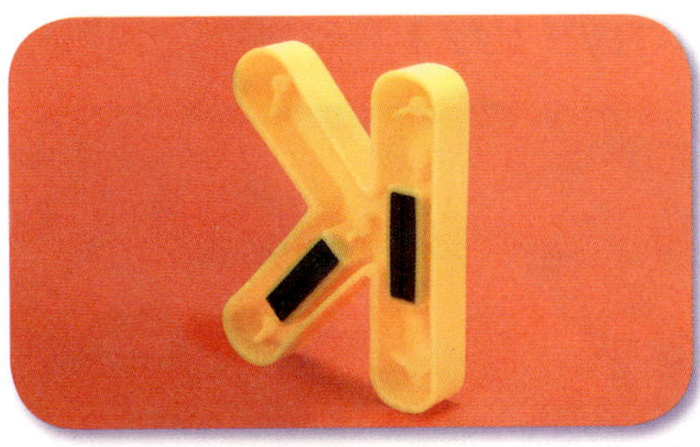

magnetic force
The pulling force of a magnet (172)

melt
To change from a solid to a liquid (102)

N

nutrients
Minerals in the soil that plants need to grow and stay healthy (197)

O

observe
To use your senses to find out about things (10)

P

pictograph
A graph that uses pictures to help you compare numbers of things (32)

pitch
How high or low a sound is (140)

pole
Near the end of a magnet where the pull is strongest (162)

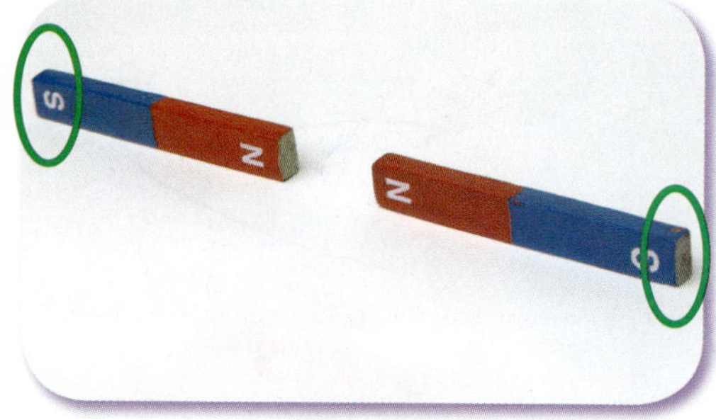

precipitation
Any form of water that falls from the sky. (90)

rain gauge
A tool you use to measure how much rain falls (77)

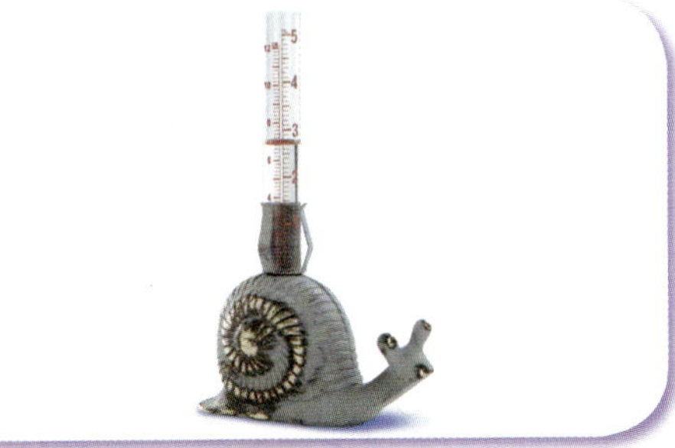

repel
To push away. Poles that are the same on a magnet repel each other. (163)

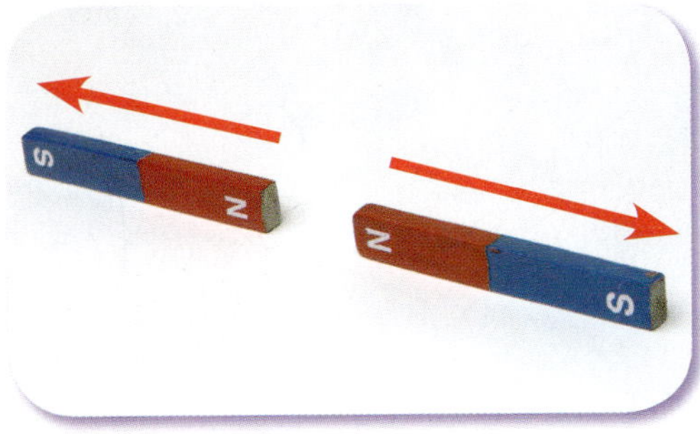

roots
The part of the plant that holds it in the soil and takes in water and nutrients (208)

science tools
Tools that scientists use to find out things (18)

season
A time of year (60)

seeds

The parts of a plant that new plants grow from (211)

shadow

A dark place made when an object blocks light (127)

shelter

A place where a person or an animal can be safe (229)

sleet

Frozen or partly frozen rain (91)

sound

A kind of energy that you hear (136)

stem

The part of the plant that holds up the plant and lets food and water move through the plant (209)

sunlight
Light that comes from the sun (194)

temperature
The measure of how hot or cold something is (75)

thermometer
A tool you use to measure temperature (75)

vibration
A movement back and forth (137)

volume
How loud or soft a sound is. A whisper is a soft sound. (138)

W

water cycle
The movement of water from Earth to the air and back again (104)

weather
What the air outside is like (48)

wind vane
A tool you use to measure the direction of the wind (76)

Index

A

B

C

KEY: (t) top, (b) bottom, (l) left, (r) right, (c) center, (bg) background, (fg) foreground

INTRODUCTION
1 (t) Imagine It! The Children's Museum of Atlanta; 14 (r) David Young-Wolff/Alamy; 26 (bl) C Squared Studios/PhotoDisc/Getty Images; 24 (bg) 4-H International & Citizenship; 26 (cl) Masterfile; 39 PhotoDisc/Getty Images;

UNIT 1
40 (bg) AmericanScapes, Inc./PhotographersDirect; 43 (t) Graeme Teague Photography; 44 (bg) Jamie Squire/Getty Images; 48 (bg) Leng/Leng/Corbis. (t) Mark Polott/Index Stock Imagery, (b) William Manning/Corbis; 50 (b) Corbis/Harcourt Index; 51 (b) Amanda Merullo/IPNStock.com; 56 (bg) Art Directors & TRIP Photo Library; 61 (all) Matheisl/Getty Images; 62 (tr) Gay Bumgarner/Getty Images; (b) PhotoDisc/Getty Images; 63 (b) Mark E. Gibson/Corbis, (tr) Gay Bumgarner/Getty Images; 64 (b) Getty Images, (tr) Gay Bumgarner/Getty Images; 65 (tr) Gay Bumgarner/Getty Images, (bl) John Henley/Corbis, (br) Jiang Jin/Superstock; 66 (bl) Journal Courier/The Image Works; 68 (bg) Alec Pytlowany/Masterfile, (tl) Birmingham Public Library; 70 (bg) Ric Feld/AP Images; 76 (b) Jim Sugar/Corbis; 77 (b) Workbookstock.com; 80 (cr) Gay Bumgarner/Getty Images, (bl) Doug Stamm/Stammphoto.com; 83 (cl) Jim Sugar/Corbis; 85 (t) Zach Holmes/Alamy; 86 (bg) Mark Barrett/Index Stock Imagery; 88 (bl) Carol Havens/Corbis; 90 (b) Georgia Department of Economic Development; 91 (br) Ric Feld/AP Images; (cl) John Howard/Photo Researchers, Inc.; 92 (c) Steve Satushek/Photographer's Choice/Getty Images; 93 (b) Ron Sherman; 96, (tr) Susan Findlay/Master file, (cl) B&C Alexander/Photo Researchers Inc., (r) Alan Fortune/Animals Animals, 97, B&C Alexander/Photo Researchers; 98 (bg) Ron Sherman; 103 (cr) (tr) SpotWorks/Alamy; 108 (bg) Andre Jenny/The Image Works; (cr) James Randklev Photography; 109 (bc) Philip Shone Photography/PhotographersDirect; 119 (t) Graeme Teague Photography; 120 (bg) Jerry Driendl/Taxi/Getty Images; 125 (b) IPS Agency/Index Stock Imagery; (cl) Garry Gay/Alamy; 130 (bg) Florida Images/Alamy; 131 (br) David Davis Photoproductions/Alamy; 132 (bg) Ron Sherman;

UNIT 2
135 (tcl) Ed Young/PictureArts, (tc) GK & Vikki Hart/Getty Images; 138 (tr) David Young-Wolff/Photo Edit, (b) Scott Barrow, Inc./SuperStock; 139 (cl) Pat LaCroix/The Image Bank/Getty Images; 140 (bl) Eduardo Garcia/Getty Images; 141 (b) Tom Carter/Photo Edit, (tr) C Squared Studios/PhotoDisc/Getty Images; 142 (bl) Spencer Grant/Photo Edit, (br) Photodisc Blue/Getty Images; 143 (br) Spencer Grant/Photo Edit; 144 (bl) C Squared Studios/Photodisc Green/Getty Images; (br) Stephen Marks/The Image Bank/Getty Images; (tr) Graeme Teague Photography; 146 (bl) Tony Freeman/Photo Edit; 150 (cl) Roy Ooms/Masterfile, (cr) Comstock/PictureQuest; 149 (bg) Zuma Press/NewsCom; (tr) MCT/NewsCom; 156 (bg) Deborah Davis/PhotoEdit; 178 (bg) Greg Janney/All You Need Photography; 179 (br)(tr) Greg Janney/All You Need Photography;

UNIT 3
189 (t) Carl Donohue/www.SkolaiImages.com; 190 (bg) Graeme Teague Photography; 194 Freeman Patterson/Masterfile; 200 (bg) John Grover Nash/Photographers Direct; (cr) age fotostock/SuperStock; 201 (br) Ping Amranand/SuperStock; (tr) Jeff Greenberg/PhotoEdit; 202 (bg) Glenn Grossman; 206 (b) Georgia Department of Economic Development; 208 (l) Visuals Unlimited, (r) Paul Souders/IPNSTOCK.com, (bg) Alamy Images;209 Gordon R. Gainer/Corbis; 211 (bl) Foods of the World/Alamy; 211 (c)(tr) Georgia Department of Economic Development 215 (b) Yva Momatiuk & John Eastcott/Minden Pictures; 219 Ken Wardius/Index Stock Imagery; 221 (t) Graeme Teague Photography; 222 (bg) blickwinkel/Alamy; 226 (b) Martin Harvey; Gallo Images/Corbis; 227 (cl) China Span/Animals Animals, (br) Gemma Giannini/Grant Heilman Photography; 228 (b) ABPL Image Library/Animals Animals/Earth Scenes; 229 (inset) W. Perry Conway/Corbis, (bg) D. Robert & Lorri Franz/Corbis; 230 Norman Owen Tomalin/Bruce Coleman, Inc., (bl) D. Robert & Lorri Franz/Corbis; 232 (br) Ric Feld/AP Images; (tl) Kimberly Smith/Atlanta Journal-Constitution; 233 (bg) ZUMA Press/NewsCom; (tr) Georgia Aquarium; 234 (bg) Dwight Kuhn Photography; 239 (bg) Stephen Dalton/Minden Pictures; 240 (b) S&D&K Maslowski/Minden Pictures.

YOUNG White-tailed deer fawns have spots on their fur.

HABITAT White-tailed deer live in Georgia and most of the United States.

BEHAVIOR The white-tailed deer eats grass, berries, leaves, and acorns.

HABITAT White-tailed deer live in forests where they can find food.

CHARACTERISTIC The white-tailed deer is named for its tail, which is white on the underside.